MW00879183

LEARN SPANISH FAST FOR ADULTS BEGINNER TO INTERMEDIATE

5 in 1 Book

Spanish Beginner to Intermediate in Just 30 Days with Essential Lessons, Stories and Simple Exercises

TABLE OF CONTENTS

Speak Abroad
Academy

DISCLAIMER NOTICE:

Please note the information contained within this document is for educational and entertainment purposes only.

All effort has been executed to present accurate, up to date, reliable, complete information. No warranties of any kind are declared or implied. Readers acknowledge that the author is not engaged in the rendering of legal, financial, medical or professional advice. The content within this book has been derived from various sources.

Please consult a licensed professional before attempting any techniques outlined in this book.

By reading this document, the reader agrees that under no circumstances is the author responsible for any losses, direct or indirect, that are incurred as a result of the use of the information contained within this document, including, but not limited to, errors, omissions, or inaccuracies.

INTRODUCTION

Let me guess: you're interested in learning Spanish, and you've tried formal lessons and apps, but you're stuck. You don't know why. No matter how excited you are at the beginning, you always end up losing your motivation. You start having difficulty finding time to sit and practice, until you finally give up. Will you ever be able to learn Spanish?

Of course, you will! While we all know that learning a new language requires effort and commitment, you will recover your motivation and look forward to learning with the right approach.

So, what is the right approach?

Scheduling a time for lessons is a great way to keep your motivation high. But this will only happen if learning is pleasant and easy; that is, if you're not overwhelmed by new information. You will be excited about new content and tasks if you feel you're in control of the process.

That is precisely what we have undertaken with this bundle by delivering micro lessons with tiny bits of information. By providing simple-to-follow lessons and lots —yes, lots!—of practice, our *Beginner to Intermediate Spanish Bundle* will help you learn Spanish quickly and thoroughly.

Our specialized easy-to-follow methodology engages readers from the very first page with short, to-the-point grammar explanations and fun exercises. We place you, the learner, at the center of the learning journey, keeping in mind that you have a long list of tasks every day competing for your time and energy.

We do not want you to place Spanish on the overflowing to-do list that fills people with stress and anxiety. Instead, we want it to be an enjoyable activity you turn to when you want to relax and distract yourself. Think of learning a language as the same as doing exercise: if you want it to stick, you need to make it pleasurable. When you're enjoying the learning process, it feels effortless —even though, many times, it isn't!— and you learn the new language more effectively.

We will help you build Spanish into your life by learning words in context, as they appear naturally, and presenting grammar explanations in real-life situations. You'll pick up your vocabulary from short stories and everyday scenes and songs. The extensive practice applies the concepts learned and reviews what you have already mastered. Our bite-sized lessons are based on gradual, cumulative learning: each new lesson builds on the previous ones to keep you from forgetting earlier concepts.

You will constantly review what you know as you take in new knowledge. This has the two-fold benefit of boosting self-confidence as you train your brain to recognize new language patterns. When you start identifying and remembering past lessons, you will feel that you're finally making progress.

So are you ready to step into the world of Spanish? Are you ready to join the countless individuals whose lives have been transformed by the magic of *our* unique approach? Picture this: within just weeks of embarking on our program, you'll find yourself effortlessly navigating the rich tapestry of Spanish-speaking countries, immersing yourself in vibrant cultures, and unlocking a realm of endless possibilities.

Imagine the thrill of enhancing your travel experiences as you confidently converse with locals, uncovering hidden gems and forging connections that transcend language barriers. Envision broadening your career horizons, seizing opportunities you once deemed out of reach, all thanks to your newfound proficiency in Spanish.

But the benefits don't end there. Dive deeper into the heart and soul of Spanish-speaking cultures as you delve into the realms of art, theater, music, film, literature, podcasts, and blogs. Feel the rhythm of flamenco pulse through your veins, lose yourself in the pages of iconic novels, and gain an insider's perspective that transcends mere language comprehension.

With our bundle as your guide, the journey to Spanish fluency becomes a gateway to a world brimming with excitement, enrichment, and endless discovery. Don't just read and write Spanish – immerse yourself in its essence and embrace a newfound appreciation for the boundless beauty it beholds.

As you begin your lessons, you will feel a sense of accomplishment because of how each class is structured. Clear explanations of grammatical rules and exercises that tie to them directly will help you make quick steps to push you forward. As you practice what you learn, you will gain confidence and feel motivated to move on to the next step. Before you know it, you will start to express your thoughts and feelings in Spanish and understand the variety of Spanish-language resources we provide: excerpts from poems, songs, and social media, among others. You will read and write in Spanish, using your newly acquired skills wherever you go.

Our approach aims to keep you focused and on track. We have also added stories for you to enjoy throughout the guide. Instead of asking you to carve out a considerable amount of time for studying, you'll be engaging in short, easy lessons. You won't feel overwhelmed because lessons are brief and focused. Each class pinpoints one grammar issue at a time and makes sure you practice it. Our exercises include a wide variety of topics and respond to current trends. In addition, each new grammar concept builds on the previous ones, making sure you review what you know before jumping into new content.

So, why wait any longer? Start right now! Boost your Spanish learning today and step into a lifetime of possibilities: new friends, exciting trips, and a host of career-growth opportunities.

BOOK I & II: BEGINNER TO INTERMEDIATE LESSONS

Welcome to our combined Beginner and Intermediate Workbook for learning Spanish! This book is the culmination of two carefully designed resources, seamlessly integrated to provide you with a comprehensive and gradual learning experience.

In this workbook, you'll find a structured progression of lessons starting from basic concepts and gradually moving towards more challenging topics. The beginner lessons lay down a solid foundation, covering essential grammar, vocabulary, and sentence structures, while the intermediate lessons build upon that foundation to further enhance your understanding and fluency.

Each lesson is crafted to reinforce previously learned concepts while introducing new ones, ensuring a smooth transition as you progress from beginner to intermediate level. Whether you're just starting your Spanish journey or looking to expand your existing knowledge, this workbook will guide you through every step of the way.

We invite you to embark on this language-learning adventure with us and discover the joy of mastering Spanish at your own pace. ¡Buena suerte! (Good luck!)

CHAPTER 1:

SUBJECT PRONOUNS, NOUNS AND ARTICLES

THE DOG, A CAT AND I

First things first! The initial step to learning any language always begins with subject pronouns. In English, these are words like 'I,' 'You,' and 'They.' They indicate *who* exactly we're talking about and they're essential for everyday conversation! Without them, it would be impossible to describe ourselves, other people, and how events have affected us. They are some of the most basic building blocks of any language.

So, let's take a look at what subject pronouns in Spanish are!

1.1 Subject Pronouns

English	Spanish	Pronunciation
I	**yo**	*[io]*
You (informal, singular)	**tú**	*[too]*
You (formal, singular)	**usted**	*[oos-tehd]*
He She	**él** **ella**	*[ehl]* *[eh-yah]*
They (masculine) They (feminine	**ellos** **ellas**	*[eh-yohs]* *[eh-yahs]*
We (masculine) We (feminine)	**nosotros** **nosotras**	*[noh-soh-trohs]* *[noh-soh-trahs]*
You (formal and informal, plural.)	**ustedes**	*[oos-the-des]*
You (inf., plural, masc.) You (inf., plural, fem.)	**vosotros*** **vosotras***	*[boh-soh-trohs]* *[boh-soh-trahs]*

* *Vosotros* and *vosotras* are only used in Spain. Although people in other Spanish-speaking countries will understand you, it will come across as unusual to them.

You'll notice that, in Spanish, there are a lot more subject pronouns than in English! Aside from *who* they reference, they're also split up based on:

- Formality of the situation.
- Genders of the people you're talking about.
- Quantity of subjects, i.e., whether you're just talking to or about one person or more.

Unlike English, there are different Spanish pronouns for 'you' and 'they' depending on how many people you're talking to or talking about. Saying *ustedes* would be like the equivalent of saying 'you all' or 'both of you.'

As you see in the table above, you'd use the word **tú** in an informal situation and **usted** in a formal situation. But what exactly constitutes an informal or formal situation?

You'd use the formal word **usted** (abbreviated as **Ud**. and always with a capital **U**) in interactions with people like:

- Your boss
- A stranger or new acquaintance (unless you dislike them and want them to know it!)
- A salesperson
- The cashier at the bank
- Older people

You'd use the informal pronoun tú with:

- Your friends
- Your family
- Children and animals
- People you intend to insult
- Other young people (if you're young, too)

> **Tip:** The masculine plural form **ellos** refers to a group of males or to a group that includes both males and females. The feminine plural form **ellas** only refers to a group of females. In other words, the default word for 'They' is **ellos**, unless you're referring to a group of people that's entirely female.

Interesting fact: In Spanish, there is no subject pronoun, **it**. You use **él** and **ella** to refer to people, and sometimes animals. You don't use él and **ella** to refer to things. It would be like calling a shoe or a potato 'he' and 'she.' Quirky, but not exactly accurate!

Let's get familiar with these pronouns, shall we?

Note on Abbreviations: masculine (m.), feminine (f.), informal (inf.), formal (form.), singular (sing.), plural (pl.)

1.1 Practice

A. Write the correct subject pronoun.

1. __________ voy a tu casa. (*I'm going to your house*)
2. __________ somos tus amigos. (*we*—m.—*are your friends*)
3. __________ sois los mejores. (*you*—m. inf. pl. in Spain—*are the best*)
4. __________ son hombres. (*you*— f. and inf. pl. in Spain and Latin America—*are men*)
5. __________ son amigos. (*they*—m.—*are friends*)
6. __________ eres mujer. (*you*—sing. inf.— *are a woman*)

B. What would you say with each of the following, **tú** or **usted**?

1. Your grandmother ______
2. A co-worker __________
3. A flight attendant ______
4. Your boss ____________
5. A little boy ____________
6. A professor ___________
7. A repair person ________
8. Your cousin ___________
9. Your best friend _______
10. Your father-in-law _____

1.2 The Gender of Nouns and Definite Articles

We covered pronouns, but what's a noun? Nouns are objects, places, and things.

Unlike English, all nouns in Spanish are either masculine or feminine. This doesn't mean that objects are perceived as having literal gender differences, of course, but rather, they are just classified into different groups.

Some of these are straightforward, such as **el hombre** and **la mujer,** which mean *the man* and *the woman* respectively. As you'd expect, **el hombre** is a masculine noun and **la mujer** is a feminine noun. Although they're different words, **el** and **la** both mean 'the' – they simply apply to different genders. You would never ever say 'la hombre' or 'el mujer' as it would be grammatically incorrect.

It's easy with people, but less easy with objects and places. To speak fluent Spanish, you'll need to remember that a book is masculine while a photograph is feminine.

The definite article (the) should always agree with the gender of the noun. This is a hard one for English speakers, because we only have one definite article—the—and don't have to worry about the rest!

Singular Masculine Nouns

The masculine singular noun uses the definite article **el**.

Most masculine nouns end in **-o**:

English	Spanish	Pronunciation
the friend (male)	**el amigo**	*[ehl ah-mee-goh]*
the boy	**el niño**	*[ehl nee-nyoh]*
the son	**el hijo**	*[ehl ee-hoh]*
the brother	**el hermano**	*[ehl ehr-mah-noh]*
the grandfather	**el abuelo**	*[ehl ah-bweh-loh]*
the uncle	**el tío**	*[ehl tee-oh]*
the cat	**el gato**	*[ehl gah-toh]*
the dog	**el perro**	*[ehl peh-rroh]*
the book	**el libro**	*[ehl lee-broh]*
the telephone	**el teléfono**	*[ehl teh-leh-foh-noh]*
the youngster	**el muchacho**	*[ehl moo-chah-choh]*

Some masculine nouns end in -e:

the tomato	**el tomate**	*[ehl toh-mah-teh]*
the coffee	**el café**	*[ehl kah-feh]*
the student	**el estudiante**	*[ehl ehs-too-dyan-teh]*

But some masculine nouns do not end in **-o**; they may end in a consonant like **l**, **r**, or **z**:

the animal	**el animal**	*[ehl ah-nee-mahl]*
the hospital	**el hospital**	*[ehl ohs-pee-tahl]*
the doctor	**el doctor**	*[ehl dohk-tohr]*
the hotel	**el hotel**	*[ehl oh-tehl]*
the train	**el tren**	*[ehl trehn]*
the pencil	**el lápiz**	*[ehl lah-peeth]*

There are also some exceptions. Here are some masculine nouns that end in **-a** or **-ma**:

English	Spanish	Pronunciation
the climate	**el clima**	*[ehl klee-mah]*
the program	**el programa**	*[ehl proh-grah-mah]*
the system	**el sistema***	*[ehl sees-teh-mah]*
the map	**el mapa**	*[ehl mah-pah]*
the language	**el idioma**	*[ehl ee-dyoh-mah]*
the planet	**el planeta**	*[ehl plah-neh-tah]*
the problem	**el problema**	*[ehl proh-bleh-mah]*
the tourist	**el turista**	*[ehl too-rees-tah]*
the sofa	**el sofá**	*[ehl soh-fah]*
the telephone	**el teléfono**	*[ehl teh-leh-foh-noh]*
the youngster	**el muchacho**	*[ehl moo-chah-choh]*

***Be careful!** Many English speakers say "la sistema," thinking this word is feminine. Remember, it's "**el sistema**."

Regardless of how the word ends, you'll still need to use **el** if it's masculine.

> **Tip**: Since there is no clear rule about what ending a noun should have to be masculine, you'll need to memorize which noun is what gender. Don't worry, this gets easier with practice!

Singular Feminine Nouns

The feminine singular noun uses the definite article **la**.

Feminine nouns usually end in **-a**:

English	Spanish	Pronunciation
the person	**la persona**	*[lah pehr-soh-nah]*
the woman	**la mujer**	*[lah moo-hehr]*
the mother	**la madre**	*[lah mah-dreh]*
the friend (female)	**la amiga**	*[lah ah-mee-gah]*
the girl	**la niña**	*[lah nee-nyah]*
the girl	**la muchacha**	*[lah moo-chah-chah]*
the daughter	**la hija**	*[lah ee-hah]*
the sister	**la hermana**	*[lah ehr-mah-nah]*
the grandmother	**la abuela**	*[lah ah-bweh-lah]*
the aunt	**la tía**	*[lah tee-ah]*
the cat (female)	**la gata**	*[lah gah-tah]*
the dog (female)	**la perra**	*[lah peh-rrah]*
the house	**la casa**	*[lah kah-sah]*
the food	**la comida**	*[lah koh-mee-dah]*
the chair	**la silla**	*[lah see-yah]*

Some feminine nouns end in **-ción, -sión, -dad, -tad, or -tud**:

the conversation	**la conversación**	*[lah kohn-behr-sah-syohn]*
the television	**la televisión**	*[lah teh-leh-bee-syohn]*
the truth	**la verdad**	*[lah behr-dahd]*
the city	**la ciudad**	*[lah syoo-dahd]*
The drugstore	**la farmacia**	*[lah fahr-mah-thyah]*
the friendship	**la amistad**	*[lah ah-mees-tahd]*

And just like the exceptions with masculine nouns, other feminine nouns end in **-o**:

the photograph	**la foto**	*[lah foh-toh]*
the hand	**la mano**	*[lah mah-noh]*
the radio	**la radio**	*[lah rrah-dyoh]*
the motorcycle	**la moto**	*[lah moh-toh]*

Since many feminine nouns don't follow a regular pattern, you need to learn each noun with its article, so you don't make mistakes like saying, "el mano," when it should be "**la mano**."

Plural Nouns

So far, we've only covered singular nouns. That is, just one object, place, or thing. But what if you wanted to refer to multiple friends, not just one friend? Or many books, not just a single book? This is where plural nouns come in.

In English, we usually indicate that there is *more* than one thing by adding 's' to the end of the word, like 'friends' or 'books.' In Spanish, plurality is also indicated by modifying the *ending* of the word.

If the Spanish singular noun ends in a vowel, like **amigo** (friend) or **mesa** (table), then we indicate plurality by ending the word with **-s.** So, in this case...

Amigo → Amigos

Mesa → Mesas

If you're referring to more than one friend, you would then use the word **amigos**, and for more than one table, you would use **mesas.**

If the Spanish singular noun ends up with a consonant (except for 'z') instead of a vowel, like **animal** (animal) or **ciudad** (city), then in this instance, we indicate plurality by ending the word with **-es.** So this would look like...

Animal → Animales

Ciudad → Ciudades

When you're talking about multiple animals, you would use the word **animales,** and for multiple cities, you would use the word **ciudades.**

Now, let's look at the final way of pluralizing a noun. If the Spanish singular noun ends in a 'z,' such as **lápiz** (pencil) or **nariz** (nose), we indicate plurality by **removing the 'z'** and ending the word with **-ces.** For example...

Lápiz → Lápices

Nariz → Narices

Hopefully, you're getting the hang of this by now! If you're referring to multiple pencils, you'd use the word **lápices.** And for multiple noses, you would use the word **narices**.

You might notice that something is missing – the definite article. How do we say 'the tables' or 'the cities?

Just like the nouns, the definite articles are also modified to indicate plurality. We must also keep in mind the gender of the noun!

The masculine definite article **el** becomes **los.**

The feminine definite article **la** becomes **las.**

For example...

El amigo → los amigos

La casa → las casas

> **Tip:** Remember that in Spanish, if we're referring to multiple people that consist of both females and males, we use the masculine plurality by default. So, you would use the term **los amigos** when referring to your friends if your friends include both males and females.
>
> To clarify...
>
> **Los amigos =** male friends OR male friends + female friends

> **Tip**: Keep in mind that, just like in English, we don't always need to use the definite article. In English, the definite article is the word 'the', and in Spanish, this is **el, la, los,** and **las.** So, when do you need to use the definite article?
>
> First, let's just quickly go over what the point of the definite article is. Let's use an English example.

If you have a salad in your fridge that you really need to eat before it goes bad, you would say "I need to eat *the* salad." Using the definite article indicates that you have a specific salad in mind. It's already there and it's just waiting to be eaten!

However, if you feel like you've been eating too much fast food lately, you might say "I need to eat *a* salad." In this case, you don't have a specific salad in mind, you just need to eat any salad. That's why we call it the *definite* article because there is more certainty and specificity implied.

These rules about when to use the definite article also apply to Spanish – but a couple of extra ones are added on top. Let's summarize!

In Spanish, the definite article (**el, la, los, las**) is used...

- To refer to a specific person or thing.
  La mujer de Adán es Eva (*Eve is Adam's woman*)
- To refer to something in a broad sense. It's the article that precedes the noun. **Me gusta la carne** (*I like meat*) or **me gusta la musica** (*I like music)*
- To refer to parts of your own body. The possessive is already established in the verb, so it's not necessary to repeat it. You only need an article. **Me rompí el brazo** (*I broke my arm*)

Time to practice what we've learned—let's dive in!

1.2 Practice

A. What's the appropriate masculine or feminine form of the definite article (the) for each noun? And while you're at it, try translating the word to see if you remember the meaning!

1. foto
2. hospital
3. televisión
4. casa
5. libro
6. ciudad
7. conversación
8. hijo
9. planeta
10. amigo
11. mapa
12. programa
13. sistema
14. problema
15. hotel
16. persona
17. animal
18. comida
19. mano
20. teléfono

> **Common Mistake**: The noun **día** (*day*) ends in **-a** but is masculine: **el día** (*the day*). So don't say, **la día**!

B. Write the plural version of each singular noun. When you finish, read each pair out loud.

1. El hombre ______________________
2. La amiga ______________________
3. La conversación ______________________
4. El animal ______________________
5. El sistema ______________________
6. El niño ______________________
7. La casa ______________________
8. El tren ______________________
9. La ciudad ______________________
10. El doctor ______________________

C. Write the singular version of each plural noun. When you finish, read each pair out loud.

1. Las verdades ______________________
2. Las televisiones ______________________
3. Las manos ______________________
4. Las perras ______________________
5. Los lápices ______________________
6. Las niñas ______________________
7. Las radios ______________________
8. Las comidas ______________________

1.3 The Indefinite Article

So, we've already talked about the definite article. What about the indefinite article? Remember when we talked about the difference between "I need to eat *the* salad" and "I need to eat *a* salad"? As you can probably guess, it's in '*a* salad' where the indefinite article is used. We use the indefinite article to refer to a thing that is non-specific.

In English, the indefinite article is *a* or *an*. In Spanish, the indefinite articles are...

Masculine, singular: **un** (*a/an*)
Masculine, plural: **unos** (*some*)

Feminine, singular: **una** (*a/an*)
Feminine, plural: **unas** (*some*)

For example:

Una amiga *[uhnah ah-mee-gah] (a female friend)* → **unas amigas** *[uhnahs ah-mee-gahs] (some female friends)*

Un hijo *[uhn ee-hoh] (a son)* → **unos hijos** *[uhnohs ee-hohs] (some sons)*

To summarize, you only use the indefinite article (**un, unos, una, unas**) when:

- You want to identify someone or something as part of a class or group: **es un animal** (*it's an animal*)
- You want to refer to something in a non-specific way: **un bote es para navegar** (*a boat is for sailing*) or **es una mujer joven** (*She's a young woman*)

Quick Recap

	MASCULINE SINGULAR NOUNS	MASCULINE PLURAL NOUNS	FEMININE SINGULAR NOUNS	FEMININE PLURAL NOUNS
DEFINITE ARTICLES	**el** amigo (the male friend)	**los** amigos (the male friends)	**la** amiga (the female friend)	**las** amigas (the female friends)
INDEFINITE ARTICLES	**un** amigo (a male friend)	**unos** amigos (some male friends or some female and male friends)	**una** amiga (a female friend)	**unas** amigas (some female friends)

Tip: Un and **una** (*a* and *an*) can mean *one* as well as *a* or *an*. You will understand which one it means based on the context. For example, **Un** niño (*a boy*) vs. Compro **un** tomate (*I buy one tomato*).

Ready to flex those newfound skills? It's practice time!

1.3 Practice

A. Turn these singular nouns with indefinite articles into plural nouns with their indefinite articles.

1. un abuelo: ____________________
2. una conversación: ____________________
3. un perro: ____________________
4. una mujer: ____________________
5. un estudiante: ____________________
6. un doctor: ____________________
7. un hotel: ____________________
8. un tren: ____________________
9. un lápiz: ____________________
10. una ciudad: ____________________

B. Complete the sentences with **el, la, los, las** or **un, una, unos, unas**

> **Tip: de + el = del.** When **de** (*of*) is followed by **el** (*the*), the words contract to **del** (*of the*), so if the question asks "**de"** followed by the answer "**el",** you can add an "**l**" in the answer space, to make it "**del**"

1. __________ casa de Juan.
2. Encontré (*I found*) __________ moneda. (*coin*)
3. Es __________ cabeza (*head*) de __________ león.
4. Eso es __________ huella. (*footprint*)
5. Son __________ amigas de mi hermana. (*they are some friends of my sisters*)
6. Me gusta __________ pollo. (I like chicken)
7. Llevo __________ pastel a tu casa. (*I'm taking a cake to your house*)
8. Pedro compra __________ bebidas para la fiesta. (*Pedro is buying the drinks for the party*)

C. Complete these sentences with the right definite or indefinite article

(**el – la – los – las – un – una – unos – unas**)

1. Washington es __________ ciudad en Estados Unidos.
2. Hudson es __________ calle *(street)* de tu casa.
3. Bogotá es __________ capital de Colombia.
4. __________ casa de Elena es grande.
5. __________ Papa *(Pope)* vive en Roma.
6. Necesito (*I need*) __________ chaqueta (*jacket*) roja.
7. ¿Tienes __________ llaves (*keys*) de la casa?
8. Vi (*I saw*) __________ león (*lion*) grande en el zoológico (*zoo*).

CHAPTER 2:

VERBS IN THE PRESENT TENSE

BACK TO BASICS

2.1 Ser and Estar *(To Be)*

In English, we use the word '**is**' (third person singular form of the verb "to be") to say both "the car is red" (description) and "the car is here" (location), even though you're describing different types of attributes about the car.

In Spanish, you wouldn't use the same word for different types of descriptions.

Yes, you can say **el coche** es **rojo** (the car is red), but you can't use the same word to indicate the location of the car.

To indicate location, you would say **el coche** está **aquí** (the car is here).

Let's look at the two verbs in these sentences, **es** and **está**. While **es** is rooted in the verb **ser**, which means 'to be,' **está** is rooted in the verb **estar**. And guess what? It also means 'to be'! That's right, in English, **ser** and **estar** both mean the same thing, but in Spanish, they describe different types of indications.

Generally, **ser** is used to describe:

- The nature of something or someone
- The identity of something or someone
- Time
- Events

ser (*to be*)			
yo	**soy**	nosotros/as	**somos**
tú	**eres**	vosotros/as	**sois**
usted él ella	**es**	ustedes ellos ellas	**son**

While, **estar** is used to talk about:

- Location
- Health
- Changing mood or condition
- Personal opinion

estar (*to be*)			
yo	**estoy**	nosotros/as	**estamos**
tú	**estás**	vosotros/as	**estáis**
usted él ella	**está**	ustedes ellos ellas	**están**

Got the concepts down? Now, let's apply them with some good old practice!

2.1 Practice

A. What are these objects made of? Example: ¿De qué es la mesa? Es de madera.

1. ¿De qué es la botella (*bottle*)? ____________________
2. ¿De qué es la silla? ____________________
3. ¿De qué es la casa? ____________________
4. ¿De qué son los zapatos? ____________________
5. ¿De qué son las ventanas? ____________________
6. ¿De qué es el piso (*floor*)? ____________________
7. ¿De qué es el coche? ____________________
8. ¿De qué es la hoja (*page*)? ____________________

B. Use the right form of the verb **ser**:

1. Usted ____________ musulmán.
2. Yo ____________ casada.
3. Nosotros ____________ solteros.
4. Martín ____________ chino.
5. Elena y Sofía ____________ brasileñas.
6. Tú ____________ blanco.

7. Vosotros _______________ cristianos.
8. María __________________ mexicana.
9. Tú y Martín _____________ amigos.

C. See if you can tell which verb to use, **ser** or **estar**, according to the meaning of each sentence, and match the verb to the subject in person and number.

   Example: María y Juan <u>están</u> tristes.

   1. La mesa y las sillas ___________ sucias.
   2. Él ___________ abogado.
   3. Nosotros ___________ cansados.
   4. ___________ importante estudiar.
   5. Vosotros ___________ en la universidad.
   6. Martín y Luis ___________ inteligentes.
   7. El café ___________ para la mujer.
   8. La ciudad ___________ hermosa.
   9. Tú ___________ una turista.
   10. Yo ___________ de Guatemala.
   11. La lección ___________ fácil.
   12. El niño ___________ en el colegio.
   13. Ustedes ___________ contentos.
   14. Nosotros ___________ italianos.
   15. Sara ___________ triste.

2.2 Tener *(To Have)*

Tener is an extremely useful verb to know as it indicates that you possess something. In English this would mean 'to have.'

tener (*to have*)			
yo	**tengo**	nosotros/as	**tenemos**
tú	**tienes**	vosotros/as	**tenéis**
usted él ella	**tiene**	ustedes ellos ellas	**tienen**

> **Tip:** The **yo** form of tener is irregular. It should be "**teno**", but it's **tengo**. In other forms, the stem vowel **e** becomes **ie**: **tienes**.

In Spanish, we also use the verb **tener** (*to have*) to say how old we are. Instead of saying you *are of* a certain age, you say that you *have* a certain number of years.

I am [number] years old = Tengo [number] años.

In Spanish, you cannot omit the word **años** in this expression.

Here are some translations of sentences expressing age:

I am thirty years old.	**Tengo treinta años.**
You are twenty-three years old.	**Tienes veintitrés años.**
He/she is forty years old.	**Tiene cuarenta años.**

Time to roll up your sleeves and practice!

2.2 Practice

A. Complete the following sentences using the correct verb form of **tener**.

1. Yo ____________________ muchos zapatos.
2. Nosotros ______________ muchos amigos.
3. Marcos ________________ un libro.
4. Tú ____________________ muchos gatos.
5. Vosotros ______________ una abuela buena.
6. Ella ___________________ un lápiz rojo.
7. Carlos y María _________ una hija.
8. Usted _________________ un sistema excelente.
9. Laura _________________ 32 años.

B. Write the correct form of **tener** to convey these people's ages:

1. Manuel y José _________ veintiún años.
2. Yo ____________________ cincuenta años.
3. Tú ____________________ dieciocho años.
4. Marina y yo ___________ treinta años.
5. Vosotros ______________ veinticinco años.

6. Mi abuelo ______________ setenta años.
7. Mi abuela ______________ sesenta y cinco años.
8. Ellas ___________________ cuarenta y dos años.

2.3 Hacer *(To do/ to make)*

Let's learn some more verbs. **Hacer** is a useful verb that allows you to say, 'to do' or 'to make.' It's helpful when we're talking about activities!

Hacer is an irregular verb, which means that it looks different depending on the pronouns that are next to it.

hacer (*to do/ to make*)			
yo	**hago**	nosotros/as	**hacemos**
tú	**haces**	vosotros/as	**hacéis**
usted él ella	**hace**	ustedes ellos ellas	**hacen**

Hacer can also be used to talk about the weather in an impersonal way. In this case, we use it as a third-person verb, just like we would use it for the pronouns for 'he' or 'she.' It looks like this...

It's cold: **hace frío**
It's hot: **hace calor**
It's windy: **hace viento**
It's sunny: **hace sol**

Vocabulary: the weather

Nubes: clouds → hay nubes/ está nublado

Lluvia: rain → hay lluvia/ está lloviendo/ llueve

Nieve: snow → hay nieve/ está nevando/ nieva

Viento: wind → hay viento/ está ventoso/ ventea

Let's spice things up with a practical exercise—time to practice!

2.3 Practice

Use the appropriate form of **hacer** (*to do/ to make*) in these sentences:

1. Nosotros ______________________ las maletas. (*suitcases*)
2. Juan e Isabel __________________ un pastel.
3. Yo ____________________________ ejercicio. (*exercise*)
4. Los niños ______________________ la tarea. (*homework*)
5. ______________________________ calor.
6. Mi hermana ____________________ yoga.
7. Tú ____________________________ deporte.
8. Vosotros _______________________ natación.
9. ______________________________ mucho frío.

2.4 Regular Verbs

Verbs in Spanish ending in **-ar, -er,** and **-ir** are called *regular verbs* because they all follow a regular pattern. As we've discussed, Spanish verbs change according to the person and the number of the subject. They're much simpler to modify when we're dealing with regular verbs!

Verbs Ending in -ar

The -ar verbs follow the pattern of **hablar.** Below are some of them:

English	Spanish	Pronunciation
to work	**trabajar**	*[trah-bah-hahr]*
to study	**estudiar**	*[ehs-too-dyahr]*
to look	**mirar**	*[mee-rahr]*
to arrive	**llegar**	*[yeh-gahr]*
to look for	**buscar**	*[boos-kahrr]*
to teach	**enseñar**	*[ehn-seh-nyar]*
to buy	**comprar**	*[kohm-prahr]*
to need	**necesitar**	*[neh-theh-see-tahr]*
to pay	**pagar**	*[pah-gahr]*
to return (to a place)	**regresar**	*[rreh-greh-sahr]*

English	Spanish	Pronunciation
to take/to drink	**tomar**	*[toh-mahr]*
to prepare	**preparar**	*[preh-pah-rahr]*
to fix	**arreglar**	*[ah-rreh-glahr]*
to travel	**viajar**	*[biah-hahr]*
to explain	**explicar**	*[ehks-plee-kahr]*

The present tense form of verbs ending in **-ar** is conjugated by removing the infinitive **-ar** ending and replacing it with an ending corresponding to the person that is performing the action of the verb. See below:

hablar (*to speak*)			
yo	**habl-o**	nosotros/as	**habl-amos**
tú	**habla-s**	vosotros/as	**habl-áis**
usted él ella	**habl-a**	ustedes ellos ellas	**habl-an**

Verbs Ending in -er

The **-er** verbs follow the pattern of **comer.** Below are some of them:

English	Spanish	Pronunciation
to learn	**aprender**	*[ah-prehn-dehr]*
to eat	**comer**	*[koh-mehr]*
to drink	**beber**	*[beh-behr]*
to understand	**comprender**	*[kohm-prehn-dehr]*
to think to believe in	**creer (en)**	*[kreh-ehr]*
should, must, ought to (do something)	**deber (+ infinitivo)**	*[deh-behr]*
to read	**leer**	*[leh-ehr]*
to sell	**vender**	*[behn-dehr]*
to put in	**meter**	*[meh-tehr]*
to turn on	**prender**	*[prehn-dehr]*

English	Spanish	Pronunciation
to run	**correr**	*[koh-rrehr]*
to break	**romper**	*[rrohm-pehr]*
to fix	**arreglar**	*[ah-rreh-glahr]*
to travel	**viajar**	*[biah-hahr]*
to explain	**explicar**	*[ehks-plee-kahr]*

You'll notice that all these verbs end in **-er**! When we're speaking in the present tense, we remove the **-er** from verbs like the ones in the table above, and we add a new ending depending on the pronoun that goes before it. See the diagram box below for the rules on how to modify the endings of these verbs for each pronoun.

comer (*to eat*)			
yo	**com-o**	nosotros/as	**com-emos**
tú	**com-es**	vosotros/as	**com-éis**
usted él ella	**com-e**	ustedes ellos ellas	**co-men**

Verbs Ending in -ir

The **-ir** verbs follow the pattern of **vivir.** Below are some of them:

English	Spanish	Pronunciation
to open	**abrir**	*[ah-breer]*
to write	**escribir**	*[ehs-kree-beer]*
to receive	**recibir**	*[rreh-thee-beer]*
to share	**compartir**	*[kohm-pahr-teer]*
to decide	**decidir**	*[deh-thee-deer]*
to describe	**describir**	*[dehs-kree-beer]*
to discuss	**discutir**	*[dees-koo-teer]*
to go up	**subir**	*[soo-beer]*
to suffer	**sufrir**	*[soo-freer]*

We talked about how to modify verbs ending in **-er**, but what about verbs that end in **-ir**? To use these verbs in the present tense, we remove the **-ir** ending and change it according to the subject. See below how these verbs are modified:

vivir (*to live*)			
yo	**vivo**	nosotros/as	**vivimos**
tú	**vives**	vosotros/as	**vivís**
usted él ella	**vive**	ustedes ellos ellas	**viven**

Tip: In English, a verb must have an expressed subject (**he** eats spaghetti). In Spanish, 'he' or 'she' is not always necessary. Why? Because it's obvious from the verb who you are referring to. People tend to omit using subject pronouns unless you want to clarify who's doing the action or place emphasis on it.

Common Mistake: You might feel it's natural to add a pronoun in Spanish but think twice before you do it. Most of the time, your verbs will do the work for you!

X DON'T SAY	✓ SAY INSTEAD
Yo quiero un café. *(I want a coffee)*	**Quiero un café.**
Nosotros queremos ir a la playa mañana. *(We want to go to the beach tomorrow)*	**Queremos ir a la playa mañana.**

Ready to play with words? Let's practice!

2.4 Practice

A. Answer these questions of conjugating the verbs ending in -ar to match the person performing the action.

1. Mi padre __________ (trabajar) de lunes a viernes.
2. Tus hijos __________ (mirar) demasiada televisión.
3. Vosotros __________ (buscar) buenos zapatos.
4. La profesora Oliva __________ (enseñar) tres clases.
5. __________ (yo/comprar) frutas y verduras todas las semanas.
6. Teresa y Pedro __________ (viajar) en tren al trabajo.
7. Nosotros les __________ (explicar) a nuestros hijos cómo comportarse (*how to behave*).
8. El señor Romanelli __________ (arreglar) carteras.

B. Complete these sentences with the appropriate form of the right verb. Use each verb once.

beber – comprender – prender – leer – correr – comer – aprender – vender

1. El niño no ____________________ la lección.
2. Luis y María ____________________ la televisión.
3. La muchacha ____________________ al colegio para (*to*) no llegar tarde (*late*).
4. Nosotros ____________________ la casa.
5. Vosotros ____________________ en ese (*that*) restaurante excelente.
6. Tú y yo ____________________ mucha agua.
7. Todos los domingos ____________ (yo) el periódico.
8. Todos los días ________________ (tú) algo (something).

C. Fill in the blanks with the correct verb form:

Infinitive	comer	vender	creer	apender
yo	como			aprendo
tú		vendes		
él/ ella/ usted			cree	
nosotros	comemos			aprendemos
vosotros		vendéis		
ellas/ ellos/ ustedes			creen	

D. Complete these sentences with the appropriate form of the correct verbs listed. Use each verb once.

vivir – subir- escribir- recibir – discutir – decidir – compartir – abrir

1. Los niños ___________ los caramelos (*candy*).
2. Todas las estudiantes ___________ las escaleras para ir a (*to go to*) la clase de matemáticas.
3. Marcos ___________ en la ciudad; María ___________ en el campo (*country*)
4. Yo ___________ la puerta (*door*).
5. Tú ___________ a tus amigos en tu casa.
6. Vosotros ___________ cartas (*letters*) a vuestros padres.
7. Nosotros ___________ las noticias (*the news*) con mi marido (*husband*).
8. Tú ___________ estudiar español.

E. Fill in the blanks with the correct verb form:

Infinitive	escribir	recibir	abrir	subir
yo	escribo			subo
tú		recibes		
él/ella/ usted			abre	
nosotros	escribimos			subimos
vosotros		recibís		
ellas/ellos/ustedes			abren	

CHAPTER 3:

SABER AND CONOCER

TO KNOW IS KNOWING YOU KNOW NOTHING

3.1 To Know: *Saber*

The verb **saber** means 'to know' in English. However, just like some of the verbs we've discussed in prior chapters, it's not the only Spanish verb that has this meaning! **Saber** refers to a very specific type of knowledge. It's only used when we're talking about knowing facts, information, and skills. It *can't* be used when talking about knowing people, places, or things.

When *know* refers to *knowing facts* and *learned skills*, use **saber**.

For example, **sé matemáticas** *(I know mathematics)* or **sé nadar** (*I know how to swim*).

saber *(to know)*			
yo	**sé**	nosotros/as	**sabemos**
tú	**sabes**	vosotros/as	**sabéis**
usted él ella	**sabe**	ustedes ellos ellas	**saben**

Saber is an irregular verb. But the only irregularity is with **sé**, which is used when talking about yourself in singular form. Normally, with verbs that end in *-er*, you would knock off the *er*, and add an *o* (**sabo** X). But with **saber**, it's just **sé** if you're talking only about yourself.

For example:

Yo sé (I know). **No sé** (I don't know).

Tip: The first person singular of **saber** is **sé** with an accent. Be careful, because there is another word in Spanish that looks the same, but it doesn't have an accent: the **se** for reflexive verbs—**se lava** (pronoun)

Theory's backstage; it's showtime for practice! Get ready to shine in the language spotlight.

3.1 Practice

Write the appropriate form of the verb **saber** in each sentence.

1. Nosotros ______________ español.
2. Tú ______________ el teléfono de Luis.
3. Vosotros ______________ la verdad.
4. ¿Elena ______________ ese poema?
5. Yo ______________ francés. (*French*)
6. María ______________ la lección.
7. Pedro y José ______________ alemán. (*German*)
8. Él ______________ bailar el vals. (*dance the waltz*)

3.2 To Know: *Conocer*

The other word for 'to know' is **conocer.** Unlike **saber,** you would use **conocer** when talking about knowing certain people or things.

When *know* refers to *being familiar or being acquainted with something or someone*, use **conocer**. For example, **conozco a Luis** (*I know Luis*).

conocer *(to be familiar with* **or** *to meet)*			
yo	**conozco**	nosotros/as	**conocemos**
tú	**conoces**	vosotros/as	**conocéis**
usted él ella	**conoce**	ustedes ellos ellas	**conocen**

Conocer is also an irregular verb. Here, too, the only irregularity is for the singular form of the first-person pronoun. Normally, with verbs that end in *-er*, you would knock off the *er*, and add an *o* (**conoco** X). But with **conocer**, you knock off the **cer** and add **zco**.

For example:

Yo conozco (*I know*). **No conozco** (*I don't know*). Every other person is the same as a regular *-er* verb: *tú conoces, él conoce, nosotros conocemos*, and so on.

The journey continues! Time to dive into the sea of practice, where each wave carries a lesson.

3.2 Practice

A. Write the appropriate form of the verb **conocer** in each sentence.

1. Elena y Pedro __________ a la profesora.
2. Juan __________________ al doctor Pérez.
3. Vosotros ______________ el sistema.
4. Nosotros ______________ la comida francesa.
5. Yo ____________________ la casa.
6. María _________________ la ciudad.
7. Tú ____________________ el Louvre.
8. Él _____________________ al turista.

B. Now let's see if you can tell when to use **saber** and when to use **conocer**. Choose one of the two and conjugate it to make it fit in the sentence.

Example: María ___________ (conocer / saber) inglés → <u>María sabe inglés</u>.

1. Tomás ________________ (conocer / saber) el sur de España.
2. Vosotros ______________ (conocer / saber) contar hasta diez en alemán.
3. Elena y Pablo __________ (conocer / saber) jugar al golf.
4. Él no _________________ (conocer / saber) si hace frío.
5. María ________________ (conocer / saber) esa avenida.
6. Tú ___________________ (conocer / saber) esa historia.
7. Yo ___________________ (conocer / saber) dónde vive Jorge (*where Jorge lives*).
8. Sara y tú ______________ (conocer / saber) las reglas del Monopoly.

C. Here, you are required to choose the right verb and conjugate it. You do not need to use the pronoun; it's just a cue to tell you how to conjugate the verb.

1. ________________________ (yo - conocer / saber) a Matías.
2. No _____________________ (nosotros - conocer / saber) dónde está el gato.

3. ________________ (vosotros - conocer / saber) muy bien las obras de Albéniz.
4. Mi hermana no ________ (conocer / sabe) ese grupo musical (*band*).
5. ¿________________ (tú - saber / conocer) a qué hora empieza (*starts*) la película?
6. Mis primos ________ (saber / conocer) cinco idiomas.
7. ________________ (yo - conocer / saber) Brasil muy bien.
8. ¿________________ (él - conocer / saber) a tu novio (*boyfriend*)?
9. Isabel y Luisa ________ (conocer / saber) la lección muy bien.

> **Tip**: When you're talking about knowing a person, in Spanish you add **a** before the person: **Conoce a María**.

D. Decide if you should add an **a** after the verb conocer, depending on if what is known is a person or something else. Write the **a** in case it's needed or an **X** when you don't need it.

Example: Tú conoces ________ Pedro → Tú conoces <u>a</u> Pedro.

1. Julia conoce ________ Italia.
2. Conozco ________ una profesora que sabe seis idiomas.
3. Conocemos ________ el camino al restaurante.
4. Conocéis ________ muchos países del mundo.
5. Mi padre conoce ________ mi novio. *(boyfriend)*
6. ¿Conoces ________ Luis?
7. Patricia y tú conocéis ________ la señorita Martí.

3.3 Saber + Infinitive: To know how to do something

We've mentioned a lot of infinitive verbs so far. In fact, **saber** itself is an infinitive verb. It's the root word of every word, which means "to know "or "to play." When you use **saber** before an infinitive verb, you're saying that you *know* how to do something.

Sé hablar francés. *(I know how to speak French*)

Here are some verbs and specific activities in the infinitive form that you can combine with **saber** to express your knowledge of a certain ability. Like, for example, **sabe nadar** *(he knows how to swim)*, **sabe hablar <u>español</u>**. (*he knows how to speak Spanish*).

Which of the following do you know how to do?

English	Spanish	Pronunciation
to swim	**nadar**	*[nah-dahr]*
to dance	**bailar**	*[bay-lahr]*
to sing	**cantar**	*[khan-tahr]*
to do artistic gymnastics	**hacer gimnasia artística**	*[ha-ther heem-nah-syah ahr-tees-tee-kah]*
to play tennis	**jugar al tenis**	*[hoo-gahr ahl teh-nees]*
to play the piano	**tocar el piano**	*[toh-kahr ehl pyah-noh]*
to play golf	**jugar al golf**	*[hoo-gahr ahl golf]*
to play football	**jugar al fútbol**	*[hoo-gahr ahl foot-bohl]*
to play basketball	**jugar al baloncesto**	*[hoo-gahr ahl bah-lohn-thehs-toh]*
to write novels	**escribir novelas**	*[ehs-kree-beer noh-beh-lahs]*
to speak	**hablar**	*[ah-blahr]*
to act	**actuar**	*[ahk-twahr]*

3.3. Practice

A. What do these people know how to do? Use the verb saber + the right infinitive and direct object to complete the sentences.

Example: Serena Williams sabe jugar al tenis.

1. Novak Djokovic ____________________
2. LeBron James ____________________
3. Tiger Woods ____________________
4. J. K. Rowling ____________________
5. Lionel Messi y Cristiano Ronaldo ____________________
6. Taylor Swift ____________________
7. Michael Phelps ____________________
8. Shakira ____________________
9. Meryl Streep ____________________
10. Simon Biles ____________________

B. Who do these famous people know? Write the appropriate sentence, picking a person from the right row and finding the correct match on the left. Remember to add the **a** after **conocer** (**conocer a + person**).

Example: El señor Increíble conoce a Elastigirl.

Sherlock Holmes	Dakota Johnson
Ashton Kutcher	Eva
Rhett Butler	Hailey Bieber
Chris Martin	Victoria Beckham
David Beckham	Watson
Adán	Scarlett O'Hara
Justin Bieber	Mila Kunis

1. ______________________________
2. ______________________________
3. ______________________________
4. ______________________________
5. ______________________________
6. ______________________________
7. ______________________________

C. Write a sentence following the cues given:

Example: (conocer)____________. (Laura/la tía Julia) → Laura conoce a la tía Julia

1. (conocer) ____________________ (yo/el profesor Blanco)
2. (conocer) ____________________ (mi hermana y yo/la madre de Juan)
3. (conocer) ____________________ (María y Luis/Sergio)
4. (conocer) ____________________(vosotros/director del área comercial)
5. (conocer) ____________________ (tú/tía Julia)
6. (conocer) ____________________ (Carlos/la tía Julia)
7. (conocer) ____________________ (Martín y Elena/la tía Julia)

D. Translate using **saber** or **conocer** depending on the context. Remember:

Conocer = to be familiar with something or someone.

Saber = to know facts and learned skills.

1. I know the truth. ______________________
2. She knows Maria. ______________________
3. They know how to swim. ______________________
4. Pedro and Elena know New York. ______________________
5. We know the answer. ______________________
6. We know the student. ______________________
7. You know my name. ______________________
8. He knows the truth. ______________________
9. The dog knows Juan. ______________________
10. I know how to play the piano. ______________________
11. We know the university. ______________________

E. **Saber or Conocer?** Choose the right verb to complete the sentence.

1. María no ______________ (sabe / conoce) nadar todavía (*yet*).
2. No ______________ (sé / conozco) esta computadora.
3. ¿______________ (sabes / conoces) Australia?
4. ¿______________ (conocen / saben) el teléfono de Luis?
5. Carlos no ______________ (conoce / sabe) al doctor.

CHAPTER 4:

NUMBERS

ONE, TWO, BUCKLE MY SHOE

If we're going to express the quantity of something, we obviously need to know our numbers. Just like in English, they're also essential for telling the date and time!

4.1 Numbers

#	English	Spanish	Pronunciation
0	zero	**cero**	*[theh-roh]*
1	one	**uno**	*[oo-noh]*
2	two	**dos**	*[dohs]*
3	three	**tres**	*[trehs]*
4	four	**cuatro**	*[kwah-troh]*
5	five	**cinco**	*[theen-koh]*
6	six	**seis**	*[seys]*
7	seven	**siete**	*[syeh-teh]*
8	eight	**ocho**	*[oh-choh]*
9	nine	**nueve**	*[nweh-beh]*
10	ten	**diez**	*[dyehth]*
11	eleven	**once**	*[ohn-theh]*
12	twelve	**doce**	*[doh-theh]*
13	thirteen	**trece**	*[treh-theh]*
14	fourteen	**catorce**	*[kah-tohr-theh]*
15	fifteen	**quince**	*[keen-theh]*
16	sixteen	**dieciséis**	*[dyeh-thee-seys]*
17	seventeen	**diecisiete**	*[dyeh-thee-syeh-teh]*
18	eighteen	**dieciocho**	*[dyeh-thee-oh-choh]*
19	nineteen	**diecinueve**	*[dyeh-thee-nweh-beh]*
20	twenty	**veinte**	*[beyn-teh]*

Ready to play with words? Let's practice!

4.1. Practice

Complete with **Uno, Una,** or **Un** according to each sentence.

Example: ________________ perro → Un perro.

1. Tiene ______________ año.
2. Tiene ______________ lápiz.
3. Tenemos ____________ gata.
4. __________________, dos, tres, cuatro.
5. __________________ hombre está caminando (*A man is walking*).
6. __________________ flor amarilla

4.2 There Is and There Are: Hay

Statements with hay

The word **hay** (pronounced like the English *eye*) means 'there is' and 'there are.' As you know, it's a useful way of describing the contents or arrangement of something. You can also use **hay** to turn something into a sentence by essentially saying 'is there?' or 'are there?'

You'll be relieved to know that **hay** is used for both singular and plural nouns. Whether you're talking about one cat in the house or more than one cat in the house, you would still use **hay** in either case.

Hay un gato en la casa (singular)

Hay gatos en la casa (plural)

Common Mistake: Don't use the Spanish definite articles **el, la, los,** and **las** (*the*) after **hay**. Use, instead, the definite articles after **hay**: **un, unos, una, unas.**

X Don't say: **Hay el lápiz en la mesa.**

✓ Say: **Hay un lápiz en la mesa** (*there is a pencil on the table*)

Tip: When **hay** is followed by a plural noun, you don't need the article:

X Don't say: **Hay las flores en el jardín**.
✓ Say: **Hay flores en el jardín**.

English	Spanish
There are fifteen dogs in the street	**Hay quince perros en la calle**
There is one person in the office	**Hay una persona en la oficina**
There is a tree in the yard	**Hay un árbol en el jardín**
There is a lot of food in the supermarket	**Hay mucha comida en el supermercado**
There are two German tourists on the train	**Hay dos turistas alemanes en el tren**

Get your learning hat on; it's time for some hands-on practice!

4.2. Practice

A. Look at these sentences and decide if you should leave them as they are (write a check mark next to them) or if they need to be changed. In that case, write the correct sentence next to them.

Example: Hay un gato en el jardín ✓

1. Hay la alfombra en la casa.____________________
2. Hay los tigres en el zoológico.____________________
3. Hay manzanas en la verdulería.____________________
4. Hay un cuadro en el museo.____________________
5. Hay las oficinas en el edificio.____________________
6. Hay muchos niños en el colegio. ____________________
7. Hay los turistas en la ciudad.____________________
8. Hay las personas en el cine. ____________________

The Negative with Hay

To make a sentence negative, just add a **no** before **hay**:

No hay quince perros en la calle. → *There are not fifteen dogs in the street.*

No hay dos turistas alemanes en el tren. →*There are not two German tourists on the train.*

The Interrogative With Hay

To ask a question with **hay**, follow the same order as with the statement, but add a question mark at the beginning and the end of the sentence, as all Spanish interrogative sentences are. If you're speaking this sentence out loud, you can use the tone of your voice to indicate that you're asking a question, just like you do in English. With a simple rising intonation, you can convey that you're asking a question, not making a statement.

English	Spanish	Pronunciation
Are there two dogs in the street?	**¿Hay dos perros en la calle?**	*[eye dohs peh-rrohs ehn lah kah-yeh]*
Is there one person in the office?	**¿Hay una persona en la oficina?**	*[eye uhnah pehr-soh-nah ehn lah oh-fee-thee-nah]*
Is there a tree in the yard?	**¿Hay un árbol en el jardín?**	*[eye uhn ahr-bohl ehn ehl hahr-deen]*
Is there a lot of food in the supermarket?	**¿Hay mucha comida en el supermercado?**	*[eye moo-chah koh-mee-dah ehn ehl soo-pehr-mehr-kah-doh]*
Are there two German tourists on the train?	**¿Hay dos turistas alemanes en el tren?**	*[eye dohs too-rees-tahs ah-leh-mahn ehn ehl trehn]*

Difference between **hay** and **estar**

Use **hay** (there is/there are) when you're talking about the existence of something/someone. For example, **hay un museo en mi ciudad** (*There is a museum in my city*)**.**

Use **estar,** which means 'to be,' when you're talking about where something or someone *is*. For example, **el colegio está en la esquina** (*The school is on the corner*)

Ready to apply what you've learned? Let's practice!

B. Translate the following to English:

Example: ¿Hay lápices en tu casa? <u>Are there pencils in your house?</u>

1. ¿Hay flores en el jardín? ____________________
2. ¿Hay sillas en la oficina? ____________________
3. ¿Hay gatos en la calle? ____________________
4. ¿Hay hoteles en la ciudad? ____________________
5. ¿Hay una televisión en la casa? ____________________
6. ¿Hay doctores en el hospital? ____________________
7. ¿Hay un perro en el coche? ____________________
8. ¿Hay una radio en el coche? ____________________
9. ¿Hay dos mujeres en la pescadería?____________________
10. ¿Hay mesas en un restaurante? ____________________

C. Turn these affirmative sentences into negative sentences. Place **no** before **hay**.

1. Hay animales en el zoológico: ____________________
2. Hay muchos niños en el parque: ____________________
3. Hay un teléfono público en la calle: ____________________
4. Hay mucha gente en el restaurante: ____________________
5. Hay un buen hotel en la ciudad: ____________________
6. Hay muchos planetas en el cielo: ____________________

D. Fill in the blanks with **hay** or **está**:

1. ¿Dónde __________ el correo?
2. En el colegio __________ un gran parque.
3. La iglesia __________ en la esquina.
4. La universidad __________ junto al parque.
5. __________ restaurantes muy buenos en mi ciudad.
6. En la plaza central __________ dos bares.
7. ¿__________ un parque allá?
8. Sí, el parque __________ allá.
9. ¿Dónde __________ el parque?
10. __________ un parque cerca.

4.3 The Interrogative ¿Cuánto/a? ¿Cuántos/as?

Questions are important! How else can we discover information from other people? Let's start off with some of the most important interrogative words for everyday life.

¿Cuánto/a? *How much?*

¿Cuántos/as? *How many?*

In English, 'much' is used for nouns that are uncountable, whereas 'many' is for nouns that *are* countable. It's the same in Spanish!

When you're asking someone how much coffee they want, you're expecting a reply like 'a lot' or 'not that much,' which is uncountable. However, if you were to phrase it as how *many* coffees they want, you're expecting a countable response like 'two cups' or 'just one.'

Keep this same rule in mind when determining whether to use **cuánto/a** (not countable) or **cuántos/as** (countable).

Put on your linguistic explorer hat—it's expedition time into the realm of practice!

4.3. Practice

A. Fill in the blanks with the right form of cuánto/a or cuántos/as.

1. ¿____________________ perros tiene usted?
2. ¿____________________ comida hay en el supermercado?
3. ¿____________________ gatos hay en el parque?
4. ¿____________________ flores hay en el jardín?
5. ¿____________________ idiomas hablas?
6. ¿____________________ café hay?

B. Now we're going to tie in **¿cuántos?** with **hay**. Answer the following questions using the written number.

Example: ¿**Cuántos** sofás **hay** en tu casa? <u>**Hay** dos sofás en mi casa.</u>

1. ¿Cuántos días hay en una semana (*week*)?

   ____

2. ¿Cuántas semanas (*weeks*) hay en un mes (*month*)?

   ____

3. ¿Cuántos días hay en un año (*year*)?

   ____

4. ¿Cuántos días hay en un fin de semana (*weekend*)?

   ____

5. ¿Cuántos días hay en el mes de febrero (*February*)?

   ____

6. ¿Cuántos dedos (*fingers*) hay en tu (*your*) mano?

   ____

7. ¿Cuántos hospitales hay en tu (*your*) ciudad?

   ____

8. ¿Cuántas televisiones hay en tu (*your*) casa?

   ____

9. ¿Cuántos árboles hay en tu (*your*) jardín?

   ____

10. ¿Cuántas sillas hay en tu casa?

   ____

C. Write sentences with the words that are suggested. Modify the words as needed to match the numbers and add articles when necessary.

   Example: Hay / tres / elefante / en / zoológico: Hay tres elefantes en el zoológico.

   1. hay / dos / universidad / en / ciudad ________________________
   2. hay / veinte / manzana / en / canasta (*basket*)________________________
   3. hay / doce / mes / en / año ________________________
   4. hay / un / Estatua de la Libertad / en / Nueva York ________________
   5. hay / dos / ojo / en / cara ________________________
   6. hay / mucho / edificio / en / ciudad________________________

4.4 Higher Numbers

You already know to count the basic numbers, how about we review something more complex?

#	English	Spanish	Pronunciation
21	twenty-one	**veintiuno**	*[beyn-teeh-oo-noh]*
22	twenty-two	**veintidós**	*[beyn-teeh-dohs]*
23	twenty-three	**veintitrés**	*[beyn-teeh-trehs]*
24	twenty-four	**veinticuatro**	*[beyn-teeh-kwah-troh]*
25	twenty-five	**veinticinco**	*[beyn-teeh-theen-koh]*
26	twenty-six	**veintiséis**	*[beyn-teeh-seys]*
27	twenty-seven	**veintisiete**	*[beyn-teeh-syeh-teh]*
28	twenty-eight	**veintiocho**	*[beyn-teeh-oh-choh]*
29	twenty-nine	**veintinueve**	*[beyn-teeh-nweh-beh]*
30	thirty	**treinta**	*[treh-eehn-tah]*
40	forty	**cuarenta**	*[kwah-reehn-tah]*
50	fifty	**cincuenta**	*[theen-kweehn-tah]*
60	sixty	**sesenta**	*[seeh-seehn-tah]*
70	seventy	**setenta**	*[seeh-teehn-tah]*
80	eighty	**ochenta**	*[oh-cheehn-tah]*
90	ninety	**noventa**	*[noh-behn-tah]*
100	one hundred	**cien**	*[syehn]*
1,000	one thousand	**mil**	*[myl]*
10,000	ten thousand	**diez mil**	*[dyehth-myl]*
100,000	one hundred thousand	**cien mil**	*[syehn-myl]*
1,000,000	one million	**un millón**	*[oon-meh-yoon]*

Now that you know more numbers, let's test your abilities.

4.4. Practice

A. Write the correspondent readings in Spanish for the following numbers.

Example: 15,678: <u>Quince mil seiscientos setenta y ocho.</u>

1. 46: ______________________________
2. 92: ______________________________
3. 160: ______________________________
4. 813: ______________________________
5. 5,209: ______________________________
6. 70,237: ______________________________
7. 805,624: ______________________________
8. 1'962,477: ______________________________
9. 34'857,090: ______________________________

B. Now let's practice a little math. You may use the calculator for this, the point of this exercise is for you to practice your numbers in Spanish.

1. 75+29 = ______________________________
2. 5+42 = ______________________________
3. 788-32 = ______________________________
4. 23,963+236 = ______________________________
5. 163,976-523 = ______________________________
6. 357+39 = ______________________________
7. 1,468-973 = ______________________________

We invite you to scan this "QR code"

By using the camera of your phone aiming at the QR code and clicking on the link that appears

to access your bonus content:

SCAN TO CLAIM YOUR BONUSES

OR

ENTER THIS URL IN YOUR WEB BROWSER:

bit.ly/speakspng

(only use lowercase letters)

CHAPTER 5:

PREPOSITIONS AND CONJUNCTIONS

THE HAT AND THE BOX ARE ON THE CHAIR

5.1 Prepositions

We use prepositions all the time and they're not complex. They're words like 'on,' 'over,' or 'until,' which are important for describing space and time.

If you're trying to help someone find something, prepositions allow you to describe to them which part of the room they would find the object in. Is it *under* the bed? *On* the table? *In* the laundry hamper?

It also describes time. If you're trying to organize plans with your friends, prepositions would help you arrange an appropriate time. Can you only hang out *at* 8 PM? *After* work? *Before* your favorite TV show starts playing? Or maybe just *until* you start feeling drunk?

The good news is that, unlike most words in Spanish, prepositions in Spanish don't change! They have no number or gender, and always remain the same. Phew!

Most Common Prepositions: en – de – con

Let's start practicing the three most common prepositions in Spanish. We will start with these three:

en	*in, on*	States the idea of remaining in a place or time	Juan está **en** su cama *(Juan is in his bed).*
de	*of, from*	Gives the idea of possession, matter, or origin	La casa es **de** Gabriela *(The house belongs to Gabriela).* La silla es **de** madera *(The chair is made of wood).*
con	*with*	Indicates company	Estoy **con** mis amigos *(I'm with my friends).*

Other Common Prepositions: a – para – sin

a	*to*	Indicates movement towards a goal, whether real or imagined. It is used before an indirect object and a direct object when it's a person.	Camino **a** mi casa (*I walk to my house*). Busco **a** mi hermana but busco los perros.
para	*for, in order to*	Indicates the aim or purpose of an action	El lápiz es **para** mi hija *(The pencil is for my daughter).*
sin	*without*	Indicates lack of	El hotel **sin** turistas *(The hotel is without tourists).*

What follows a preposition?

- In Spanish, prepositions can be followed by verbs in the infinitive form (the verbs that usually end in **-r**!): **Tomás estudia para aprender** (*Tomas studies to learn*) or **Martín habla sin pensar** (*Martin speaks without thinking*).
- Prepositions can be followed by nouns: **María compra una flor para su madre** (*María buys a flower for her mother*).
- Prepositions can be followed by pronouns: **El libro es para ella** (*The book is for her*). In Spanish, the pronouns that follow prepositions are **subject pronouns**, except for **mí** and **ti** (instead of **yo** and **tú**): **El café es para mí** and **El té es para ti**.

Tip: When you use the preposition **con** together with the **1st and 2nd subject pronoun**, the result is **conmigo** and **contigo**. In fact, **con** is the only preposition that combines with a pronoun. Example: **Mi esposo siempre viaja conmigo** (*My husband always travels with me*) or **Hablo en el parque contigo** (*I talk with you in the park*).

Other Common Prepositions: hasta – por – según – para – contra

hasta	*until, up to, as far as*	Expresses a limit	Camina **hasta** la cocina *(He/she walks up to the kitchen).*
por	*by, for*	Describes the means or cause for something. Also precedes a quantity of time.	Viaja **por** barco *(He/she travels by boat).* Camina **por** dos horas *(She walks for two hours).*
según	*according to*	Used to describe the opinion of others. It's used before names and pronouns.	**Según** mi mamá, la película es mala *(According to my mom, the film is bad).*
para	*for, in order to*	Used for deadlines, and to indicate purpose and destination	El regalo es **para** mi amiga *(The present is for my friend)*
contra	*against*	Describes opposition	La lucha **contra** el cambio climático *(The battle against climate change)*

Excited to play with sentences? Let's do it!

5.1. Practice

A. Complete the following sentences with the prepositions **en**, **de**, or **con**:

1. Luis vive __________ una ciudad grande.
2. María viaja siempre __________ su hermana.
3. La casa es __________ color amarillo.
4. Los zapatos son __________ cuero (*leather*).
5. Ustedes están __________ el jefe.
6. Hay parques hermosos __________ París.
7. El gato es __________ Pedro.
8. Mi sobrina trabaja __________ su padre.
9. Soy __________ Inglaterra.
10. Flavia cumple el cuatro __________ abril __________ 2000.
11. Me gustaría un café __________ leche.
12. Esta cartera es __________ Simón.

13. Regresa de la oficina __________ bicicleta.
14. Tengo una buena relación __________ mis padres (*my parents*).
15. Tengo una casa __________ ocho ventanas.

B. Complete the following sentences with the prepositions **a, para**, or **sin**.

1. El regalo es __________________ Juan.
2. Me gusta el café ______________ azúcar.
3. El padre regresa ______________ su casa a las 9:00 p.m.
4. Ella estudia __________________ aprender.
5. Mi mamá corre ________________ la sala.
6. Elena aprende alemán _________ profesores.
7. Mi tío entra __________________ la oficina a las 8:00 p.m.
8. Tomás viaja __________________ mapas.

C. See if you can complete these sentences with the right preposition from this last group: **hasta – para – por – según – contra**

1. El hombre salta _______________ la ventana.
2. El regalo es __________________ su hijo.
3. _____________________________ mi amiga, el restaurante es malo.
4. Caminamos ___________________ el parque.
5. Ella mira televisión ____________ una hora.
6. Estoy _______________________ las ideas de ese profesor.
7. Está en mi casa _______________ el martes.
8. Hay una habitación ___________ dos personas.
9. _____________________________ el doctor, debes comer muchas verduras y frutas.

5.2 Coordinating Conjunctions

Don't be intimidated by that big word! Conjunctions are some of the most common components of everyday language. They connect other words, phrases, and clauses. For example, in that last sentence 'and' was the conjunction, because it unites the rest of the sentence.

Some other examples of conjunctions are 'or' and 'but.' They allow us to say things like "She came by, but she didn't come in."

By learning conjunctions in Spanish, you'll be able to construct slightly more complex sentences. Although they aren't hard to construct, they can convey a whole new layer of meaning.

In Spanish, there are two types of conjunctions:

Coordinating conjunctions ('but,' 'and,' 'or')

Subordinating conjunctions ('because,' 'although')

What's the difference?

Coordinating conjunctions join two parts of a sentence that are equal in importance.

E.g. "Tina loves Instagram and Bob loves Facebook." You know they're equal because if you removed the conjunction, you would still understand that Tina loves Instagram and Bob loves Facebook.

Subordinating conjunctions, on the other hand, connect parts of a sentence that don't convey the same message when they're independent. E.g. "Tina loves Instagram because she's a fan of photography." If you removed the conjunction in this sentence, you wouldn't understand that the reason Tina loves Instagram is because she's a fan of photography.

These same differences apply to coordinating and subordinating conjunctions in Spanish. Understanding their purpose will help you navigate them.

Coordinating Conjunctions			
Combine Elements Together (Copulative Conjunctions)	**y**	*and*	Come **y** bebe. *(He eats and drinks)*
	e	*and* (used when the word following the copulative conjunction 'y' begins with 'i' or the silent letter 'h' followed by the vowel 'i')	Andrés **e** Inés bailan en la fiesta. *(Andres and Ines dance at the party.)*
	ni	*nor*	No come **ni** pan **ni** galletitas. *(He doesn't eat bread nor crackers.)*

Coordinating Conjunctions			
Show an Opposition or Difference (Adversative Conjunctions)	**pero**	*but*	Es inteligente **pero** perezoso. *(He's intelligent but lazy.)*
	mas	*but*	Tiene un trabajo **mas** no es feliz. *(She has a job but isn't happy.)*
	sin embargo (usually used after a semi-colon)	*however, nevertheless, but*	Tiene mucho dinero; **sin embargo**, no lo comparte. *(She has a lot of money but doesn't share it.)*
	aunque	*even if, though, although*	La película es buena, **aunque** larga. *(The movie is good, even if it's long.)*
	sino	*but*	No come carne **sino** pescado.
Show Options (Disjunctive Conjunctions)	**o**	*or*	María regresa a las 12:00 p.m. **o** a la 1:00 p.m. *(María comes back at 12:00 p.m. or at 1:00 p.m.)*
	u	*or* (used when the word following the disjunctive conjunction "**o**" begins with the vowel "o" or the silent letter "h" followed by the vowel "o")	Laura organiza **u** ordena los papeles. *(Laura organizes or arranges the papers.)*

Coordinating Conjunctions			
Show Alternation (Distributive Conjunctions)	**o... o**	*either... or*	**O** estudias **o** no miras televisión. *(Either you study, or you don't watch TV.)*
	bien... bien	*either... or*	**Bien** estudian en el parque, **bien** en la biblioteca. *(Either they study in the park or in the library.)*
	tanto... como	*both*	**Tanto** Pedro **como** María son buenos estudiantes. *(Both Pedro and María are good students.)*
	ya... ya	*whether... or*	El matrimonio es compartir la vida **ya** en las alegrías, **ya** en las tristezas. *(Marriage is sharing life whether in happiness or in sorrow.)*

Tip: The conjunction **y** is replaced by **e** before words starting with **i** or **h**i for reasons of pronunciation.

Example: **Tomates e higos.** (*tomatoes and figs*)

For the same reason, **o** is replaced with **u** before words starting with **o** or **ho**. Example: **Apartamentos u hoteles**.

Theory, step aside; it's practice time!

5.2. Practice

A. Find the right conjunctions: **y** – **e** – **o** – **u**. Go ahead and translate the sentence.

1. María and Inés are friends since childhood.

   ____

2. There are ten or eleven children in the store.

   ____

3. Get the key and try to open the door.

   ____

4. He calls and invites us to his party.

   ____

5. She sees something or hears a noise.

   ____

6. She knows how to read and write very well.

   ____

B. Fill in the blanks with the conjunctions **y, o**, or **pero**

1. El niño come una banana __________ una manzana.
2. ¿Martín trabaja __________ estudia?
3. Busco a mi perro __________ no lo encuentro.
4. Lo repito dos __________ tres veces.
5. Cantasteis __________ bailasteis toda la noche.
6. Soy francés __________ vivo en Italia.
7. Llegas a las ocho __________ nueve de la mañana.
8. Luisa trabaja mucho __________ gana poco.

C. Let's practice adversative conjunctions: **pero, más, sin embargo, aunque, sino.** Fill in the blanks with the right conjunction:

1. Como poco __________ estoy gordo.
2. No trabaja hoy en la oficina __________ mañana
3. Tomás sabe mucho __________ es una persona humilde.
4. Tiene coche; __________ le gusta caminar.
5. Viaja mucho, __________ no tiene mucho dinero.
6. __________ yo no recibo el periódico, lo leo todos los días.

D. Circle the right conjunction in each sentence. Then, translate the sentences to English.

1. Camino todos los días { porque – sin embargo } es bueno para la salud.

   ____

2. Ellos comen en un restaurante todos los días { pero – ni } nosotras comemos en casa.

   ____

3. Teresa aprende alemán { ni – aunque } no lo necesita.

   ____

4. { Aunque – Ni } Elena { aunque – ni } Cristián beben vino.

   ____

5. Elena { y – e } Hilario son abogados.

   ____

6. { Aunque – Tanto } Pedro { como – ni } Sofía son franceses.

   ____

7. Compramos { y – pero } vendemos ropa usada.

   ____

8. Estudia mucho; { aunque – sin embargo } no aprende mucho.

   ____

5.3 Subordinating Conjunctions

As we mentioned earlier, subordinating conjunctions connect parts of a sentence that are dependent on each other.

Subordinating Conjunctions			
Showing Cause (Cause Conjunctions)	**porque**	*because*	Ella está cansada **porque** trabaja mucho. *(She's tired because she works a lot.)*
	pues	*since, as, because*	Estoy en casa **pues** llueve. *(I'm home because it's raining.)*
	como	*since, as, because*	**Como** está ocupado, no tiene tiempo. *(Since he's busy, he doesn't have any time.)*

Subordinating Conjunctions			
Elaborating (Relative Conjunctions)	**que**	*that*	Me dijo **que** soy su mejor amigo. *(He told me that I was his best friend.)*
Making Comparisons (Comparative Conjunctions)	**así como**	*just as*	José es alto, **así como** su hermana. *(José is tall, just as his sister.)*
	así también	*so to*	Sabe francés, **así también** alemán. *(He knows French, so too German.)*
	tal como	*as*	María es simpática **tal como** Clara. *(Maria is as nice as Clara.)*
To Show an Obstacle Doesn't Prevent Action (Concessive Conjunctions)	**aunque**	*although, even though, though*	La biblioteca está cerrada, **aunque** son las 12:00 p.m. *(The library is closed, even though it's 12:00 p.m.)*
	a pesar de que	*even though, despite the fact that*	Está triste, **a pesar de que** tiene muchos amigos. *(He's sad, despite the fact that he has lots of friends.)*
To Show Conditions (Conditional Conjunctions)	**si**	*if*	Pago con tarjeta **si** lo necesito. *(I pay with a credit card if I need to.)*
	a menos que	*unless*	Corro todos los días **a menos que** llueva. *(I run every day unless it rains.)*
To Give a Sense of Time and Order (Time Conjunctions)	**mientras**	*while, meanwhile*	Camina **mientras** habla por teléfono. *(She walks while she talks on the phone.)*

Common Mistakes: The conjunction **que** is essential in Spanish, even though it is often not translated in English. **Que** as a conjunction which means *that*.

Creo que ella es feliz (*I believe that she is happy*)

Note that in English, you can say, *I believe she is happy* (without the "that"). Be careful! You can't say **Creo es feliz** in Spanish, omitting the **que**. You absolutely need the **que**.

X Creo la niña es feliz
✓ Creo que la niña es feliz

Ready to flex those newfound skills? It's practice time!

5.3 Practice

A. Let's practice the relative conjunction **si**. Join these sentences and conjugate the verbs. **Example: María / no / saber / si / Juan / necesitar / algo: <u>María no sabe si Juan necesita algo.</u>**

1. Pedro y Luis / no / saber / si / sus amigos / regresar / hoy:

   ____

2. Mirta / pregunta (*ask*) / si / hay / examen / mañana:

   ____

3. José / decidir / si / subir / el monte Fitz Roy:

   ____

4. Vosotros / no / saber / si / Paula / necesitar / algo / para la fiesta:

   ____

5. Usted / preguntar / si / los empleados / trabajar / bien:

   ____

6. Tú / decidir / si / beber / café / o / té:

   ____

B. Let's practice the relative conjunction **que**. Remember? The one you should never omit in Spanish. Join these sentences.

Example: Tenemos una fiesta. Me dice. → Me dice que tenemos una fiesta.

1. Vivimos en la calle Oro. Ella sabe: ______________________
2. Viajamos todo el año. Juan piensa: ______________________

3. El señor Ortiz arregla hornos. Yo creo: ______________________
4. A José le gusta comer. Juana dice: ______________________
5. Es tarde. La profesora nos dice: ______________________
6. Los niños necesitan lápices nuevos. La madre dice: ____________

C. Join both sentences with a subordinate conjunction: **porque – pero – aunque – que. Example: Es un buen profesor. Yo creo → <u>Yo creo que es un buen profesor</u>.**

1. Me gusta. Mis hijos ordenan solos.

   ____

2. Trabajo mucho. Gano poco.

   ____

3. Hace frío. Hay sol.

   ____

4. Martín cree. Está demasiado ventoso para correr.

   ____

5. El verdulero me explica. Los tomates están verdes.

   ____

6. Llegas temprano. Sales temprano.

   ____

5.4 Indefinite Adjectives

An indefinite adjective is an adjective used to describe a noun in a non-specific way. It agrees with the noun in number and sometimes gender. Many indefinite adjectives in Spanish are identical to Spanish indefinite pronouns.

Examples of indefinite adjectives are:

Hay **pocas** manzanas. (*There are a few apples*)
Tiene **alguna** posibilidad (*possibility*) de viajar (*travel).*
Hay **mucho** sol.
Es la **misma** casa.
Necesito **algún** vestido.
El profesor explica **todos** los ejercicios.

Se pueden anexar algunos ejemplos de adjetivos indefinidos que no concuerdan con el género, por ejemplo: Nunca vi semejante cosa, Elige cualquier camisa, Tengo bastante comida. Cada perro tiene su collar. Tal experiencia causó mucho revuelo.

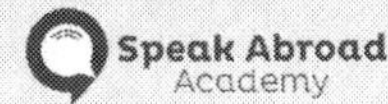

SINGULAR		PLURAL		
masculine	**feminine**	**masculine**	**feminine**	
algún	**alguna**	**algunos**	**algunas**	*some, a few*
ningún	**ninguna**	-	-	*none, neither*
cada	**cada**	-	-	*each*
cierto	**cierta**	**ciertos**	**ciertas**	*certain*
mismo	**misma**	**mismos**	**mismas**	*same*
mucho	**mucha**	**muchos**	**muchas**	*many, much, a lot*
otro	**otra**	**otros**	**otras**	*other*
poco	**poca**	**pocos**	**pocas**	*few, a little*
tal	-	**tales**	-	*some, any*
tanto	**tanta**	**tantos**	**tantas**	*so many, so much*
todo	**toda**	**todos**	**todas**	*all*
-	-	**varios**	**varias**	*several, some*

Agregar algunos adjetivos indefinidos sin distinción de género: tal, bastante, cualquier, cada, semejante, etc.

Common Mistake:

Indefinite adjectives are used in place of an article, **not with one**.

X Don't say: **Hay las algunas manzanas**.

✓ Say, instead: **Hay algunas manzanas**.

Rules, step aside; it's practice time!

5.3 Practice

A. Complete the sentences with the right indefinite adjective.

Example: **Pablo solo compra __________ manzanas. → <u>Pablo solo compra unas manzanas</u>.**

1. __________ personas trabajan en su casa.
2. Hay __________ pájaros que parece una selva.
3. Es el __________ sombrero que tiene Juan.
4. Susana tiene __________ casa en la playa.
5. __________ personas comparten apartamento con amigos.
6. __________ día que pasa es peor.
7. Ese cantante compuso __________canciones parecidas.
8. Llueve__________ la semana.

B. Translate the following sentences with conjunctions and indefinite adjectives:

1. Ella tiene muchos perros y gatos en su casa.

   ____

2. María tiene varias hijas, pero no tiene hijos, quiere tener uno pronto.

   ____

3. Tanto Luis como Juan tienen pocos amigos en el colegio.

   ____

4. No lee ni revistas ni periódicos.

   ____

5. Conoce otros países, pues viaja mucho. Su favorito es Uruguay.

   ____

6. Tiene el mismo coche que Laura.

   ____

7. Conoce cada calle de París, pero no conoce su propia ciudad.

   ____

8. Habla algunos idiomas, pero no habla inglés.

   ____

9. Es la misma amistad, aunque somos más viejos.

 ____

10. Todos los idiomas son útiles, aunque algunos son más útiles que otros.

 ____

C. Elena has a positive outlook on life. Roberto has a negative outlook on life. Change Elena's statements to the opposite to know what Robert thinks.

Example: Tengo pocos problemas. → <u>Tengo muchos problemas</u>.

1. Todos los días son hermosos. → ______________
2. Tengo pocas tristezas. → ______________
3. Hay tantas cosas lindas en la vida. → ______________
4. Tengo muchos amigos. → ______________
5. Ciertos días son malos. → ______________
6. Ninguna tarea es imposible. → ______________

CHAPTER 6:
POSSESSIVE ADJECTIVES
YOUR BALL, MY BALL

Possessive Adjectives

Mi árbol tenía **sus ramas de oro.**	*My tree used to have* *branches of gold.*
Un viento envidioso **robó mi tesoro.**	*An envious wind* *stole my treasure.*
Hoy no tiene ramas. **Hoy no tiene sueños**	*Today it has no branches.* *Today it has no dreams*
mi árbol callado, **mi árbol pequeño.**	*my silent tree,* *my small tree.*

This poem is by Antonio García Tejeiro (1952), one of the great Galician poets and narrators of children and young adult's literature. It's about a tree stripped off its branches by a strong wind which robbed its dreams.

This poem contains a couple of possessive adjectives: **Mi** árbol and **sus** ramas de oro, illustrating a deep personal connection between the poet and the tree, which adds more emotion to the poetry.

Here is a complete list of possessive adjectives that will help you add depth to your own conversations:

POSSESSIVE ADJECTIVES		
mi	*my*	mi casa
mis		mis tías
tu	*your*	tu libro
tus		tus mochilas
su	*your, his, her, its*	su foto
sus		sus amigas

POSSESSIVE ADJECTIVES		
nuestro	*our*	nuestro escritorio
nuestros		nuestros lápices
vuestro	*your*	vuestro reloj
vuestros		vuestras mochilas
su	*your, their*	su casa
sus		sus pelotas

Possessive adjectives are placed before a noun.

The possessive adjectives **mi, tu**, and **su** agree only in number with the nouns they modify. Instead, **nuestro and vuestro** agree in both number and gender, like all adjectives.

Tip: Possessive adjectives must match the thing possessed, not the possessor, in gender and number. So what happens if you're referring to your books? You say **mis libros,** even if there's only one of you. And if the person with the books is your friend? It's **tus libros**, even if he's one person holding the books.

Tip: The possessive adjective **su** is hard to keep straight! In English, it has several equivalents:

su:	your (sing.)	=	su hija *(your daughter)*
su:	his (sing)	=	su hija *(his daughter)*
su:	her (sing)	=	su hija *(her daughter)*
su:	its (sing)	=	su comida *(its food)*
su:	your (pl.)	=	su hija *(your daughter)*
su:	their (pl)	=	su hija *(their daughter)*

How to tell which one it is? Well, the meaning will be clear from the context. For example:

If you are standing with your friend and talking about his/her book, you would say, "**tu libro**." But if you're with a group of people referring to their book, you would say "**su libro**" (your, pl.).

Tip: Thought we were done with possessive adjectives in Spanish? Think again! We've got another set in the game called stressed possessive adjectives. These bad boys can even pull double duty as nouns – think **mío**, **tuyo**, **suyo**, and so on.

For instance, check this out: "Esta maleta es mía." Here, "mía" steps in for "mi maleta." But don't stress; we'll dive into this in our more advanced grammar workbook. Stay tuned!

Common Mistake:

Don't use possessive adjectives with body parts. Only use definite and indefinite articles.

X Don't say: **Tiene su pelo largo**. *(She has long hair.)*

✓ Say, instead: **Tiene el pelo largo**. *(She has long hair.)*

Vocabulario: the family

English	Spanish	Pronunciation
the mother (mom)	**la madre (mamá)**	*[lah mah-dreh]*
the father (dad)	**el padre (papá)**	*[ehl pah-dreh]*
the daughter	**la hija**	*[lah ee-hah]*
the son	**el hijo**	*[ehl ee-hoh]*
the sister	**la hermana**	*[lah ehr-mah-nah]*
the brother	**el hermano**	*[ehl ehr-mah-noh]*
the wife	**la esposa**	*[lah ehs-poh-sah]*
the husband	**el esposo**	*[ehl ehs-poh-soh]*
the grandmother	**la abuela**	*[lah ah-bweh-lah]*
the grandfather	**el abuelo**	*[ehl ah-bweh-loh]*
the granddaughter	**la nieta**	*[lah nyeh-tah]*
the grandson	**el nieto**	*[ehl nyeh-toh]*
the cousin (female)	**la prima**	*[lah pree-mah]*
the cousin (male)	**el primo**	*[ehl pree-moh]*

English	Spanish	Pronunciation
the aunt	**la tía**	*[lah tee-ah]*
the uncle	**el tío**	*[ehl tee-oh]*
the niece	**la sobrina**	*[lah soh-bree-nah]*
the nephew	**el sobrino**	*[ehl soh-bree-noh]*

Here are a few more adjectives to help you with the exercises below (see Lesson 4 for other lists).

English	Spanish	Pronunciation
long	**largo**	*[lahr-goh]*
varied	**variado**	*[bah-ryah-doh]*
wide	**ancho**	*[ahn-choh]*
complete	**completo**	*[kohm-pleh-toh]*
elegant	**elegante**	*[eh-leh-gahn-teh]*
peaceful	**tranquilo**	*[trahn-kee-loh]*
impressive	**impresionante**	*[eem-preh-syoh-nahn-teh]*
prestigious	**prestigioso**	*[prehs-tee-hyoh-soh]*
gorgeous	**precioso**	*[preh-thyoh-soh]*
ancient	**antiguo**	*[ahn-tee-gwoh]*
generous	**generoso**	*[heh-neh-roh-soh]*
selfish	**egoísta**	*[eh-goh-ees-tah]*

6 Practice

A. Let's practice with the members of the family. Complete these sentences.

1. El padre de mi padre es mi ____________________.
2. La hija de mi tío es mi ____________________.
3. La hermana de mi padre es mi ____________________.
4. El hijo de mi hermana es mi ____________________.
5. La mujer de mi padre es mi ____________________.
6. La hija de la hija de mi abuela es su ____________________.

B. Now describe these people.

Example: sobrino: es el hijo de mi hermano o hermana.

1. abuela: ______________________________.
2. prima: ______________________________.
3. tío: ______________________________.
4. nieto: ______________________________.
5. hermano: ______________________________.

C. Look at the list of adjectives we just covered in this chapter and complete these sentences matching the adjectives to the noun. Make sure they agree in gender (masculine or feminine) and number (singular or plural).

1. Ese vestido de fiesta es muy ____________________.
2. Tu profesor es ____________________.
3. Tomás colecciona coches ____________________.
4. Es un lugar donde no hay ruido y es muy ____________.
5. Una piscina olímpica (*Olympic pool*) es ______ y ________.
6. El menú (*menu*) de ese restaurante es muy ____________.

D. Describe the family members of these different people using the right possessive adjective. If it looks a little confusing, it's quite easy. Remember to find the possessive adjective that refers to whatever is between parenthesis. Also, make sure the adjective matches the noun!

Example: hermano / simpático (el hermano de Martín y Susana) Su hermano es simpático. ("su" refers to Martín and Susana. It works as "their": *Their brother is funny*).

Another example: primo / joven (yo): mi primo es joven ("mi" refers to "yo." It works as "my": *My cousin is young.*

1. tía / delgada (yo)

   ____

2. padre / deportista (Elena)

   ____

3. abuela / interesante (Carlos y María)

   ____

4. sobrinos / soltero (tú)

   ____

5. primo / rubio (you're talking to several people)

   ____

6. nietas / pequeño (Pedro y yo)

   ____

7. esposo / guapo (yo)

   ____

8. hermana / casado (Tomás)

   ____

9. madre / bueno (tú)

   ____

E. Complete the sentences with the right possessive adjective.

1. Mi padre es abogado; __________ oficina está en la ciudad.
2. Vosotros vendéis flores; __________ flores son muy bonitas.
3. La hermana de Cecilia es profesora; __________ alumnos son inteligentes.
4. Mi sobrino vive en Inglaterra; __________ esposa vive en Francia.
5. Ustedes están ocupados. __________ trabajo es difícil.
6. Me gustan las frutas. __________ fruta preferida (*favorite fruit*) es la manzana.
7. Nuestro primo es ingeniero. __________ padres también son ingenieros.
8. Mi esposa viaja esta noche. __________ maletas están listas (*ready*).
9. Juan está en el parque con __________ hijos.
10. Tus primos trabajan mucho. __________ trabajo no es fácil.

F. What are Elena's relatives like? Answer using the possessive adjectives following the example (remember to make the adjective match the noun!).

Example: prima María / soltero: <u>Su prima María es soltera</u>.

1. abuela Marta / anciano: ______________________.
2. padre Roberto / trabajador: ______________________.
3. hermanitos (*little brothers*) / traviesos: ______________________.
4. madre Julia / generoso: ______________________.

5. primo Martín / delgado: ______________________________.
6. tíos / simpático: ______________________________.
7. sobrina Ana / bonito: ______________________________.
8. hermano Pablo / inteligente: ______________________________.

G. Now imagine they are your relatives and describe them using the same words as above.

Example: Mi prima María es soltera.

1. ______________________________.
2. ______________________________.
3. ______________________________.
4. ______________________________.
5. ______________________________.
6. ______________________________.
7. ______________________________.
8. ______________________________.

H. Now describe what the town is like for a friend who lives in a different country. Again, match the adjectives to the noun!

Example: calle / grande: Nuestras calles son grandes. (*Our streets are big.*)

1. avenidas / largo: ______________________________.
2. supermercados / completo: ______________________________.
3. teatros / grande: ______________________________.
4. parques / precioso: ______________________________.
5. universidades / prestigioso: ______________________________.
6. museos / interesante: ______________________________.
7. restaurantes / variado: ______________________________.
8. edificios / elegante: ______________________________.
9. monumentos / antiguo: ______________________________.

I. Replace **de + name** with the appropriate possessive adjective.

Example: Los zapatos de María son elegantes: Sus zapatos son elegantes.

1. La ciudad de mi familia es grande: ______________________.
2. La casa de mi amiga es elegante: ______________________.
3. Los coches de José son negros: ______________________.
4. La gata de los señores Pérez es blanca: ________________.
5. Los zapatos de Elena son viejos: ______________________.

J. A friend is asking about your town. Answer using possessive adjectives and follow the example. If the question is to a collective you (**vuestro/a**), answer with **nuestro/a** (*our*); if the question is addressed to a singular you (**tu**), answer with **mi** (*my*).

Make sure the adjectives agree with the noun!

Example: ¿Cómo son vuestras calles? (ancho): Nuestras calles son anchas.

1. ¿Cómo son vuestras avenidas? (largo) vuestras → nuestras

   ____.

2. ¿Cómo son vuestros edificios? (alto) vuestros → nuestros

   ____.

3. ¿Cómo es tu oficina? (grande) tú → yo

   ____.

4. ¿Cómo son vuestros parques? (precioso) vuestros → nuestros

   ____.

5. ¿Cómo es tu universidad? (prestigioso) tu → yo

   ____.

CHAPTER 7:

THE INDICATIVE MOOD: REFLEXIVE VERBS & VERB IR + INFINITIVE

SHE BATHES HERSELF

7.1 Reflexive Verbs

Reflexive verbs are kind of weird for English speakers because in English the reflexive trait is indicated with pronouns like *myself, yourself, herself, himself, itself, oneself, ourselves, themselves*: *I shower myself*. In Spanish, the reflexiveness is indicated with a pronoun: **me, te, se, nos, os, se**. And this pronoun goes **before the verb** when conjugated: **yo me ducho** (*I shower myself*), depending on who the subject is.

Check out the description below. The highlighted verbs are the **reflexive verbs**. Remember, when a subject is doing anything for himself/herself/itself, the verb is reflexive.

A Typical Day

El señor García **se despierta** todos los días a las 7:00 a.m. **Se levanta** de la cama a las 7:15 a.m. y **se lava** los dientes. Luego **se baña** o **se ducha**. Después, **se afeita** y **se viste**. **Se pone** los zapatos. Después desayuna y **se va** a la oficina.

Glossary

despertarse: *to wake up*
levantarse: *to get up*
cama: *bed*
lavarse: *to wash*
bañarse: *to take a bath*
ducharse: *to take a shower*
afeitarse: *to shave oneself*
vestirse: *to get dressed*
ponerse: *to put on*
zapatos: *shoes*
desayunar: *to have breakfast*
irse: *to go*

When there is a **no** in a sentence, the possessive pronoun goes after the **no**:

No se peinan. (*They don't brush their hair.*)

Spanish Reflexive Pronouns

English	Spanish	Pronunciation
myself	**me**	*[meh]*
yourself	**te**	*[teh]*
yourself/ himself/ herself/ itself/ oneself	**se**	*[seh]*
ourselves	**nos**	*[nohs]*
yourselves	**os**	*[ohs]*
themselves	**se**	*[seh]*

Some verbs have a different meaning, whether they have the pronoun attached to them or not. Take a verb like **lavar** *(to wash):*

Lavo los platos is, *I wash the dishes*. See what the verb means when it stands by itself.
Me lavo la cara is, *I wash my face*. Here **lavarse** means something slightly different. It's used for washing one's body parts.

Remember, though, don't use a possessive adjective next to the body part like you do in English:

✓ **Se lava los brazos.**
X **Se lava sus brazos.**

These are some reflexive verbs:

English	Spanish	Pronunciation
to wake up	**despertarse**	*[dehs-pehr-tahr-seh]*
to get up	**levantarse**	*[leh-bahn-tahr-seh]*
to wash oneself	**lavarse**	*[lah-bahr-seh]*
to take a bath	**bañarse**	*[bah-nyahr-seh]*
to take a shower	**ducharse**	*[doo-chahr-seh]*
to shave oneself	**afeitarse**	*[ah-fey-tahr-seh]*
to comb oneself	**peinarse**	*[pey-nahr-seh]*
to dress oneself	**vestirse**	*[behs-teer-seh]*
to put on (clothing)	**ponerse**	*[poh-nehr-seh]*
to take off (clothing)	**quitarse**	*[kee-tahr-seh]*

English	Spanish	Pronunciation
sit down	**sentarse**	*[sehn-tahr-seh]*
to leave	**irse**	*[eer-seh]*
to be called	**llamarse**	*[yah-mahr-seh]*

To make a normal verb reflexive, just add **se** to the infinitive ending: **lavar + se.** Once you conjugate the verb, the **se** turns into the pronoun belonging to the person who is doing the action.

For example: **amar** (*to love*) → **amarse** (*to love oneself*) → **se ama**. And if it's María getting dressed, the conjugated form is **María se viste** *(María dresses herself).*

Common Mistake: Some verbs only have a reflexive form. Even if the English doesn't have it, you have to use the reflexive pronoun in Spanish. One of these verbs is **ducharse**.

✓ You need to say: **Me ducho**.

X Don't say: **Ducho.** [by itself]

7.1 Practice

A. Answer the questions according to the example to practice **llamarse**.

Example: ¿Cómo te llamas? → yo (Juana) Me llamo Juana.

1. ¿Cómo me llamo? → tú (Tomás) ____________
2. ¿Cómo te llamas? → yo (José) ____________
3. ¿Cómo se llama? → ella (Elena) ____________
4. ¿Cómo nos llamamos? → ustedes (Paula y Teo) ____________
5. ¿Cómo os llamáis? → nosotros (Martín y Laura) ____________
6. ¿Cómo se llaman? → ellos (Pablo y Mirta) ____________

B. The following schedule belongs to Daniel. Answer the questions below using it as a guide.

8:00 a.m.: Despertarse

8:10 a.m.: Lavarse los dientes

8:15 a.m.: Bañarse

8:25 a.m.: Afeitarse

8:30 a.m.: Peinarse

8:45 a.m.: Vestirse

9:00 a.m.: Sentarse a desayunar

9:30 a.m.: Irse al trabajo

1. ¿A qué hora se despierta Daniel?

____

2. ¿A qué hora se lava los dientes?

____

3. ¿A qué hora se baña?

____

4. ¿A qué hora se afeita?

____

5. ¿A qué hora se peina?

____

6. ¿A qué hora se viste?

____

7. ¿A qué hora se sienta a desayunar?

____

8. ¿A qué hora se va al trabajo?

____

C. Use one of the reflexive pronouns (**me – se – te – nos – os**) to complete the sentences.

1. Yo __________ llamo Juan y mi hermana __________ llama Carola.
2. Roberto __________ pone las medias (*socks*).
3. Mis hermanos __________ llaman Victoria y Luis.
4. Tú __________ duchas por la mañana.
5. Nosotros __________ sentamos delante de la televisión.
6. ¿A qué hora __________ despiertan durante la semana?
7. Claudia __________ pone los zapatos fuera de la casa.
8. Vosotros __________ laváis los dientes en el baño.

D. Now try to conjugate the reflexive verbs (don't forget to add the right pronoun!)

1. Yo __________ todos los días. (afeitarse)
2. Tú __________ las manos después de entrar (*come in*) en tu casa. (lavarse)
3. Marcos __________ a las 10:00 de la mañana los sábados. (despertarse)
4. Elena __________ los zapatos para subir a su habitación. (quitarse)
5. Vosotros __________ en las sillas de plástico. (sentarse)
6. Teresa y Cecilia __________ en su baño. (bañarse)

E. Now answer questions about your own habits.

Example: ¿A qué hora se despierta los días de semana? <u>Me despierto a las 6:00 a.m. los días de semana</u>.

1. ¿A qué hora se levanta usted los sábados?

   ____

2. ¿Cuándo se lava el pelo usted?

   ____

3. ¿Le gusta a usted ducharse o bañarse?

   ____

4. ¿Dónde se sienta usted para ver televisión?

   ____

5. ¿Se peina usted en la peluquería (*hairdresser*)?

   ____

7.2 The Verb Ir (to go) and the Verb Ir +a + Infinitive (*will + infinitive*)

The verb **ir** is a completely irregular verb. ***Ir*** doesn't work like *bailar → yo bailo, ir → yo iro. Bailar* is a regular verb and the conjugation is fine, this isn't the case for *ir*. But don't worry! It's such a common verb, you'll have a lot of practice and will soon master it.

ir *(to go)*			
yo	**voy**	nosotros/as	**vamos**
tú	**vas**	vosotros/as	**vais**
él ella usted	**va**	ellos ellas ustedes	**van**

The verb **ir** is also used as an auxiliary to express actions in the near future by adding a + the infinitive of the action that will be done, like in continuous tenses.

Voy a correr. *(I'm going to run.)*
Van a comprar. *(They're going to buy.)*
Vais a ir. *(You all are going to go.)*
Vamos a comer. *(We're going to eat.)*
Vas a beber agua. *(You're going to drink water.)*
Va a caminar al colegio. *(He's going to walk to school.)*
Va a ir a Francia. *(He's going to go to France.)*

Notice how these sentences have none of the subject pronouns (yo, tú, él, ella, etc.).

Tip: Voy a ir and the preposition that follows it.

When saying you're going to a place, you need to use a preposition + an article (**el/la**): **Vamos al parque.** (*We're going to the park.*)

In this case, remember the preposition contracts with the article: **al/ el**: **Voy al supermercado** (voy a + el supermercado). Or **Voy a la casa de Juana.**

On the other hand, when you're going to a city/country, you **don't add the el/ la**:

✓ **Voy a España.** (*I'm going to Spain.*)
X **Voy a la España.**

7.2 Practice

A. Say where these people will be next summer using **ir + a + infinitive.**

Example: Marta / España: <u>Marta va a ir a España</u>. (*Marta is going to go to Spain.*)

1. Yo / Estados Unidos ______________________________
2. Martín / Inglaterra ______________________________
3. Sofía / Italia ______________________________
4. Teresa y yo / Francia ______________________________
5. Usted y José / España ______________________________
6. Tú / México ______________________________
7. Pablo y María / Canadá ______________________________

B. Fill in the blanks with the correct form of **voy a + infinitive, vas a + infinitive, etc.**

1. ¿Qué ____________ (ustedes/ hacer) estas vacaciones (*vacations*)?
2. Estas vacaciones ____________ (nosotros/ ir) a Alemania.
3. ____________ (yo/ bañarse) en ese baño.
4. ____________ (vosotros/ leer) un libro para el colegio.
5. Karina y Pablo ____________ (viajar) en tren.
6. ____________ (yo/ buscar) un médico para la rodilla.
7. María ____________ (encontrarse) con su amiga en el parque.
8. El profesor y yo ____________ (hablar) después de la clase.

C. Use these verbs with the **ir a + infinitive**, choosing the ones that correspond to each situation, to express the consequence of the first part. Remember in Spanish you don't need to add a pronoun because it is implicit in the verb.

Example: The boy is learning Chinese. → <u>Va a entender el idioma</u>.

chocar (*crash*) – **leer** – **ganar** – **volar** – **caerse** – **casarse** – **buscar** – **pedir** – **entender**

1. The runner is about to get to the finish line: ____________ la carrera.
2. The student doesn't understand the exercise: ____________ ayuda.
3. The boy is walking on the roof: ____________
4. The bird is posed on the edge of the nest: ____________
5. The girl is climbing the ladder to pick apples: ____________ manzanas.

6. Two cars are racing toward a corner from opposite sides: ___________
7. Tom got a letter in the mailbox: ___________
8. El novio y la novia ___________ en la iglesia.

D. Fill in the blanks with ir a + the infinitive between parenthesis.

1. Mañana mi padre ____________________ (visitar) al abuelo.
2. ¿Adónde ____________________ (vosotros/ ir) este sábado?
3. ¿Qué ____________________ (vosotros/ cocinar) para la cena?
4. ¿Cómo ____________________ (yo/ cuidar) a este perro?
5. Martín y yo ____________________ (salir) este viernes.
6. Tú ____________________ (ser) un gran deportista.
7. ____________________ (yo/ estar) ocupada este lunes.
8. Pilar ____________________ (ayudar) a sus abuelos.

E. The García family are going to the beach. Complete the sentences with **ir a + infinitive** to know what they will do there.

La familia García ___________ [1] (ir) a la playa este verano. ___________ [2] (ellos/ viajar) en coche durante todo el día. La señora García ___________ [3] (conducir) un rato y el señor García ___________ [4] (manejar) otra parte del viaje. ___________ [5] (ellos/llegar) a las ocho de la noche. ___________ [6] (ellos/estar) cansados por el viaje. Luego ___________ [7] (ellos/cenar) algo rápido y ___________ [8] (ellos/ irse) a la cama.

CHAPTER 8:
COMPARISONS
THIS BOOK IS BETTER THAN THAT ONE

8.1 Comparing Adjectives

Comparative adjectives are used to contrast differences between two objects of persons they modify. Read the following story about three sisters. Notice the comparisons made by Susana. In this lesson, we are going to study how to compare in Spanish!

Me llamo Susana. Tengo dos hermanas: Teresa y Sofía. Somos muy diferentes. Yo soy la mayor. Soy más estudiosa que mis hermanas. También soy más introvertida que ellas. Mi hermana Teresa es más deportista que mi hermana Sofía y yo, pero es menos estudiosa que yo. Mi hermana Sofía es más extrovertida que mi hermana Teresa y yo. Tiene muchos amigos, pero es menos estudiosa que yo y menos deportista que Teresa.

Tip: También is an adverb that means *too, also, as well.*

Mi hermana también es estudiosa. *(My sister is also studious.)*

More adjectives

English	Spanish	Pronunciation
sporty	**deportista**	*[deh-pohr-tees-tah]*
introvert	**introvertido**	*[een-troh-behr-tee-doh]*
extrovert	**extrovertido**	*[ehks-troh-behr-tee-doh]*
studious	**estudioso**	*[ehs-too-dyoh-soh]*
delicious	**rico**	*[rree-koh]*
stimulating	**estimulante**	*[ehs-tee-moo-lahn-teh]*

8.1 Practice

A. Let's see if you understood the relationships between the siblings. Join the part on the right to the one on the left.

1. Sofía es	más introvertida que Sofía
2. Susana es	menos deportista que Teresa
3. Teresa es	menos estudiosa que Susana

In English we use the suffixes **-er** and **-est** to compare two different adjectives (*Mary is taller than Alice*). In Spanish you need to say **más... que** (*more... than*) and **menos... que** (*less... than*): **María es más alta que Alicia** or **Alicia es más baja que María.**

As you see, Spanish uses the adverbs **más** and **menos** before an adjective to say if there is more or less or a specific quality.

Examples:
Fabián es más guapo que Raúl. (*Fabian is more handsome than Raul.*)
María es menos inteligente que Elena. (*Maria is less intelligent than Elena.*)

B. Comparing people

Roberto: Es moreno. Es serio y le gusta estudiar (estudioso). Es un poco introvertido.
Marta: Es morena. Le gusta jugar al tenis (deportista). No le gusta tanto estudiar.
Laura: Es rubia. Le gusta estudiar y tiene muchos amigos. Es extrovertida.

Answer the questions comparing these kids' traits, using **más que** or **menos que**. Of course, we are assuming things here, but it's just for the purposes of the exercise!
Example: Roberto / Marta (estudioso): Roberto es más estudioso que Marta.

1. Marta / Laura (deportista) ____________________
2. Roberto /Marta (deportista) ____________________
3. Laura / Marta (estudiosa) ____________________
4. Roberto / Laura (introvertido) ____________________
5. Laura / Roberto (extrovertido) ____________________
6. Marta / Laura (morena) ____________________
7. Marta / Roberto (seria) ____________________

8.2 Irregular Comparatives

While the most common way of comparing things in Spanish is with **más... que or menos... que**, there are irregular forms of comparatives as well. They apply to the adjectives **bueno** (*good*) and **malo** (*peor*). Check this out:

Bueno → Mejor (*better*) :
Este libro es mejor que ese. (*This book is better than that one.*)

Malo → Peor *(worse*) :
Este restaurante es peor que aquel. (*This restaurant is worse than that one.*)

Other irregular forms of comparatives are with the adjectives **mayor** (*older*) and **menor** (*younger)* when referring to age:

Mayor (older)	**Tomás es mayor que Sofía.** *(Tomás is older than Sofía)*
Menor (younger)	**Mi abuelo es menor que mi abuela.** *(My grandfather is younger than my grandmother.)*

8.2 Practice

A. Complete these sentences by comparing terms.

1. Estos chocolates son buenos, pero esos son ______________
2. Esta película es mala, pero aquella es ______________
3. Sandra Bullock es buena actriz, pero Meryl Streep es ______________
4. Yo tengo 29 años. Mi hermano Ricardo tiene 25. Él es ______________que yo.
5. Mi mamá tiene 50 años. Mi tía tiene 52. Mi tía es ______________ que mi mamá.

B. Write the opposite of these statements.

1. Los peores colegios. ______________
2. Alicia es mayor que Paula. ______________
3. Es el peor restaurante de la ciudad. ______________
4. Juan es menor que Tomás. ______________
5. Ese museo es mejor que aquel. ______________

C. Complete these short paragraphs with the appropriate form of **mayor, menor, mejor,** and **peor**.

1. Hoy voy de compras. Hay un vestido rojo, uno azul y uno amarillo. El vestido rojo tiene buen precio, pero el vestido azul tiene ____________ precio. El vestido amarillo cuesta mucho. Tiene el ____________ precio.
2. Ana tiene 15 años. Su hermano Ariel tiene 12 años. Es ____________ que Ana. Su hermano Leo tiene 17 años. Es ____________ que Ana y Ariel.

8.3 Comparing Equal Adjectives

In Spanish, when you want to compare two equal adjectives, you use **tan... como**. For example, **ella es tan inteligente como su hermana** (*She is as intelligent as her sister*). Notice how in English, comparisons just need the word **as** twice. But in Spanish, you need **tan** and **como**. And the adverb **tan** never changes, regardless of whether the adjective es feminine or masculine, singular or plural. It remains invariable.

María es tan estudiosa como Pedro. (*Maria is as studious as Pedro*).

Elena es tan deportista como Juan. (*Elena is as sporty as Juan*)

8.3 Practice

Complete the following with **tan... como**. Example: mi cuarto /el cuarto de mi hermano (limpio): **Mi cuarto es tan limpio como el cuarto de mi hermano.** (*My room is as clean as my brother's room.*) Remember to use the definite article or the possessive in each case!

1. cuerpo / mente (importante): ____________________________
2. bananas / manzanas (ricas): ____________________________
3. café / té (estimulante): ____________________________
4. carne / pescado (sana): ____________________________
5. Tomás / Sara (simpático): ____________________________
6. mi coche / tu coche (rápido): ____________________________
7. París / Londres (hermoso): ____________________________
8. gatos / perros (fieles): ____________________________

8.4 Comparing Nouns

To compare nouns in Spanish you need to use **tanto... como**. Only in this case, **tanto** has to match the noun:

Hay tantas personas como ayer.	*(There are as many people as yesterday.)*
Hay tanta comida en esta mesa como en esa.	*(There is as much food on this table as on that one.)*
Hay tantas flores en este jardín como en ese.	*(There are as many flowers in this garden as in that one.)*
Hay tanto café en esta taza como en esa.	*(There is as much coffee in this cup as in that one.)*
Hay tantos parques en esta ciudad como en aquella.	*(There are as many parks in this city as in that one.)*

Remember:

with adjectives use:	**with nouns use:**
más /menos... que	más / menos... que
tan... como	tanto / tantos / tanta / tantas... como

8.4 Practice

A. Complete these sentences using **tanto / tanta / tantos / tantas.**

1. Martín estudia ______________ horas como Javier.
2. Estela come ______________ pan como Susana.
3. En ese parque hay ______________ flores como en aquel.
4. En ese vaso hay ______________ agua como en este.
5. En mi ciudad hay ______________ bares como en tu ciudad.
6. José tiene ______________ amigos como Fran.
7. María hace ______________ ejercicio como Manuel.

B. Now answer negatively to these statements. **For example:**

—Tengo muchas bananas.
—Yo no tengo tantas bananas.

1. —En mi colegio hay muchos estudiantes.
   —En mi colegio no _______________________________.
2. —Juan come mucha carne.
   —Esteban no _______________________________.
3. —Martín estudia muchas horas por día.
   —Teresa no _______________________________.
4. —Pedro mira muchas películas por televisión.
   —Carlos no _______________________________.
5. —Bebo mucho café.
   —Tú no bebes _______________________________
   como Fernando.

CHAPTER 9:
HOW TO ASK QUESTIONS
HOW ARE YOU?

9.1 Interrogative Pronouns

The interrogative pronoun replaces the subject when you ask a question. They are used in learning information, and it's important to remember that they always have the graphic accent called **tilde**. A tilde is a diacritical mark (~) placed above certain letters, such as in Spanish, where it indicates a change in pronunciation or emphasis. In Spanish, the tilde is commonly used with vowels (á, é, í, ó, ú) and the letter ñ

Furthermore, they come with the question marks ¿? Remember that both of them are used when you ask questions in Spanish.

English	Spanish	Pronunciation
What?	**¿Qué?**	*[keh]*
For what?	**¿Para qué?**	*[pah-rah keh]*
Why?	**¿Por qué?**	*[pohr-keh]*
How? / What?	**¿Cómo?**	*[koh-moh]*
When?	**¿Cuándo?**	*[kwahn-doh]*
Where?	**¿Dónde?**	*[dohn-deh]*
From where?	**¿De dónde?**	*[deh dohn-deh]*
To where?	**¿Adónde?**	*[ah dohn-deh]*
Who? (singular)	**¿Quién?**	*[kyehn]*
Who? (plural)	**¿Quiénes?**	*[kyeh-nehs]*
Whose? (singular)	**¿De quién?**	*[deh kyehn]*
Whose? (plural)	**¿De quiénes?**	*[deh kyeh-nehs]*
Which one?	**¿Cuál?**	*[kwahl]*
Which ones?	**¿Cuáles?**	*[kwah-lehs]*

English	Spanish	Pronunciation
How much? (masculine)	**¿Cuánto?**	*[kwahn-toh]*
How much? (feminine)	**¿Cuánta?**	*[kwahn-tah]*
How many? (masculine)	**¿Cuántos?**	*[kwahn-tohs]*
How many? (feminine)	**¿Cuántas?**	*[kwahn-tahs]*

Examples:
¿Qué es esto? (*What is this?*)
¿Para qué necesitas trabajar? (*What do you need to work for?*)
¿Quién es tu mejor amigo? (*Who is your best friend?*)
¿Cómo está tu abuela? (*How is your grandmother?*)
¿Cuándo viene (*to come*) **Tomás?** (*When is Tomas coming?*)
¿Dónde compras el pan? (*Where do you buy the bread?*)
¿Quién es esa chica? (*Who is that girl?*)
¿Por qué estás triste? (*Why are you sad?*)
¿Cuántos libros lees en un mes? (*How many books do you read in a month?*)
¿Cuánta leche hay en el refrigerador? (*How much milk is there in the refrigerator?*)
¿Cuál es el padre de Sofía? (*Which one is Sofía's father?*)
¿Cuáles son tus libros favoritos? (*Which are your favorite books?*)

Tip: What can be translated for **¿qué?** and **¿cuál?**

¿Qué? tackles general questions, like asking:

"**¿Qué restaurante te gusta?**" (*What restaurant do you like?*)

Meanwhile, **¿Cuál?** steps up when you're choosing between two options, as in: "**¿Cuál es el edificio más grande?**" (*Which one is the biggest building?*)

Vocabulary: meals of the day

El desayuno *[ehl dehs-ah-yoo-noh]* : breakfast
La hora del té *[lah ohrah dehl teh]* : tea time
El almuerzo *[ehl ahl-mwehr-thoh]* : lunch
La cena *[lah theh-nah]* : dinner

9.1 Practice

A. Complete these sentences with the right interrogative pronoun. Make sure not to repeat any: **cuándo – quiénes – cuántos – cuánta – cuál – para qué – por qué – cómo – qué – dónde**

1. ¿________________ azúcar hay?
2. ¿________________ vamos al parque?
3. ¿________________ vive tu abuela?
4. ¿________________ es esto?
5. ¿________________ es tu habitación?
6. ¿________________ debo ir a la universidad?
7. ¿________________ es tu cumpleaños? *(birthday)*
8. ¿________________ son esos hombres?
9. ¿________________ es el amigo de Juana?
10. ¿________________ años tienes? (*How old are you?*)

B. Try to decide which to use, **¿qué?** or **¿cuál?** In each case. Remember **¿qué?** is used for general questions and **¿cuál?** is used for specific choices between objects or people.

1. ¿____________ es tu parque favorito?
2. ¿____________ vestido te gusta más, el azul o el amarillo?
3. ¿____________ es esto?
4. ¿____________ son los abuelos de Laura?
5. ¿____________ bebida te gusta?
6. ¿____________ computadora usas, la nueva o la vieja?

C. Fill in with **¿dónde? ¿de dónde? or ¿adónde?**

1. ¿____________ eres?
2. ¿____________ vas?
3. ¿____________ está mi mamá?
4. ¿____________ está Bangkok?
5. ¿____________ son tus abuelos?
6. ¿____________ está tu hermano?
7. ¿____________ va ese tren?

8. ¿_____________ vienen (*to come*) esas bananas?
9. ¿_____________ vas a ir?
10. ¿_____________ es tu esposo?

D. Choose between **¿cuánto? ¿cuánta? ¿cuántos? ¿cuántas?**

1. ¿_____________ amigas tienes?
2. ¿_____________ dinero tienes en tu billetera (*wallet*)?
3. ¿_____________ coches tiene Martín?
4. ¿_____________ pelotas tiene ese chico?
5. ¿_____________ azúcar hay en el frasco (*jar*)?
6. ¿_____________ bebes tú por día?
7. ¿_____________ años tienes?
8. ¿_____________ pescado comes por semana?

E. Now think of the question based on the answer. Use **¿Dónde? ¿Adónde?** and **¿De dónde?**

Example: ¿_________________________? Viene de Cuba. Answer: ¿De dónde viene?

1. ¿_________________________? Somos de Inglaterra.
2. ¿_________________________? Vamos al parque.
3. ¿_________________________? Los niños están en el colegio.
4. ¿_________________________? Voy a la biblioteca a estudiar.
5. ¿_________________________? Vienen (*to come*) de Italia.
6. ¿_________________________? Mi mamá está en clase de yoga.

F. Here, think of the question based on the answer. This time choose between:

¿De quién? ¿De quiénes? ¿Quién? ¿Quiénes?

1. ¿_____________? Esta casa es de mis abuelos.
2. ¿_____________? Julia Roberts es una actriz famosa.
3. ¿_____________? Estas medias son de Pablo.
4. ¿_____________? Esa niña es la hija de María.
5. ¿_____________? Los mejores jugadores de tenis son Medvedev y Zverev.
6. ¿_____________? Ese libro es de Marcos.

G. Read the text in the box and answer the questions below. Be sure to give a complete answer, using the verb provided.

Example: ¿A qué hora almuerza Pilar en la cafetería? Almuerza a las 12:00 del mediodía.

Pilar es profesora. Tiene 30 años. Vive en Madrid. Trabaja en un colegio. Entra a su trabajo todos los días a las 7:45 de la mañana. Llega en tren al colegio y camina unas cuadras. A veces, la acompaña una amiga desde la estación de tren. Pilar enseña geografía. A las 12:00 del mediodía almuerza en la cafetería del colegio. Le gusta comer un sándwich y una ensalada. A las 3:00 de la tarde, Pilar toma el tren y regresa a su casa.

1. ¿Qué hace Pilar? ______________________________
2. ¿Cuántos años tiene? ______________________________
3. ¿Cómo llega Pilar al colegio? ______________________________
4. ¿A qué hora llega al colegio? ______________________________
5. ¿Cuándo almuerza Pilar? ______________________________
6. ¿Dónde trabaja Pilar? ______________________________
7. ¿Qué hace Pilar en el colegio? ______________________________
8. ¿Quién acompaña a veces a Pilar desde la estación de tren? ______
9. ¿Qué come Pilar? ______________________________

9.2 The verb Venir (*to come*)

The verb "venir" in Spanish means "to come." Here's how it is conjugated in different forms. These conjugations are used to express various forms of *coming* in different contexts and subjects.

venir *(to come)*			
yo	**vengo**	nosotros/as	**venimos**
tú	**vienes**	vosotros/as	**venís**
él ella usted	**viene**	ellos ellas ustedes	**vienen**

Venir is an irregular verb in the yo form: **yo vengo** (*I come*), tú form: **tú vienes** (*you come*), usted/él/ella form: **él viene** (*he comes*), and the ustedes/ellos/ellas form: **ellas vienen** (*they come*)**.** Notice how the **e** from the stem changes to **ie**.

9.2 Practice

A. Give the right form of **venir**. Match the adjective to the noun provided and add the missing articles if needed.

Example: Mirta / venir / a / universidad / todo / días: **Mirta viene a la universidad todos los días.**

1. Susana / venir / de / Italia / en / avión
2. José y Tomás / venir / a / buscar / manzanas
3. Tú / venir / a / mi / fiesta
4. Tú y yo / venir / a / restaurante / todos / martes
5. Yo / venir / de / trabajar
6. Ellos / venir / a / París / a / ver / Torre Eiffel
7. Laura / venir / hospital / para / ver / a / médico

B. Now complete each sentence with the correct form of **venir.**

1. Yo no ________________ a la oficina hasta las 10:00 de la mañana.
2. Ellos no ______________ al restaurante hasta la hora de comer.
3. Tú no ________________ a mi casa todos los días.
4. Juana ________________ tarde (*late)* a clase.
5. Vosotros _____________ temprano (*early*) a la reunión.
6. Nosotros _____________ a la cita por la mañana.

C. Translate the following to Spanish:

1. Marcos comes to school in the morning.

   ____

2. You and I come to the university every Tuesday and Wednesday.

   ____

3. They come to our house for dinner.

   ____

4. You (plural) come to the doctor in the summer.

   ____

5. María comes to the restaurant to eat fish.

   ____

6. I come to the party happy.

   ____

CHAPTER 10:

USING ADVERBS TO DESCRIBE OUR ACTIONS

HOW DO YOU DO?

Adverbs

Adverbs are words that modify verbs, adjectives, and other adverbs, like *quickly, soon, a lot, and few*. In Spanish and English, adverbs are invariable. They don't change, regardless of whether the adjective they modify is feminine or masculine, singular or plural.

You might not have realized it, but you already know some of the most common adverbs. Here are some additions to the ones you've already been working with.

10.1 Adverbs of Quantity

Spanish	English	Example (Translation)
muy	very	Esas flores son **muy** hermosas. *(Those flowers are very beautiful.)*
mucho	a lot	Carlos viaja **mucho**. *(Carlos travels a lot.)*
bastante	quite/ quite a lot	Ella camina **bastante** rápido. *(She walks quite fast.)*
poco	not a lot	Martín come **poco**. *(Martín doesn't eat a lot.)*
demasiado	too much	Elena habla **demasiado**. *(Elena talks too much.)*
más	more	Ella corre **más** rápido. *(She runs faster.)*
menos	less	Tomás estudia **menos**. *(Tomás studies less.)*
muy	very	El plato está **muy** caliente. *(The plate is very hot.)*

10.2 Adverbs of Denial

Spanish	English	Example (Translation)
no	no, not	Ella **no** estudia. *(She doesn't study.)*
ni	nor, neither	No compra **ni** vende. *(He doesn't buy nor sell.)*
nunca	never	Juan **nunca** viene. *(Juan never comes.)*
tampoco	either	Leo **tampoco** mira televisión. *(Leo doesn't watch TV either.)*
jamás	never, ever	**Jamás** visitamos a mi tío. *(We never visit our uncle.)*

10.3 Adverbs of Time

Spanish	English	Example (Translation)
antes	before	Ella bebe agua **antes** de correr. *(She drinks water before running.)*
después	after	El estudia **después** de cenar. *(He studies after eating dinner.)*
luego	after, then	**Luego** me explicas el libro. *(After, you explain the book to me.)*
entonces	then	**Entonces**, viajé a Milán. *(Then, I traveled to Milan.)*
mientras	while	**Mientras** estudio, miro televisión. *(While I study, I watch TV.)*
pronto	soon	**Pronto** leeré ese libro. *(I'll soon read that book.)*
a tiempo	in time	El escribe la nota **a tiempo**. *(He writes the note in time.)*
tarde	late	Ella viene a mi casa **tarde**. *(She comes home late.)*

Spanish	English	Example (Translation)
temprano	early	Se levanta muy **temprano**. *(He wakes up very early.)*
siempre	always	**Siempre** compra pan negro. *(She always buys dark bread.)*
nunca	never	Marta **nunca** discute. *(Marta never argues.)*

10.4 Adverbs of Affirmation

Spanish	English	Example (Translation)
también	as well, also	Pedro **también** aprende chino. *(Pedro also learns Chinese.)*
sí	yes	**Sí**, quiero ir. *(Yes, I want to go.)*
ciertamente	certainly	**Ciertamente**, no lo conozco bien. *(I certainly don't know him well.)*
seguramente	surely	**Seguramente** sabe inglés. *(Surely, he knows English.)*

10.5 Adverbs of Manner

Spanish	English	Example (Translation)
bien	well	Conoce **bien** a Pablo. *(She knows Pablo well.)*
mejor	better	Esa clase es **mejor**. *(That class is better.)*
mal	badly	Martín arregla **mal** el coche. *(Martin fixes the car badly.)*
peor	worse	Pedro cocina **peor**. *(Pedro cooks worse.)*
solamente/solo	only	**Solo** bebe vino blanco. *(She only drinks white wine.)*

Now, let's dive into the realm of adverbs ending in -mente. These adverbs, also known as adverbs of manner, shed light on how you perform an action. Get ready to unravel the nuances of expressing the manner in which things are done!

How do you form them? The suffix **-mente** is added to the **feminine singular form of adjectives**. If an adjective has only one form for masculine and singular (**fácil**), then you simply add **-mente** to it: **fácilmente** *(easily)*

ADJECTIVE	ADVERB
rápido *(fast)*	**rápidamente** *(rapidly)*
perfecto *(perfect)*	**perfectamente** *(perfectly)*
libre *(free)*	**libremente** *(freely)*
alegre *(cheerful)*	**alegremente** *(cheerfully)*

When an adverb modifies a verb in Spanish, it's placed directly after the verb it modifies, or as close to the verb as possible: **Susana canta hermosamente** (*Susana sings beautifully*).

When an adverb modifies an adjective or adverb, it is placed directly before these: **El programa es menos eficiente** (*The program is less efficient*).

Some adjectives double as adverbs. For example, you can say **El tren corre rápidamente** or **El tren corre rápido**. Other examples of adjectives used as adverbs:

El hombre habla **fuerte**

La anciana habla **bajo**

La niña dibuja **bonito**

Los niños saltan **alto**

Practice 10

A. Complete these sentences with the right adverb of quantity

1. Los jóvenes comen ______________ (*a lot*)
2. Sofía estudia ____________________ (*quite a lot*)
3. Su gato come ___________________ (*too much*)
4. José habla _____________________ (*a lot*)

5. Elisa lee ____________ de noche (*more*)
6. Felipe está ____________ estresado (*very*)
7. Tu profesora es ____________ simpática que mi profesora (*less*)

B. Translate the following sentences into Spanish:

1. His brother is not here.

   ____

2. He doesn't like apples nor oranges.

   ____

3. They never go to the movie theater.

   ____

4. She doesn't like exercise either.

   ____

5. We never study together.

   ____

C. Complete this paragraph with adverbs of time

__________[1] *(always)* llego a la oficina a las 7:00 de la mañana. Es muy __________[2] *(early)*. __________[3] *(then)* trabajo dos horas. La gente __________[4] *(never)* llega __________[5] *(before)* de las 9:00 de la mañana. __________[6] *(while)* trabajo, escucho la radio. __________[7] *(soon)* es la hora de almorzar. Llego al comedor __________[8] *(in time)* para comer un rico plato de comida. No me voy muy __________[9] *(late)* de la oficina. Me gusta llegar __________[10] *(early)* a mi casa.

D. Turn these adjectives into adverbs. **Example: fiel → fielmente**

1. Inteligente → ____________________
2. Difícil → ____________________
3. Débil → ____________________
4. Feliz → ____________________
5. Rápido → ____________________
6. Furioso → ____________________
7. Nervioso → ____________________
8. Sincero (*sincere*) → ____________________
9. Verdadero (*true*) → ____________________
10. Normal (*normal*) → ____________________

E. Complete these sentences by turning the feminine form of the adjective next to them into an adverb.

Example: El avión no viaja ___________ a Brasil (directo) → El avión no viaja directamente a Brasil. Here, we took "directo" and changed it to the feminine "directa" and then added -mente: directamente.

1. ___________, no me gustó (**sincero**)
2. Está ___________ sucio (**total**)
3. Es ___________ interesante **(verdadero**)
4. Mira ___________ a su hija (**cariñoso**)
5. ___________, Martín viaja mañana (**posible**)
6. El coche gira ___________ (**rápido**)
7. Viene ___________ a mi casa (**directo**)
8. El padre explica ___________ el ejercicio a su hija (**paciente**)
9. Mi prima siempre come ___________ a las 12:00 del mediodía (**puntual**)
10. En esa ciudad, la gente vive ___________ (**tranquila**)

F. Complete these sentences turning the adjective in parentheses to an adverb and translating it.

1. Me preparo ____________________ para empezar a trabajar. (*happy*)
2. Su perro come ____________________. (*a lot*)
3. La cama entra ____________________ por la puerta de la habitación. (*difficult*)
4. Sofía mira ____________________ por la ventana. (*sad)*
5. Luisa viaja ____________________ a ver a su madre. (*fast*)
6. El nadador (*swimmer*) nada ____________________ hacia la orilla *(shore)*. *(weak)*
7. Los niños descansan ____________________. (*peaceful*)
8. ____________________ subimos al tren después de esperar tres horas. (*final*)
9. ____________________ vienen mis padres a almorzar. (*possible*)
10. Es ____________________ la una de la tarde. (*approximate*)

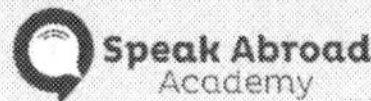

G. Give the opposite of these adverbs. **Example: fácilmente → difícilmente**

1. Débilmente → ______________________________
2. Rápidamente → ______________________________
3. Tristemente → ______________________________
4. Mucho → ______________________________
5. Mejor → ______________________________
6. Menos → ______________________________
7. Nunca → ______________________________

H. Now give an answer turning the adjective in the questions to an adverb.

Example. Julio responde a sus hermanos (*Julio answers his brothers*).

¿Está furioso? (*Is he furious?*) **→ Sí, responde furiosamente a sus hermanos** (*Yes, he answers his brothers furiously)*.

1. Elena trabaja en su casa. ¿Está tranquila?

   ____
2. La madre espera a su hijo. ¿Está nerviosa?

   ____
3. El periodista *(journalist)* critica las noticias. ¿Es duro?

   ____
4. Sandra organiza los cajones (*drawers*) de su habitación. ¿Es eficiente?

   ____
5. Fernando gana la carrera (*race*). ¿Está feliz?

   ____

I. These sentences are all mixed up! Sort the elements to come up with a real sentence. **Example: avanza / tren / el / rápidamente / muy: El tren avanza muy rápidamente.**

1. muy / trabajo / responsablemente ______________________________
2. cocinan / muy / Tomás y José / rico ______________________________
3. mal / profesora / problemas / los / la / explica ______________________________
4. bien / equipo / juega / fútbol / ese /al ______________________________
5. ocupados / estamos / hoy / muy ______________________________
6. rápidamente / del / salgo / taxi ______________________________

J. Translate the following sentences:

1. Luisa is more tired than you. ______________________________
2. Pedro speaks more clearly than Tomás. ___________________
3. This class is better than that one. _________________________
4. The president speaks passionately. ________________________
5. I know her mother well. ___________________________________
6. He never wakes up early. __________________________________
7. The dog always eats his food. _____________________________
8. While Susana works, Teresa studies. ______________________

CHAPTER 11:

INDICATIVE MOOD – PRESENT TENSE OF IRREGULAR VERBS

DO YOU PREFER CHICKEN OR PASTA?

11.1 Expressing Actions: Preferir (*To Prefer*), Querer (*To Want*), and Poder (*To be Able, Can*)

	preferir *(to prefer)*	**querer** *(to want)*	**poder** *(to be able)*
yo	**prefiero**	**quiero**	**puedo**
tú	**prefieres**	**quieres**	**puedes**
él, ella	**prefiere**	**quiere**	**puede**
usted	**prefiere**	**quiere**	**puede**
nosotros/as	**preferimos**	**queremos**	**podemos**
vosotros/as	**preferís**	**queréis**	**podéis**
ellos, ellas	**prefieren**	**quieren**	**pueden**
ustedes	**prefieren**	**quieren**	**pueden**

Preferir, querer, and **poder** are irregular because the stem vowel changes in the **yo, tú, él, ella**, and **usted**, as well as in **ellos, ellas,** and **ustedes.** In fact, the only people that keep the same stem are **nosotros** (*preferimos*) and **vosotros** (*preferís*).

Pre**fe**rir → yo pre**fie**ro

Querer → ellos **quie**ren

P**od**er → tú **pue**des

11.1 Practice

A. Answer these questions about your preferences.

Example: ¿Prefieres los perros o los gatos? Prefiero los gatos.

1. ¿Prefieres la televisión o el cine?
2. ¿Prefieres aprender español o francés?
3. ¿Prefieres estudiar lenguas o matemáticas?
4. ¿Prefieres comer en un restaurante o en tu casa?
5. ¿Prefieres vivir en el campo o en la ciudad?
6. ¿Prefieres la pasta (*pasta*) o el pollo (*chicken*)?

B. You're a storekeeper and are asking your client about a series of choices.

Example: ¿Quiere jamón o queso? Quiero queso.

1. ¿Quiere mantequilla (*butter*) o margarina?
2. ¿Quiere gelatina (*jello*) o flan (*custard*)?
3. ¿Quiere sal (*salt*) o pimienta (*pepper*)?
4. ¿Quiere ravioles (*ravioli*) o ñoquis (*gnocchi*)?
5. ¿Quiere carne (*meat*) o pescado (*fish*)?
6. ¿Quiere queso brie (*brie cheese*) o queso gruyère (*gruyère cheese*)?
7. ¿Quiere jugo de manzana (*apple juice*) o jugo de naranja (*orange juice*)?

C. You're describing your new baby's recent developments. Your friend asks you what she can do. **Example: ¿Puede gatear *(crawl)*? No, no puede gatear.**

1. ¿Puede comer sola? ______________________
2. ¿Puede pararse sola? ______________________
3. ¿Puede caminar sola? ______________________
4. ¿Puede subir las escaleras sola? ______________________
5. ¿Puede subirse a una silla sola? ______________________
6. ¿Puede beber leche sola? ______________________

D. Fill in the blanks with the right form of the verb in parenthesis

1. Mariana ______________ muchos exámenes. (tener)
2. Pedro y Hernán ______________ las manzanas a las bananas. (preferir)
3. Alicia ______________ esta noche a mirar televisión. (venir)
4. Nosotros ______________ ir al cine, pero no hay nada para ver. (querer)
5. Rubén y Sara ______________ tres perros en su casa. (tener)
6. Tú ______________ viajar en tren que viajar en avión. (preferir)
7. Yo ______________ dos veces por semana a la universidad. (venir)
8. Vosotros ______________ un regalo demasiado caro. (querer)

11.2 Other Stem-Changing Verbs: Pensar (*To Think*), Pedir (*To Ask*), Volver (*To Return*)

11.2 Practice

A. Reading Comprehension. Check this dialogue out and see if you can answer the questions below.

MAMÁ: Juan, **cierra** los ojos y **duerme**. Mañana **tienes** tu primer día de colegio.

JUAN: No **puedo** dormir. Estoy nervioso. Mañana **empieza** el colegio.

MAMÁ: ¿No **quieres** ver a tus amigos?

JUAN: Sí, **quiero** ver a mis amigos, pero **prefiero** verlos en el parque. Allí siempre jugamos al fútbol.

MAMÁ: **Pueden** venir el sábado a nuestra casa.

JUAN: ¡Qué buena idea!

1. ¿Qué tiene Juan mañana?
2. ¿Cómo está Juan?
3. ¿Quiere ver a sus amigos?
4. ¿Qué prefiere Juan?
5. ¿Cuándo pueden venir los amigos a la casa de Juan?

Here is a list of stem-changing verbs. Notice how in the **yo, tú él/ella/usted**, and **ellos** persons, the stem changes.

	e → ie	e → i
	pens-ar *(to think)*	ped-ir *(to ask for)*
	Other verbs like *pensar:* *cerrar, comenzar, despertarse, empezar, entender, perder, preferir, sentir*	Other verbs like *pedir:* *elegir, conseguir, corregir, despedir, freír, impedir, medir, perseguir, reír, repetir, seguir, servir, sonreír, vestirse*
yo	p**ie**n-so	p**i**d-o
tú	p**ie**n-sas	p**i**d-es
él/ella	p**ie**n-sa	p**i**d-e
usted	p**ie**n-sa	p**i**d-e
nosotros/as	pen-samos	ped-imos
vosotros/as	pen-sáis	pedís
ellos/ellas	p**ie**n-san	p**i**d-en
ustedes	p**ie**n-san	p**i**d-en

	o → ue		u → ue
	volv-er *(to return)*	dorm-ir *(to sleep)*	jug–ar *(to play)*
	Other verbs like *volver:* *acordarse, acostarse, contar, costar, encontrar, recordar, soñar, volar, devolver, llover, morder, poder, morir*		
yo	v**ue**lv-o	d**ue**rm-o	j**ue**g-o
tú	v**ue**lv-es	d**ue**rm-es	j**ue**g-as
él/ella	v**ue**lv-e	d**ue**rm-e	j**ue**g-a
usted	v**ue**lv-e	d**ue**rm-e	j**ue**g-a
nosotros/as	volv-emos	dorm-imos	jug-amos
vosotros/as	volv-éis	dorm-ís	jug-áis
ellos/ellas	v**ue**lv-en	d**ue**rmen	j**ue**g-an
ustedes	v**ue**lv-en	d**ue**rmen	j**ue**g-an

B. Complete these sentences with the right verb form.

Example: La profesora __________ el examen (corregir) → La profesora corrige el examen.

1. Elisa ________________ en su hijo. (pensar)
2. Nosotros ____________ un café. (pedir)
3. Tomás y Juan ________ de la ciudad. (volver)
4. Yo __________________ con mi hermana. (dormir)
5. Tú __________________ con la pelota. (jugar)
6. Vosotros _____________ de Francia. (volver)

C. Now answer complete sentences with the verb provided in the question.

Example: ¿Vosotros entendéis este problema? No, no entendemos ese problema.

1. ¿Tienes un jardín grande?

   Sí, yo ____.

2. ¿Vosotros preferís la carne o el pescado?

   Nosotros ____. (pescado)

3. ¿Laura consigue pan?

   No, Laura ______________________.

4. ¿Ellos duermen mucho?

   Sí, ellos ______________________.

5. ¿Qué restaurante elige Daniel?

   Daniel ______________________. (chino)

6. ¿Vosotros venís al museo?

   No, nosotros no ______________________.

7. ¿Cuánto mides tú?

   Yo ______________________. (1.70 m)

8. ¿Puede ayudarme, señor Pérez?

   Sí, ______________________.

D. Write negative sentences.

Example: (Francia, tener) __________ el Big Ben → <u>Francia no tiene el Big Ben.</u>

1. (Elsa/soñar) ______________ con su exnovio (*ex boyfriend*).
2. (Nosotros/dormir) ______________ mucho.
3. (Teresa y Miguel/jugar) ______________ siempre al tenis.
4. (Tú/empezar) ______________ a cocinar temprano.
5. (Vosotros/querer) ______________ una casa moderna.
6. (Yo/volver) ______________ tarde del trabajo.

E. Complete these sentences using the right form of the existing verb in the first part.

Example: Juana quiere té, pero yo __________ café → <u>Juana quiere té, pero yo quiero café</u>.

1. Ellos piensan en la comida, pero nosotros __________ en el deporte.
2. Yo prefiero jugar al golf, pero tú __________ jugar al tenis.
3. Zara cierra a las 8:00 p.m., pero las otras tiendas __________ a las 10:00 p.m.
4. Ustedes sirven comida china, pero nosotros __________ comida tailandesa (*Thai*).
5. Nosotros jugamos al Monopoly, pero vosotros __________ a las cartas (*cards*).

6. José duerme siete horas, pero los niños ___________ diez horas.
7. Tú vuelves a tu casa el viernes, pero yo ___________ el sábado.
8. Andrés piensa poco, pero sus padres ___________ demasiado.

F. Translate the following sentences. Try not to use the pronoun when it's already implicit in the verb form and you don't have to specify any name.

Example: We serve wine at dinner: <u>Servimos vino en la comida</u>.

1. I close the window in the living room.

   ____.

2. She starts her classes in the morning.

   ____.

3. You (plural) have lunch in a French restaurant.

   ____.

4. Roberto and Maria remember their grandfather.

   ____.

5. You (singular) play tennis on Sundays.

   ____.

6. María always thinks of her children.

   ____.

Common Mistake: The verbs **empezar** (*to begin/to start*) and **comenzar** (*to begin/to start*) need the preposition **a** when followed by an infinitive.

For example: **Empiezo a estudiar a las 8:00 p.m.**

X Don't say: **Empiezo estudiar.**

✓ Say instead: **Empiezo a estudiar.**

CHAPTER 12:

INDICATIVE MOOD – PAST TENSE OF REGULAR VERBS

I WASN'T BORN YESTERDAY

12.1 The Preterite Tense of Ser (*to Be*) and Ir (*to Go*)

The two main past tenses in Spanish are the **preterite** and the **imperfect**. The preterite refers to actions that are over and have ended. Instead, the imperfect refers to an action in the past that wasn't completed.

The preterite is usually used in narrations and descriptions, habitual actions, or continuous actions in the past: **Juana se levantaba a las ocho de la mañana todos los días** (*Juana used to wake up at 8:00 a.m. every morning*). Many times, the translation from the Spanish imperfect to English sounds better with "used to..."

Even if **ser** (*to be*) and **ir** (*to go*) are both irregular verbs, we will start with their preterites since they're such important verbs. Funnily enough, the preterite of **ser** *(to be)* is exactly the same as the preterite of **ir** *(to go)*. Do you think that confuses things more or less? In any case, the only way to tell the difference is by context. Don't worry. You'll get the hang of it!

	ser *(to be)*	**ir** *(to go)*
yo	fui	fui
tú	fuiste	fuiste
él, ella	fue	fue
usted	fue	fue
nosotros/as	fuimos	fuimos
vosotros/as	fuisteis	fuisteis
ellos, ellas	fueron	fueron
ustedes	fueron	fueron

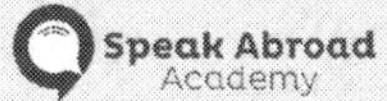

12.1 Practice

Fill in the blanks with the correct preterite form of **ser** or **ir**, and say which of the two you're using. **Example: __________ una sorpresa:** **<u>Fue una sorpresa</u>** (verbo **ser**)

1. Matisse y Monet __________ pintores.
2. ¿__________ (tú) al Burj Khalifa en Dubai?
3. Vosotros __________ muy inteligentes.
4. Elsa __________ muy buena con sus nietos.
5. Yo no __________ a la fiesta anoche.
6. Tú __________ generosa con tu dinero.
7. No __________ (nosotros) al supermercado ayer.
8. Luisa, ¿adónde __________ el sábado pasado?
9. Tú y Pedro __________ los mejores amigos de mi hijo.
10. Tomás y Germán __________ al monte Washington.

12.2 The Preterite of Regular Verbs Hablar (*to Talk*), Comer (*to Eat*), and Vivir (*to Live*)

	habl-ar *(to talk)*	**com-er** *(to eat)*	**viv-ir** *(to live)*
yo	habl-é	com-í	viv-í
tú	habl-aste	com-iste	viv-iste
él, ella	habl-ó	com-ió	viv-ió
usted	habl-ó	com-ió	viv-ió
nosotros/as	habl-amos	com-imos	viv-imos
vosotros/as	habl-asteis	com-isteis	viv-visteis
ellos, ellas	habl-aron	com-ieron	viv-ieron
ustedes	habl-aron	com-ieron	viv-ieron

Tip: Verbs ending in **-ar** and **-ir** have the same form for the first-person plural **(nosotros)** preterite as for the present. You'll know if the verb is in the present or past from context: **Todos los días caminamos al colegio** (present) vs. **Ayer caminamos al colegio** (past).

Here are some examples of the use of the preterite:

Anoche, ella **estudió** tres horas.	Last night, she studied three hours.
Ayer, Marcos y Fabián **cocinaron** para sus amigos.	Yesterday, Marcos and Fabian cooked forsome friends.
El domingo pasado **corrí** una maratón.	Last Sunday, I ran a marathon.
Elisa **jugó** al golf el martes pasado.	Elisa played golf last Tuesday.
Nosotros **vivimos** muchos años en África.	We lived many years in Africa.
¿**Viste** a María en el centro comercial?	Did you see Maria at the shopping center?

12.2. Practice

A. Reading Comprehension

Caperucita Roja

Una niña llamada Caperucita Roja **fue** a ver a su abuela. Pero **se encontró** con el lobo en el bosque. El lobo **corrió** a la casa de la abuela. **Tocó** la puerta, **entró** y **se comió** a la abuela. Luego, Caperucita **llegó** a la casa de su abuela. **Creyó** que el lobo era su abuela. **Tenía** los ojos, las orejas y los dientes muy grandes. Entonces, el lobo **quiso** comer a Caperucita. Un cazador **pasó** por la casa y **vio** al lobo por la ventana. **Entró** rápidamente y **mató** al lobo con su escopeta. La abuela de Caperucita **salió** del estómago del lobo. Todos **vivieron** muy felices.

Glossary:

llamada: called

se encontró: she met (*encontrarse*)

bosque: forest

tocó: knocked (*tocar*)

quiso: wanted (*querer*)

cazador: hunter

mató: killed (*matar*)

escopeta: shotgun

estómago: stomach

Answer the following questions:

1. ¿Adónde fue Caperucita Roja?

    ____

2. ¿Con quién se encontró en el bosque?

    ____

3. ¿Quién pasó por la casa?

    ____

4. ¿Qué hizo el cazador?

    ____

5. ¿De dónde salió la abuela de Caperucita?

    ____

B. Complete the sentences with the correct preterite form. To make this easier for you, you'll find the infinitive in parenthesis to know what group it belongs to! Remember not to include the subject pronouns. **Example: Ayer _________ (vosotros/estudiar) hasta la medianoche → <u>Ayer estudiasteis hasta la medianoche</u>.**

1. _________ a tu amigo. (tú /llamar)
2. _________ un vaso de agua. (yo/beber)
3. _________ la puerta. (nosotros /abrir)
4. Tomás y Mariana _________ a la anciana a cruzar la calle. (ayudar)
5. Anoche, los invitados _________ hasta tarde. (bailar)
6. En la universidad, Luisa _________ biología (estudiar)
7. _________ una invitación (*invitation*) para ir a la fiesta (vosotros/recibir)
8. _________ a Estela en el parque. (ustedes/ver)
9. _________ un vaso de agua al corredor (*runner*). (vosotros/ofrecer)
10. Anoche _________ con nuestro padre (nosotros /soñar)

12.3 The Preterite of Regular Verbs with a Spelling Change

These verbs have a spelling change for the preterite in the first person singular: Yo

	habl-ar *(to talk)*	**com-er** *(to eat)*	**viv-ir** *(to live)*
yo	habl-é	com-í	viv-í
tú	habl-aste	com-iste	viv-iste
él, ella	habl-ó	com-ió	viv-ió
usted	habl-ó	com-ió	viv-ió
nosotros/as	habl-amos	com-imos	viv-imos
vosotros/as	habl-asteis	com-isteis	viv-visteis
ellos, ellas	habl-aron	com-ieron	viv-ieron
ustedes	habl-aron	com-ieron	viv-ieron

12.3 Practice

A. Complete these sentences choosing one verb from the list (each verb is used once). Remember you don't need to add the pronoun because it's already included in the verb's conjugation.

Example: Anoche ___________ (yo) el timbre *(doorbell)* de tu casa: Anoche toqué el timbre en tu casa.

abrazar – publicar – empezar – pagar – alcanzar – buscar – llegar – tocar

1. Ayer ___________ (vosotros) a estudiar para el examen de Geografía.
2. ___________ (yo) mis zapatos debajo de la cama.
3. Karina y Pablo ___________ a la cena muy tarde.
4. ___________ (yo) el primer puesto (*the first place*)
5. ___________ (tú) mucho dinero.
6. ___________ (yo) mi libro el año pasado.
7. ___________ (yo) a mis hijos.

B. Complete Shakira's biography

Shakira nació (nacer) en Colombia en el año 1977. A los ocho años __________ (escribir) [1] su primera canción. __________ (empezar) [2] su carrera musical en 1991 y __________ (publicar) [3] el álbum *Pies descalzos*. __________ (vender)[4] cuatro millones de álbumes. Su álbum *¿Dónde están los ladrones?* la __________ (convertir) [5] en la artista más popular de Latinoamérica. __________ (ganar) [6] muchos premios, entre ellos, tres Grammy Award y doce Latin Grammy. En febrero de 2020, Shakira __________ (cantar) [7] en el Super Bowl. Mucha gente __________ (ver) [8] ese show.

C. Who says this? Give the right subject pronoun for each verb.

Example: vivisteis: vosotros

1. Ayudó ______________________________
2. Fumé ______________________________
3. Escuchamos ______________________________
4. Viví ______________________________
5. Comencé ______________________________
6. Pagaste ______________________________
7. Pagasteis ______________________________
8. Bebieron ______________________________
9. Estudió ______________________________
10. Busqué ______________________________

D. Fill in the missing squares with the appropriate verb form:

Infinitive form of the verb >>>	hablar	comer	vivir
yo		comí	
tú	hablaste		
él, ella, usted	habl-ó		
nosotros	hablamos		vivimos
vosotros			vivisteis
ellas, ellos, ustedes		comieron	

E. Remember reflexive verbs in Lesson 17? They have the same past tense as regular verbs, but you have to place the pronoun **befor**e the verb. Turn these infinitive forms into the preterite. **For example: Despertarse (ella)→ se despertó.**

1. Levantarse (nosotros) ______________________________
2. Lavarse (tú) ______________________________
3. Bañarse (vosotros) ______________________________
4. Ducharse (yo) ______________________________
5. Afeitarse (ellos) ______________________________
6. Prepararse (él) ______________________________

F. What did these people do on Saturday? Write the verbs in parenthesis in the preterite matching the pronoun.

yo: El domingo pasado (despertarse) __________[1] temprano y (tomar) __________[2] el desayuno. (beber) __________[3] café y (comer) __________[4] tostadas. Por la mañana (estudiar) __________.[5] Después (preparar) __________[6] el almuerzo y (almorzar) __________.[7] Luego, (lavar) __________[8] y (secar) __________[9] los platos. Por la tarde (jugar) __________[10] al golf. (acostarse) __________[11] temprano.

nosotros: El domingo pasado (despertarse) __________[12] temprano y (tomar) __________[13] el desayuno. (beber) __________[14] café y (comer) __________[15] tostadas. Por la mañana (estudiar) __________.[16] Después (preparar) __________[17] el almuerzo y (almorzar) __________.[18] Luego, (lavar) __________[19] y (secar) __________[20] los platos. Por la tarde (jugar) __________[21] al golf. (acostarse) __________[22] temprano.

G. Change the sentences to the past. **Example: Me levanto temprano: Me levanté temprano.**

1. Busco un empleado: ______________________________
2. Empieza el día: ______________________________
3. Sacamos el pastel (*cake*) del horno (*oven*): ______________
4. Usan un lápiz: ______________________________
5. Os bañáis en la piscina: ______________________________
6. Elena y Luis hablan por teléfono: ____________________
7. Ofrece sus servicios: ______________________________
8. Viven bien: ______________________________

CHAPTER 13:

INDICATIVE MOOD – PAST TENSE OF IRREGULAR VERBS

YOU DID IT

13.1 The Preterite Tense of Irregular Verbs Dar (*to Give*), and Hacer (*to Do*)

In this lesson, we are going to practice the preterite form of two more irregular verbs.

	dar *(to give)*	**hacer** *(to do)*
yo	di	hice
tú	diste	hiciste
él, ella	dio	hizo
usted	dio	hizo
nosotros/as	dimos	hicimos
vosotros/as	disteis	hicisteis
ellos, ellas	dieron	hicieron
ustedes	dieron	hicieron

13.1 Practice

A. Make a sentence joining the fragments and conjugating the verb to match its subject. **Example: Escocia / a / hacer / nosotros / viaje / un: Nosotros hicimos un viaje a Escocia**.

1. dar / regalo / a / un / sábado / el / mi / amigo (yo)
   ______________________________.
2. concierto / un / dar / Teresa y Julio / piano / de
   ______________________________.
3. largo / un / viaje / Canadá / por / hacer / nosotros
   ______________________________.
4. parque / vosotros / un / dar / paseo / por / el
   ______________________________.

5. pastel / ayer / para / Luisa / hacer / (yo) / un
   ____.
6. dar / pastel / un / nosotros / le (to him)
   ____.

B. Cecilia's vacation. Change the verbs in parenthesis to the preterite and make them match the pronoun they're referring to. **Example: Anoche __________ (yo/ estudiar) para el examen: <u>Anoche estudié para el examen</u>.**

El año pasado, mi amigo Pedro y yo __________ (ir)[1] a Francia y __________ (vivir) [2] con una familia francesa. __________ (visitar) [3] los museos y los parques y __________ (ir) [4] a clases de francés en la universidad. __________ (aprender) [5] a hablar francés y __________ (practicar) [6] con muchos franceses. También __________ (hacer) [7] viajes a otras ciudades de Francia. __________ (ver)[8] lugares preciosos. Además, __________ (visitar)[9] Lyon y Avignon. __________ (comer) [10] muchas baguettes y __________ (beber)[11] vinos muy ricos.

Glossary:

Lugares: *places*

Baguettes: *long, thin piece of French bread*

C. Change the verbs to the preterite.

Example: Yo __________ (levantarse) tarde el sábado. Yo <u>me levanté</u> tarde el sábado.

1. 1 El lunes yo ________________ (ir) al trabajo.
2. 2. El martes tú _______________ (jugar) al tenis.
3. 3. El miércoles ella ____________ (hacer) un pastel.
4. 4. El jueves nosotros __________ (dar) un concierto (*concert*) de piano.
5. 5. El viernes ustedes __________ (ir) al cine.
6. 6. El sábado vosotros __________ (descansar).

13.2 The Preterite Tense of More Irregular Verbs

Have you mastered the previous verbs? Let's learn five more that will be helpful to your Spanish. The best way to remember the conjugations of irregular verbs is to practice and study!

	est-ar *(to be)*	**pod-er** *(to be able to)*	**pon-er** *(to put)*	**sab-er** *(to know)*	**quer-er** *(to want)*
yo	estuve	pude	puse	supe	quise
tú	estuviste	pudiste	pusiste	supiste	quisiste
él, ella	estuvo	pudo	puso	supo	quiso
usted	estuvo	pudo	puso	supo	quiso
nosotros/as	estuvimos	pudimos	pusimos	supimos	quisimos
vosotros/as	estuvisteis	pudisteis	pusisteis	supisteis	quisisteis
ellos, ellas	estuvieron	pudieron	pusieron	supieron	quisieron
ustedes	estuvieron	pudieron	pusieron	supieron	quisieron

	ten-er *(to have)*	**ven-ir** *(to come)*	**de-cir** *(to say)*	**tra-er** *(to bring)*
yo	tuve	vine	dije	traje
tú	tuviste	viniste	dijiste	trajiste
él, ella	tuvo	vino	dijo	trajo
usted	tuvo	vino	dijo	trajo
nosotros/as	tuvimos	vinimos	dijimos	trajimos
vosotros/as	tuvisteis	vinisteis	dijisteis	trajisteis
ellos, ellas	tuvieron	vinieron	dijeron	trajeron
ustedes	tuvieron	vinieron	dijeron	trajeron

If you look closely, you'll see that all these verbs have the same endings for the preterite.

estar:	**estuv-**	
poder:	**pud-**	**-e**
poner:	**pus-**	**-iste**
querer:	**quis-**	**-o**
saber:	**sup-**	**-imos**
tener:	**tuv-**	**-isteis**
venir:	**vin-**	**-ieron**
decir:	**dij-**	
traer:	**traj-**	**-e, -iste, o- imos- isteis, eron**

13.2 Practice

A. Fill in the missing squares with the appropriate verb form:

Infinitive >>>	dar	hacer	estar	poder	poner	saber
yo		hice				supe
tú	diste			pudiste		
él, ella, usted		hizo			puso	
nosotros			estuvimos			supimos
vosotros				pudisteis		
ellas, ellos, ustedes	dieron		estuvieron		pusieron	

B. Complete this paragraph with the appropriate preterite irregular verb form:

El año pasado __________ (venir)[1] todos mis hermanos a Bogotá. __________ (nosotros/poder)[2] vernos después de muchos años. __________ (nosotros/tener)[3] suerte. Mi madre y mi padre también __________ (estar) [4] presentes. Mis hermanos __________ (traer) [5] regalos para todos. __________ (ser) [6] muy lindo. Mi hermana Mariana y yo __________ (hacer)[7] una comida especial. __________ (nosotros/poner)[8] la mesa en el jardín y __________ (nosotros/reunirse)[9] para comer. Todos __________ (contar) [10] anécdotas de su vida. Luego, __________ (ir)[11] a visitar a mis abuelos.

Glossary:

suerte: *luck*

regalos: *presents*

anécdotas: *anecdotes*

comida: *dinner* (as well as food)

C. Fill in the blanks with the appropriate preterite irregular verb form:

1. Ayer, Matías __________ (ir) al banco.
2. Rosa y Teresa __________ (ser) grandes amigas.
3. ¿Cómo __________ (estar) la fiesta?
4. Te __________ mucho. (yo/querer)
5. __________ un gran año. (vosotros/tener)
6. __________ a Canadá para ver a tu padre. (tú/venir)
7. __________ que no quiere comer (ella/decir)
8. No __________ venir por el trabajo (yo/poder)
9. La reunión __________ muy buena (estar)
10. Ayer __________ que Fernando no vino (vosotros/saber)

D. Complete the blank spaces in this dialogue.

Tomás: Oye (*hey*), ¿por qué no __________ (tú/venir) [1] ayer a la universidad?

Pedro: __________ (yo/estar) [2] en el hospital. __________ (yo/tener) [3] cita (*appointment*) con el médico (*doctor*).

Tomás: ¿__________ (tú/estar) [4] enfermo (sick)?

Pedro: No, me dolía el hombro *(my shoulder hurt*).

Tomás: ¿Y qué te __________ (dar) [5] el médico?

Pedro: Me __________ (dar) [6] una crema (*cream*) para calmar (*calm*) el dolor (*pain*).

E. What happened last night? Turn the sentences from the present to the preterite

1. El hijo de Elena viene a visitarnos.

   ____

2. Está en nuestra casa durante una hora.

   ____

3. Nos trae un regalo.

   ____

4. No puede estar mucho tiempo.

   ____

5. Nos dice adiós y se va.

   ____

13.3 The Preterite Tense of Stem-Changing Verbs

Did you know that not all verbs in Spanish change their stem in the preterite tense? It's true! Both -ar and -er stem-changing verbs, like **recordar** and **perder,** maintain their original stem in the preterite.For example, **recordar** (that changes its stem to **-ue** in the present: **recuerdo**) and **perder** (that changes its stem to **-ie** in the present: **pierdo**) do not change their forms when conjugated in the preterite.

	recordar *(to remember)*	**perder** *(to lose)*
yo	recordé	perdí
tú	recordaste	perdiste
él, ella	recordó	perdió
usted	recordó	perdió
nosotros/as	recordamos	perdimos
vosotros/as	recordasteis	perdisteis
ellos, ellas	recordaron	perdieron
ustedes	recordaron	perdieron

Instead, **-ir** stem-changing verbs do have a stem change in the preterite, but only in the third person singular and plural. For example, **pedir → él pidió/ellos pidieron** or **dormir(se) → él durmió/ellos durmieron.** Other -ir stem-changing verbs are **preferir, reír(se), sentir(se), servir, sonreír,** and **vestir(se).**

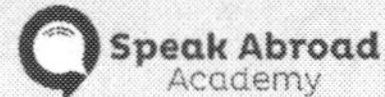

	pedir *(to ask for)*	**dormir(se)** *(to sleep)*
yo	pedí	dormí
tú	pediste	dormiste
él, ella	pidió	durmió
usted	pidió	durmió
nosotros/as	pedimos	dormimos
vosotros/as	pedisteis	dormisteis
ellos, ellas	pidieron	durmieron
ustedes	pidieron	durmieron

13.3 Practice

A. Make sentences with the words suggested, and conjugate the infinitive in the preterite

1. Martín / reírse / de mis planes

   ____

2. Mi mamá / me / pedir / un favor (*a favor*)

   ____

3. Yo / preferir / el helado de chocolate (*chocolate ice cream*)

   ____

4. Tomás y Juana / dormir / muy bien

   ____

5. El profesor / sentirse / contento / con / las notas (*grades*) / de / los alumnos

   ____

6. Vosotros / servir / una sopa / de tomate

   ____

7. Tú / sonreír / cuando (*when*) / ver / a / tu amigo

   ____

B. Complete these sentences with one of the verbs suggested in the preterite:

pedir – dormir(se) – preferir – reír(se) – sentir(se)
servir – sonreír – vestir(se) – entender

1. Yo __________ con un vestido largo para ir a la fiesta.
2. Tú __________ delante del televisor.
3. Marta __________ un favor.
4. El niño no __________ porque no __________ la broma (*the joke*).
5. Julio y yo __________ ir en coche que caminar.
6. El camarero me __________ la comida muy rápido.
7. El bebé vio a su madre y __________.
8. Vosotros __________ muy mal después de comer tanto.

CHAPTER 14:

INDICATIVE MOOD – IMPERFECT PAST

WHEN I WAS YOUNG

14.1 The Imperfect Past Tense

Unlike the preterite past tense, which talks about an action that happened at a specific point in the past and finished, in Spanish the **past imperfect tense** is used to describe things in the past that happened over a period of time. The imperfect indicates an action that was habitual or was in progress.

El día que conocí al amor de mi vida

Cuando conocí a mi novia, **creía** que era la mujer más perfecta del mundo. **Llevaba** su foto en mi billetera y la **miraba** todo el día. Todas las tardes la **visitaba** y **hablábamos** mientras **caminábamos** por el parque. Yo **tenía** dieciocho años y ella **tenía** diecisiete. No **teníamos** dinero, pero no lo **necesitábamos**. **Era** una joven muy linda. **Tenía** el pelo rubio y los ojos azules. **Era** simpática y divertida. **Olía** a rosas. O eso **creía** yo en ese momento. Yo le **regalaba** flores y chocolates. Todavía recuerdo ese amor. Y todavía puedo oler el perfume de las rosas que **adornaban** su pelo.

hablar (*to speak*)			
yo	**hablaba**	nosotros/as	**hablábamos**
tú	**hablabas**	vosotros/as	**hablabais**
él ella usted	**hablaba**	ellos ellas ustedes	**hablaban**

comer (*to eat*)			
yo	**comía**	nosotros/as	**comíamos**
tú	**comías**	vosotros/as	**comíais**
él ella usted	**comía**	ellos ellas ustedes	**comían**

vivir (*to live*)			
yo	**vivía**	nosotros/as	**vivíamos**
tú	**vivías**	vosotros/as	**vivíais**
él ella usted	**vivía**	ellos ellas ustedes	**vivían**

Tip: REMEMBER that in the conjugation of verbs in Spanish, the persons corresponding to the pronouns ***he***, ***she*** and ***you*** are conjugated the same. The same thing happens with ***they***, ***them*** and ***you***. As you can see, the imperfect does not escape this grammatical rule.

Good news: No stem change is needed in the imperfect tense.

There are only three verbs that are irregular in the imperfect: **ir, ser,** and **ver**

	ir (*to go*)	**ser** (*to be*)	**ver** (*to look*)
yo	**iba**	**era**	**veía**
tú	**ibas**	**eras**	**veías**
él,ella,usted	**iba**	**era**	**veía**
nosotros/as	**íbamos**	**éramos**	**veíamos**
vosotros/as	**ibais**	**erais**	**veíais**
ellos,ellas,ustedes	**iban**	**eran**	**veían**

Here are some examples of the imperfect:

Siempre íbamos al mismo hotel.
(We always went to the same hotel.)

Todos los inviernos visitábamos a mi abuela.
(Every winter we visited my grandmother.)

Yo leía mientras tú escribías.
(I read while you wrote.)

La quería mucho.
(I loved her a lot.)

Tenía treinta años.
(She was thirty years old.)

14.1 Practice

A. Give the imperfect of the following verbs according to the pronoun:

1.
   a. Yo (cerrar) ______________________
   b. Yo (escuchar) ______________________
   c. Yo (mirar) ______________________
   d. Yo (querer) ______________________
   e. Yo (recibir) ______________________

2.
   a. Tú (pedir) ______________________
   b. Tú (visitar) ______________________
   c. Tú (pensar) ______________________
   d. Tú (entrar) ______________________
   e. Tú (tener) ______________________

3.
   a. usted/ él/ ella (preguntar) ______________
   b. usted/ él/ ella (abrir) ______________
   c. usted/ él/ ella (comprar) ______________
   d. usted/ él/ ella (enseñar) ______________
   e. usted/ él/ ella (volver) ______________

B. Fill in the blanks with the imperfect of **ir, ser,** or **ver**

1. Marta __________ televisión todas las noches.
2. Jorge y Tomás __________ a jugar al tenis todos los sábados.
3. De joven, __________ (yo) muy deportista.
4. Vosotros __________ los mejores profesores de la universidad.
5. De niño, tú __________ mucho al cine.
6. Todos los martes, vosotros __________ vuestro programa favorito.

C. Now and Before. Times Change. Turn the sentence in the present tense into a past tense statement, describing how things were in the past. You'll get some helpful hints in parenthesis. **Example: Ahora guardamos la comida en el refrigerador. <u>Antes guardábamos la comida con sal</u>.**

1. Ahora lavamos la ropa en la máquina de lavar. (antes/lavar a mano)

   ____

2. Ahora viajamos en coche. (antes/en carreta)

   ____

3. Ahora hablamos por teléfono celular (antes/cara a cara(*face to face*))

   ____

4. Ahora vivimos en casas. (antes/en chozas)

   ____

5. Ahora escribimos con computadora. (antes/máquina de escribir)

   ____

6. Ahora cocinamos con horno eléctrico. (antes/fogatas)

   ____

D. Now try to answer these questions about your past.

1. ¿Dónde vivías de niño?

   ____

2. ¿A qué colegio ibas?

   ____

3. ¿Cuántos amigos o amigas tenías?

   ____

4. ¿Eras un niño tranquilo o inquieto?

   ____

5. ¿Practicabas algún deporte? ¿Cuál?

 ____

6. ¿Tenías un perro o un gato?

 ____

E. Fill in the blanks with the right form of the imperfect. The pronoun is only indicated to match the verb to the person.

1. De niño, mi familia y yo __________ (pasar) los veranos en la playa.
2. Nuestra casa __________ (estar) sobre la arena.
3. Mis primos también __________ (ir).
4. Todos __________ (nosotros/jugar) al fútbol sobre la arena.
5. Después __________ (nosotros/almorzar) sandwiches y limonada (*lemonade*).
6. Por la tarde __________ (ver) la puesta de sol (*sunset*) sobre el mar.
7. __________ (nosotros/volver) a casa cuando las estrellas __________ (brillar) en el cielo.

F. Make a sentence reordering the fragments and conjugating the verb to match its subject. **Example: de niña/ tener / Mariana / un hámster: <u>De niña, Mariana tenía un hamster</u>**.

1. de joven / jugar / fútbol / al / pedro

 ____

2. vivir / mis primos / lejos / muy / casa / de / mi / de niño

 ____

3. los veranos / durante / en la piscina / vosotros / club / del / nadar

 ____

4. beber / abuela / leche / mi / dormir / para

 ____

5. veranos / la casa / pasar / yo / los / en / tíos / mis / de

 ____

6. domingos / los / abuelo / siempre / un restaurante / ir / mi / a / yo / y / a almorzar

 ____

14.2 The Imperfect Tense Used Together with the Indefinite Tense

You also use the imperfect tense when you're describing a situation in which suddenly—an action in the preterite tense—interrupts it.

Here are some examples:

Estaba durmiendo cuando mi mamá me despertó.
(*I was sleeping when my mom woke me up.*)
Llovía cuando salimos del cine.
(*It was raining when we came out of the movie theater.*)
Estabais en el supermercado cuando se fue la luz.
(*You were in the supermarket when the lights went out.*)
Laura manejaba el coche cuando tuvimos el accidente.
(*Laura was driving the car when we had the accident.*)
Cuando llegó Juan, Elena estaba durmiendo.
(*When Juan arrived, Elena was sleeping.*)

Notice that in all these sentences, there is a background action that is happening when a sudden situation interrupts it.

14.2 Practice

A. Choose between the preterite and the imperfect to complete the blanks. Remember, if it's an event that happened at a specific point in time, it goes in the preterite. If it's something that has some duration, it goes in the imperfect.

ir – sacar – abalanzarse (*throw oneself*) – **sujetar** (*restrain*) – **querer – estar - apuntar** (*aim*) – **aparecer** (*appear*) – **quitar** (*take away*)

El martes Josefina __________[1] al banco para sacar dinero del cajero. Cuando __________[2] en la cola (*line*), una de las personas __________[3] una pistola (*gun*) y __________[4] hacia el policía. El ladrón __________[5] robar. Pero, de pronto, un guardia __________[6] desde atrás y __________[7] sobre el ladrón. Le __________[8] el arma (*weapon*) y le __________[9] las manos.

B. Choose among the preterite and the imperfect with these verbs:

moverse – gritar – entrar – quedarse – salir – oír – dejar – ver (x2) – **bajar – tener – ser**

De niño, Juan ___________ [1] muchas veces solo en su casa. Sus padres ___________ [2] mucho y lo ___________ [3] solo. Una noche, ___________ [4] un ruido abajo. ___________ [5] las escaleras y ___________ [6] una sombra (*shadow*) a través de la puerta de la cocina. ___________ [7] miedo (*fear*). De pronto, la sombra ___________ [8] y Juan ___________ [9], pero ___________ [10] un niño valiente. Cuando ___________ [11] en la cocina, ___________ [12] que era solo un gato.

C. Write sentences using the imperfect for background information and preterite for things that happened. Remember, you don't need to use the subject pronouns: they're implicit in the verb forms. But if you do, it's no big deal!

Example: El esposo /estar de viaje /la mujer / enfermarse (cuando): Mientras su esposo estabade viaje, la mujer se enfermó. (*When the husband went on a trip, his wife got sick.*)

1. La familia / pasear en el parque / el ladrón / entrar / para robar (cuando)

   ____

2. Vosotros / hacer las compras / vuestros hijos / estar / en el colegio (mientras)

   ____

3. Tú / estar de viaje / recibir / una oferta laboral (cuando)

   ____

4. (yo) / estar / en el parque / empezar / a llover (cuando)

   ____

5. Nosotros / pasear / por el bosque / empezar / un incendio (mientras)

   ____

6. Horacio / estudiar / en la universidad / sus padres / vender / su ropa (mientras)

   ____

14.3 The Imperfect Tense to Tell time

The imperfect tense is also used to tell the time in the past. For example: **¿Qué hora era? (What time was it?) Era la una en punto. (It was one o'clock sharp).**

14.3 Practice

A. Write sentences using the third person singular imperfect tense to speak about the time and the preterite tense to refer to the activity carried out. Use the adverb **cuando** to connect both parts. **Example: las tres / vosotros / salir a caminar: Eran las tres cuando vosotros salisteis a caminar.**

1. La una en punto / Tomás y Daniel / encontrarse / para almorzar:

 ____

2. Muy temprano / Teresa / salir a correr

 ____

3. Las ocho y media / nosotros / llegar a la fiesta

 ____

4. Las cinco menos cuarto / los niños / empezar las clases de tenis (*tennis lessons)*

 ____

5. Nueve / llamar (yo) /al taxi

 ____

6. Las seis de la tarde / Roberto / apareció / en la reunión

 ____

Throughout the remainder of the book, interspersed between the upcoming chapters, you'll encounter captivating short stories in Spanish. These stories serve as valuable opportunities for you to practice and reinforce your comprehension of the language, complementing the grammar concepts you've just learned. But for now, let's immerse ourselves in the first story!

STORY #1 Cristina y El Gato Poeta

(Cristina and Poeta, The Cat)

Cristina adora a los animales. Tiene tres gatos, un perro y una **tortuga**. Un día salió a comprar alimento para sus **mascotas**. Caminaba por la calle cuando vio que algunas personas **discutían alrededor** de un árbol. Se dio cuenta de que un **gatito maullaba** en la **rama** más alta y de que había **cables eléctricos** muy cerca de esa rama. Una **anciana** lloraba al pie del árbol y Cristina **entendió** que era la **dueña** del gatito. Un hombre trajo una **escalera de mano** y la **apoyó** contra el tronco del árbol, pero nadie se **atrevía** a subir porque la rama estaba muy arriba y los cables eléctricos son **peligrosos**.

Sin pensarlo, Cristina entregó su bolsa de compras a una **vecina** y subió por la escalera. Varios hombres sujetaron la escalera para mantenerla **estable**. Desde **abajo**, la anciana le decía que fuera **cuidadosa** y que estaba muy **agradecida** con ella por intentar **rescatar** a su gatito. Cristina se **estiró**, pero no alcanzaba al gatito, así que subió hasta el escalón más alto.

Intentó coger al gatito con una mano, pero el animal estaba **asustado** y se alejó de ella. Decidida a cumplir su **misión**, Cristina subió un poco más, apoyó el **pie izquierdo** en una rama firme y **rodeó** otra rama con la **pierna derecha**, para poder utilizar sus dos manos. "Se llama Poeta y es muy **nervioso**. Ten cuidado. No quiero que te **lastime**," le gritó la anciana.

Asustado y **furioso**, Poeta lanzó algunos **zarpazos** y hacía ruidos **amenazantes**. ¡Toda una pequeña **fiera**! **Afortunadamente**, Cristina sabía cómo tratar animales **alterados**, así que conservó la calma. **Muy suavemente,** Cristina empezó a hablarle al gatito por su nombre y le acercó sus manos para que pudiera **olerlas**. Ella pensó que Poeta identificaría el olor de sus gatos y se sentiría más **confiado**.

Por suerte, ella tuvo razón. Poeta permitió que lo **acariciara** y dejó de **defenderse**. Cristina pudo **por fin** coger al gatito y acercarlo a su **pecho**. La gente en la **acera aplaudió**, pero la anciana pidió **silencio** para que Poeta se mantuviera **tranquilo**.

Contento, Poeta se abrazó al **cuello** de Cristina y comenzó a **ronronear**. Cristina logró sujetarse del árbol para comenzar a bajar **muy despacio** por la escalera. Poeta no quería **soltarse** del cuello de Cristina.

Poco a poco, Cristina bajó hasta que pudo poner sus dos pies en **tierra firme.** Poeta **accedió** a soltar a Cristina para **acurrucarse** en los brazos de su dueña. La anciana agradeció Cristina, se **despidió** de sus vecinos y se **apresuró** a entrar a su casa para que Poeta no **escapara** otra vez.

Todos **felicitaron** a Cristina y ella se puso **como un tomate.** Cuando **recuperó el aliento**, Cristina levantó la vista hasta donde rescató a Poeta. ¡Y fue entonces cuando sintió **temor** al **peligro**, a la **altura** y a los cables eléctricos que estuvieron tan cerca de ella!

"¿Cómo pude hacer eso?", se preguntaba **una y otra vez.** Ella nunca se había sentido **capaz** de hacer algo así. Cuando contó su **aventura** a sus amigos, nadie le creyó porque sabían que ella no era tan **valiente**; pero Cristina descubrió que sí lo era, gracias a Poeta. Ahora es **rescatista** de animales y vive aventuras increíbles.

GLOSSARY	
Tortuga	Tortoise
Mascota	Pet
Discutir	Argue
Alrededor	Around
Gatito	Kitty
Maullar	Meow
Rama	Branch
Cables eléctricos	Electric wires
Anciana	Old lady
Dueña	Owner
Escalera de mano	Ladder
Apoyar	To lean against
Atrever	Dare
Peligroso	Dangerous
Vecina	Neighbor
Estable	Stable
Abajo	Below
Cuidadosa	Careful
Rescatar	To rescue

GLOSSARY	
Oler	To smell
Confiado	Confident
Acariciar	To caress
Defender	To defend
Temblorosa	Shaky
Por fin	Finally
Pecho	Chest
Acera	Sidewalk
Aplaudir	To clap the hands
Silencio	Silence
Tranquilo	Calmed
Cuello	Neck
Ronronear	To purr
Muy despacio	Very slowly
Recibir	To receive
Soltar	To let go of
Poco a poco	Little by little
Tierra firme	Solid ground
Acceder	To agree

GLOSSARY	
Estirar	To stretch
Asustado	Scared
Misión	Mission
Pie izquierdo	Left foot
Rodear	To surround
Pierna derecha	Right leg
Nervioso	Nervous
Lastimar	Hurt
Furioso	Furious
Zarpazo	Swipe of a paw
Amenazante	Threatening
Fiera	Wild beast
Afortunadamente	Fortunately
Alterado	Disturbed
Muy suavemente	Very softly

GLOSSARY	
Acurrucar	To snuggle up
Despedir	To say goodbye
Apresurar	To hurry
Escapar	To escape
Felicitar	To congratulate
Como un tomate	To blush (like a tomato)
Recuperar el aliento	To catch one's breath
Temor	Fear
Peligro	Danger
Altura	Height
Una y otra vez	Over and over
Capaz	Able, capable
Aventura	Adventure
Valiente	Brave
Rescatista	Rescuer

CHAPTER 15:
THE VERB SER (TO BE)
TO BE OR NOT TO BE

Past Tense of Ser

Before starting to conjugate other verbs in the past tense, let's remember how the verb be is conjugated in this tense. Chapter 2 has taught you how to use it in the present, such as **ella es ingeniera** or **nosotros somos inteligentes**. But what if you wanted to say, 'we were' or 'I was'?

Let's roll up our sleeves to get some practice in!

Mini Challenge

Read the following dialogue and use the table below (past tense of 'ser') to identify exactly what they're saying.

En la fiesta

TOMÁS:	Disculpe, ¿a qué se dedica?
LUIS:	Yo **fui** doctor en Madrid.
TOMÁS:	Ah, ¿**fue** doctor?
LUIS:	Así es, antes de eso **fui** actor, pero **fallé**.
TOMÁS:	Lamento oír eso, ¿qué hace ahora?.
LUIS:	**Actúo** de nuevo. ¿Y usted?
TOMÁS:	Yo soy actor, también.
LUIS:	Ah. Somos dos actores. Aquella señora **es** cantante, pero **era** maestra.

Glossary:

Fallé: *failed*

Actúo: *act*

Cantante: *singer*

ser (*to be* - preterite)			
yo	**fui**	nosotros/as	**fuimos**
tú	**fuiste**	vosotros/as	**fuisteis**
usted él ella	**fue**	ustedes ellos ellas	**fueron**

ser (*to be* - imperfect)			
yo	**era**	nosotros/as	**eramos**
tú	**eras**	vosotros/as	**erais**
usted él ella	**era**	ustedes ellos ellas	**eran**

We mentioned that verbs meaning 'to be' are used to describe things in different ways. So, let's review when exactly is **ser** (**fui, fuimos, fuiste, era, eras, eran** etc) used?

These are ten situations where you would use **ser**:

1. To *describe*

Yo **fui** rubia.	=	*I was blond.*
Tú **eras** delgado.	=	*You used to be thin.*
Él **fue** joven.	=	*He was young.*
Ella **era** inteligente.	=	*She used to be intelligent.*
Fuimos simpáticos.	=	*We were nice.*
Vosotros **erais** solteros.	=	*You all used to be single.*
Ustedes **fueron** románticos.	=	*You all were romantic.*
Ellos **eran** morenos.	=	*They used to be dark-haired.*

Tip: Remember that in Spanish you do not need to add the pronoun to a sentence—unless you want to stress it—because it is already included in the verb: **fuimos** simpáticos (*we were nice*).

2. To *indicate a profession*

Marcos **fue** abogado.	=	*Marcos was a lawyer.*
Yo **era** estudiante.	=	*I used to be a student.*
Ella **fue** arquitecta.	=	*She was an architect.*
Eramos doctores.	=	*We used to be doctors.*
Fuisteis profesores.	=	*You were professors.*
Ustedes **eran** gerentes.	=	*You used to be managers.*
Ellos **fueron** ingenieros.	=	*They were engineers.*

Tip: Unlike English, Spanish omits the indefinite article **un/una** before an unmodified profession. For example: **Ellas fueron doctoras**. But if you modify the profession, you need to add the indefinite article: **Ellas fueron unas doctoras excelentes**.

3. To *indicate where someone came from*

In this case, when we want to refer to the place where someone is from, in the past tense, we use the imperfect. Usually, the sentence is accompanied by another indicating something specific about the individual we are referring to. For example: The boy I met yesterday was from Mexico. We do not say in any case, The boy I met yesterday was from Mexico.

Yo **era** italiano antes de conseguir la nacionalidad francesa.

¿Tú **era**s italiano?

El joven (Él) que me llamó por teléfono **era** mexicano.

La chica que ganó el concurso **era** hondureña.

Nosotros **eramos** mexicano antes de conseguir la nacionalidad francesa.

¿Vosotros **erais** franceses?

Los muchachos (Ellos) de la orquesta **eran** dominicanos.

However, to indicate where someone comes from, or what nationality they have, the tense that is commonly, if not always, used in Spanish: I am Mexican, He is from the Dominican Republic, Are you Venezuelan?, etc.

4. To *identify specific attributes about a person, such as relationship, nationality, race, or religion*

Yo **era** católica, pero ahora soy budista.	=	*I used to be Catholic, but now I'm Buddhist.*
Tú **fuiste** su jefa.	=	*You were their boss.*
Él **era** su esposo.	=	*He used to be their husband.*
Fuimos solteros.	=	*We were single.*
Vosotros **erais** estudiantes y amigos.	=	*You used to be students and friends.*
Marcos y Luisa **fueron** amigos.	=	*Marcos and Luisa were friends.*

5. To say *what material something was made of*

La mesa **era** de madera.	=	*The table was of wood. (The table was made of wood)*
La casa **era** de ladrillos.	=	*The house was of bricks. (The house was made of bricks)*
La silla **era** de plástico.	=	*The chair was of plastic. (The chair was made of plastic)*
Los zapatos **eran** de cuero.	=	*The shoes were of leather. (The shoes were made of leather)*
Las ventanas **eran** de vidrio.	=	*The windows were of glass. (The windows were made of glass)*

6. To say *who something belonged to*

El perro **fue** de María.	=	*The dog was of María. (The dog belonged to Maria)*
Los amigos **era** mios.	=	*The friends were mine. (The friends belonged to me)*
El libro **fue** del muchacho.	=	*The book was of the boy. (The book belonged to the boy)*

La foto **era** de ella.	=	*The photograph was of her. (The photograph belonged to her)*
La moto **era** de ellos.	=	*The motorcycle was of them. (The motorcycle belonged to them)*

7. To say for *whom or for what something was intended*

La televisión **fue** para ella.	=	*The television was for her.*
El lápiz **era** para ellos.	=	*The pencil was for them.*
La gata **fue** para mi hermano.	=	*The cat was for my brother.*

8. To describe *where an event took place*

Las fiestas **eran** en la casa de María.	=	*The parties were in Maria's house.*
La ceremonia **fue** en la universidad.	=	*The ceremony was at the university.*

9. To *indicate a generalization*

Fue necesario estudiar mucho.	=	*It was necessary to study a lot.*
Era muy facil portarse bien.	=	*It was very easy to behave well.*

10. To express time, dates, and days of the week

Fueron las 3:00 p.m.	=	*It was 3:00 p.m.*
Fue el 14 de agosto.	=	*It was August 14th.*
Era lunes cuando me enamoré.	=	*It was Monday when I fell in love.*

Now that you know how to conjugate the verb **ser** in the past tense, it's important to have some things in mind. The main differences between these two tenses are:

1. If you want to **describe objects**, you're going to use the imperfect and not the preterit. For example: La mochila **era** blanca. And **not**: La mochila **fue** blanca.
2. The imperfect is used on incomplete actions, when something hasn't finished or repetitive events. If you say: **De niño, mis cumpleaños eran lo mejor** (*As a kid, my birthdays used to be the best*), means that happened more than once. If you say: **De niño, mi cumpleaños 8 fue el mejor** (*As a kid, my 8th birthday was the best*), you refer to a specific event in the past.

So! If you have a hard time figuring out when to use the imperfect or the preterit, just keep in mind what you're trying to convey.

The moment of truth has arrived—let's practice what we've learned!

Practice 15

A. Answer these questions about the dialogue "La fiesta" at the beginning of the lesson:

1. ¿Qué fue Luis? ______________________________
2. ¿Qué es Tomás? ______________________________
3. ¿En dónde están? ______________________________
4. ¿Qué son Luis y Tomás? ______________________________
5. ¿Qué es la señora? ______________________________
6. ¿Qué era la señora? ______________________________

B. Where were these famous people from? Use the 3rd person singular of **ser** *(to be)* in past tense to say where they were from and what nationality they were.

Inglaterra (*England*)

Francia (*France*)

Colombia (*Colombia*)

Argentina (*Argentina*)

Paises Bajos (*Netherlands*)

México (*Mexico*)

Estados Unidos (*United States*)

Alemania (*Germany*)

Example: David Bowie: Fue de Inglaterra. Era inglés.

1. Elvis Presley ______________________________
2. Frida Kahlo ______________________________
3. Vincent Van Gogh ______________________________
4. Albert Einstein ______________________________
5. Coco Chanel ______________________________
6. Freddy Ricón ______________________________
7. Maria Kodama ______________________________
8. John Lennon ______________________________

C. Complete the following sentences with the appropriate form of **ser** and include in parentheses *why* you're using this verb:

- Description
- Profession
- Origin
- Identification
- Possession
- Material something was made of
- For whom something was intended
- Generalizations
- Where an event took place
- Time, date, or day of the week

Example: El muchacho <u>era</u> simpático (description)

1. Amy Winehouse ___________ inglesa. (________________________)
2. Las sillas ___________ de plástico. (________________________)
3. Ellos ___________ de Colombia. (________________________)
4. Las mesas ___________ de madera. (________________________)
5. La comida ___________ para la niña. (________________________)
6. ___________lunes. (________________________)
7. Marcos y Luis ___________ abogados. (________________________)
8. La fiesta ___________ en el club. (________________________)
9. El perro ___________ de María. (________________________)
10. El libro ___________ amarillo. (________________________)
11. ___________el 14 de febrero. (________________________)

D. Complete with the right form of the verb ser: **era/fue** or **eran/fueron**, depending on the subject.

1. El perro ________________ de María.
2. Los amigos _____________ de Marcos.
3. La casa ________________ de Teresa.
4. Las fotos ______________ de los abuelos.
5. Los coches _____________ de los tíos.
6. El gato _________________ de María.

E Complete the sentences with the right form of the verb "to be" (**ser**) and the place suggested in each case. **Example: Mi abuela (Perú) Mi abuela era/fue de Perú, pero ya murió.**

1. Ellos (Alemania) ________________
2. Felix y Alejandra (Argentina) ________________
3. Ellas (Colombia) ________________
4. José (México) ________________
5. María (Francia) ________________
6. Felipe (Brasil) ________________

F. Translate the following sentences. Remember that you use **era/fue** or **eran/fueron** to express time, dates, and days of the week.

1. It was three o'clock in the afternoon: ________________
2. It was first of May: ________________
3. It was November 3rd: ________________
4. It was Wednesday: ________________
5. It was ten o'clock in the morning: ________________
6. It was Sunday: ________________

G. Answer these questions with the appropriate form of **ser**:

1. ¿Fue usted simpático de niño?(Sí) ________________
2. ¿Ellos eran estudiantes? (Sí) ________________
3. ¿Era pequeña la casa de Mariana? (No) ________________
4. ¿De dónde era Elena? (Inglaterra) ________________
5. ¿Qué fue importante? (estudiar) ________________
6. ¿Qué hora era? (4:00 p.m.) ________________

H. Rewrite these sentences contracting de + el. **Example: El coche era de el señor Pérez: El coche era del señor Pérez**.

1. Los perros eran de el niño: ________________
2. El libro era de el colegio: ________________
3. Aquella casa fue de el hombre rico: ________________
4. La moto era de el joven: ________________
5. La comida era de el restaurante: ________________
6. El coche fue de el muchacho: ________________

STORY #2 El Éxito de Alberto

(Alberto's Success)

Alberto es **diseñador gráfico**. Ahora ocupa un **puesto** muy importante en una empresa **trasnacional** y es un **directivo** muy **exitoso**, pero **hubo un tiempo** en que tuvo dificultades para encontrar **empleo**. Llamó a todos sus **conocidos**, se anunció en los **periódicos**, envió su **currículum vitae** a todas las empresas donde quería trabajar y trató **por todos los medios** de que lo contrataran, pero no tuvo mucha **suerte**.

Tuvo algunas **entrevistas**, pero ninguna **oferta** se concretaba porque le faltaba o le sobraba experiencia, **como siempre sucede.** Él es muy **talentoso** en su profesión, pero comenzaba a **desesperarse** porque necesitaba dinero. En su casa hacía falta su **ingreso** y además tenía **novia**.

Sus amigos le decían que fuera **paciente**, que ya tendría una **oportunidad** y que alguna compañía valoraría su talento y su **responsabilidad**. Cuando ya empezaba a perder la **esperanza** y estaba **a punto de** aceptar un empleo que no quería, se le ocurrió una **idea brillante** y se encerró en su habitación para **llevarla a cabo.**

Varias semanas después llamó a Laura, su **mejor amiga,** y le pidió ayuda. Como no podía pagar un **servicio de mensajería,** decidió hacer las entregas él mismo. Alberto conduciría su auto y Laura entregaría misteriosos paquetes en las oficinas de las empresas donde él quería trabajar. Laura aceptó, se puso **sus mejores ropas,** se arregló como alta ejecutiva y partió con Alberto.

Alberto dedicó un día entero a cada zona de la ciudad, con Laura entregando los paquetes etiquetados con el nombre del **director creativo** de cada **agencia de publicidad.** Laura entraba a la **recepción** con seguridad y elegancia, le daba el sobre cerrado a la recepcionista y le pedía entregárselo al director **sin demora.**

Durante una semana, Alberto y Laura entregaron los sobres. Cuando por fin terminaron, decidieron **celebrar** con una **comida sencilla** en una **taquería** de su **vecindario**. Fue entonces cuando Alberto confesó a Laura que los sobres contenían un cómic estilo vintage, totalmente diseñado por él, donde contaba su **trayectoria estudiantil y laboral** y terminaba con la **petición** de que el director creativo le

concediera una entrevista. “Todo este talento estará **a su servicio.** Sea inteligente y tome la **decisión estratégica** de aprovecharlo”, concluía la **historieta**. El personaje de Alberto era **simpatiquísimo** y se parecía mucho a él. Laura reconoció que su gran amigo había tenido una **idea genial** y se alegró de haberlo ayudado.

Alberto sabía que la siguiente **etapa** era **la peor:** esperar a que le llamaran. **Por fortuna,** en **un par de días** concertó más de diez citas y recibió varias ofertas. Incluso pudo elegir en cuál empresa trabajar. Los directores lo felicitaron por su **creatividad,** su **iniciativa** y su excelente manera de demostrar que era un diseñador gráfico extraordinario.

Ahora que Alberto es el jefe, **lo que más valora** de sus colaboradores es justo eso: creatividad, iniciativa y ganas de **hacer que las cosas sucedan.**

GLOSSARY	
Diseñador gráfico	Graphic designer
Puesto	Job position
Trasnacional	Transnational
Directivo	Manager
Exitoso	Successful
Hubo un tiempo	There was a time
Empleo	Job
Conocidos	Acquaintances
Periódicos	Newspapers
Currículum vitae	Resume
Por todos los medios	By all means
Suerte	Luck.
Entrevistas	Interviews
Oferta	Offer
Como siempre sucede	As it always happens
Mejor amiga	Best friend
Servicio de mensajería	Delivery service
Sus mejores ropas	Her best clothes
Director creativo	Creative Director
Agencia de publicidad	Advertising agency
Recepción	Reception area
Sin demora	Without delay
Celebrar	To celebrate
Comida sencilla	Simple lunch
Taquería	Taco shop
Vecindario	Neighborhood
Trayectoria estudiantil y laboral	Student and work trajectory
Petición	Petition
A su servicio	At your service
Decisión estratégica	Strategic decision

GLOSSARY	
Talentoso	Talented
Desesperar	To get desperate
Ingreso	Income
Novia	Girlfriend
Paciente	Patient
Oportunidad	Opportunity
Responsabilidad	Responsibility, reliability
Esperanza	Hope
A punto de	About to
Idea brillante	Brilliant idea
Llevar a cabo	To carry out

GLOSSARY	
Historieta	Comic
Simpatiquísimo	Very funny
Idea genial	Great idea
Etapa	Stage
La peor	The worst
Por fortuna	Fortunately
Un par de días	A couple of days
Creatividad	Creativity
Iniciativa	Initiative
Lo que más valora	What he values the most
Hacer que las cosas sucedan	To make things happen

CHAPTER 16:

ESTAR (TO BE) AND TENER (TO HAVE)

I HAVE YOUR LOVE

16.1 Past Tense of Estar (*To Be*)

As we said in the previous chapter, **estar** also means 'to be.' However, it's used in different types of contexts and situations.

- Ella **estuvo** en la casa. (*She was in the house.*) = location
- Él **estuvo** enfermo. (*He was sick.*) = health
- **Estaba** feliz. (*I was happy.*) = changing mood
- La comida **estaba** deliciosa. (*The food was delicious.*) = personal opinion

Notice that what most of these situations have in common is that they are changeable. He was sick, but he might not be sick anymore. It was a temporary state, not a permanent one. 'Sick' is his condition, but it's not his nature.

Remember, the main difference between the preterit and the imperfect is that the first talks about a finished action in the past. The second one refers to an action that lasted in the past. **Both might be right in your answers**, it all depends on what you're trying to say!

> **Tip:** When using **estar** for location, use the preposition **en + the article** (**el, la, los, las**): **Sara estuvo en la casa.**

estar *(to be -preterit)*			
yo	**estuve**	nosotros/as	**estuvimos**
tú	**estuviste**	vosotros/as	**estuvisteis**
usted él ella	**estuvo**	ustedes ellos ellas	**estuvieron**

estar *(to be - imperfect)*			
yo	**estaba**	nosotros/as	**estábamos**
tú	**estabas**	vosotros/as	**estabais**
usted él ella	**estaba**	ustedes ellos ellas	**estaban**

16.1 Practice

A. Write the appropriate form of **estar**. Say why you chose that option:

- location
- health
- changing mood or condition
- personal opinion

1. Mi casa __________ en Francia. (________________)
2. La niña __________ enferma. (________________)
3. __________ triste. (________________)
4. Juan __________ delgado. (________________)
5. Nosotros __________ aquí. (________________)
6. La comida __________ deliciosa. (________________)
7. Vosotros __________ contentos. (________________)
8. Tú __________ cansada luego del ejercicio. (________________)

B. Make complete sentences using the appropriate form of **ser** or **estar** + the words between the parentheses.

Example: La abuela (enferma) <u>La abuela estuvo enferma</u>

1. Tim (español) ______________________________
2. El restaurante (cerrado) ______________________________
3. Las hijas de Pedro (rubias e inteligentes) ______________
4. El problema (muy fácil) ______________________________
5. El libro (interesante) ______________________________
6. Tú (furioso) ______________________________

7. La banana (amarilla) ______________________________
8. Nosotros (felices) ______________________________
9. La foto (silla) ______________________________

Common Mistake: Of course, since English speakers only have one verb (*to be*) to express all these situations, it's completely normal to be confused about when to use each verb when speaking or writing in Spanish. You'll get the hang of it with more practice!

X Don't say : **Yo fui contenta.**

✓ Say it the right way: **Yo estuve contenta.**

C. Write **ser** or **estar** according to whether the adjective refers to an inherent feature or a changing condition. **Example: Él __________ triste → Él <u>estaba</u> triste.** (changing condition)

1. Ella __________________ inteligente.
2. Él ____________________ estudioso.
3. Paula _________________ furiosa.
4. Las abogadas __________ ocupadas.
5. La mesa _______________ sucia.
6. El anciano _____________ cansado.
7. El anciano _____________ simpático.
8. La niña ________________ nerviosa.

Summary of the Uses of Ser	
➲ To describe	**La flor es hermosa.**
➲ To indicate a profession	**Yo fui abogada.**
➲ To indicate someone's origin/nationality	**Ellos eran de México.**
➲ To identify inherent qualities about a person	**Él era inteligente.**
➲ To say what material something is made of	**La silla era de plástico.**
➲ To say who something belongs to	**El libro era de la niña.**
➲ To say for whom something is intended	**El perro fue para él.**
➲ To describe where an event takes place	**La fiesta fue en la casa.**
➲ To use a generalization	**Era importante estudiar.**
➲ To express time, dates, and days of the week	**Fue martes** (*It's Tuesday*).

Summary of the Uses of Estar	
➲ To express location	**Yo estuve en el restaurante.**
➲ To describe health	**María estuvo enferma.**
➲ To express a changing mood or condition	**Luis estaba muy ocupado.**
➲ To express a personal opinion	**La comida estaba buena.**

Common Mistake:

Keep in mind that **ser** is used to express **inherent** qualities of a person, such as...

Luisa fue cariñosa. Luisa had a sweet-loving character. That was her nature. She was nice because that's who she was.

Estar is used to express a **transitory** condition, such as...

Luisa estaba cansada. Luisa used to be tired now, but she recovered. ✓

X Don't say:	✓ Say This:
Luisa estuvo cariñosa.	Luisa fue cariñosa.
Luisa era cansada.	Luisa estaba cansada.
Yo fui cansado.	Yo estuve cansado.
Mi papá era en el supermercado.	Mi papá estaba en el supermercado.
Él estuvo un doctor.	Él fue un doctor.

Then again, many adjectives can be used with either **ser** or **estar**, depending on the exact message that you're trying to convey. But as a rule, **ser** is used for unalterable qualities (**fue rubia**) and **estar** is used for variable qualities (**estuvo triste**).

D. Say if these sentences are right (✓) or wrong (**X**) according to their use of ser or estar. **Example: X Él fue cansado.**

1. __________ Teresa y Miguel eran en el cine.
2. __________ Vosotros fuisteis enfermos.
3. __________ La universidad estuvo buena.
4. __________ Tú eras buen estudiante.
5. __________ Tú estabas buena abogada.
6. __________ Yo estuve de Perú.
7. __________ Las flores eran amarillas.
8. __________ Las sillas estuvieron de plástico.

9. ___________ Susana estaba inteligente.
10. ___________ Miguel y Juan fueron profesores.
11. ___________ La moto estuvo de Federico.
12. ___________ Ayer estuvo miércoles.

E. Now take the ones that are wrong and rewrite them with the right verb:

____

____

____

____

____

____

16.2 Past Tense of Tener (*to have*)

Now that we're getting the hang of different verbs. Let's practice another one! **Tener** is an extremely useful verb to know as it indicates that you possess something. In English this would mean 'to have.'

tener *(to have -preterit)*			
yo	**tuve**	nosotros/as	**tuvimos**
tú	**tuviste**	vosotros/as	**tuvisteis**
usted él ella	**tuvo**	ustedes ellos ellas	**tuvieron**

tener *(to have - imperfect)*			
yo	**tenía**	nosotros/as	**teníamos**
tú	**tenías**	vosotros/as	**teníais**
usted él ella	**tenía**	ustedes ellos ellas	**tenían**

Mucho and Poco

You can also describe nouns by saying something about their quantity. In English, we might say something like 'many dogs' or 'a few dogs.' There are words for these descriptors in Spanish, too. Unlike regular adjectives, they go *before* the noun instead of after.

Mucho/a/os/as (*a lot, many*)

This word must agree in gender and plurality with the noun they're in front of.

E.g. **Tuve muchos perros.** *(I had many dogs.)*

Mucho can also be an adverb, and remains invariable. Adverbs are words that describe verbs: **Lee mucho.** *(He reads a lot.)*

Poco/a/os/as (*little, few, not many*)

This word also must agree in gender and plurality with the noun, too!

E.g. **Tenía pocos vestidos.** *(I used to have few dresses.)*

Poco can also be an adverb, which means that it describes a verb, not just a noun.

E.g. **Martín come poco.** *(Martín doesn't eat much.)*

Let's make it real! Time for some practical exercises to solidify your skills.

16.2 Practice

A. Complete the sentences with the correct form of **tener**.

Example: Vosotros __________ muchas fiestas → Vosotros teníais muchas fiestas.

1. Nosotros __________ una casa muy linda.
2. Sofía y Pablo __________ seis televisiones.
3. Tú y Sara __________ muchos libros.
4. La abuela __________ pocos problemas.
5. Yo __________ dos manos, antes de perder una.
6. Ese cine __________ muchos asientos.

7. Aquel jardín __________ muchos árboles dos años atrás.
8. Roberto y yo __________ un restaurante.
9. Tú __________ un jardín muy hermoso.
10. Ese museo __________ muchos cuadros interesantes.

Tener to Express Age

In Spanish, we use the verb **tener** (*to have*) to say how old we are. Instead of saying you *are of* a certain age, you say that you *have* a certain number of years.

I am [number] years old = Tengo [number] años.

In Spanish, you cannot omit the word **años** in this expression.

Common Mistake: Of course, English speakers tend to translate the structure they use in English directly into Spanish. This doesn't always work! In Spanish, you never use the verbs **ser** (*to be*) or **estar** (*to be*) to talk about age. You use the verb **tener**.

X	Don't say :	**Yo era veinte años.**
X	Don't say :	**Yo estuve veinte años.**
✓	Say it this way :	**Yo tuve veinte años.**

Time to roll up your sleeves and practice some further!

B. Write the correct form of **tener** to convey these people's ages from last year.

1. Manuel y José __________ veintiún años.
2. Yo __________ cincuenta años.
3. Tú __________ dieciocho años.
4. Marina y yo __________ treinta años.
5. Vosotros __________ veinticinco años.
6. Mi abuelo __________ setenta años.
7. Mi abuela __________ sesenta y cinco años.
8. Ellas __________ cuarenta y dos años.

C. Indicate if these sentences are right (✓) or wrong (X). Remember, to express age in Spanish you use the verb **tener**, not **ser** or **estar** like in English. **Example: X Él estuvo veinte años. ✓ Él tuvo veinte años.**

1. __________ Nosotros fuimos sesenta años.
2. __________ Ustedes estuvimos cuarenta años.
3. __________ Yo tenía cincuenta y dos años.
4. __________ José y Daniel tenían treinta y cinco años.
5. __________ Tú eras quince años.
6. __________ María estaba seis años.
7. __________ Tú y Miguel eran setenta años.
8. __________ Josefina estuvo veintitrés años.

D. Now take the ones that were wrong and rewrite them with the correct verb:

____

____

____

____

____

E. Complete the following sentences using the correct verb form of **tener**.

1. Yo __________ muchos zapatos.
2. Nosotros __________ muchos amigos.
3. Marcos __________ un libro en mecánica.
4. Tú __________ muchos gatos.
5. Vosotros __________ una abuela buena.
6. Ella __________ un lápiz rojo.
7. Carlos y María __________ una hija.
8. Usted __________ un sistema excelente.
9. Laura __________ 32 años.

STORY #3 Nadando en El Arcoíris

(Swimming in the Rainbow)

Campeche es una ciudad pequeña del **sureste** de la República Mexicana. El **clima** siempre es **cálido**, incluso en **invierno** y cuando hay **tormentas**. La **lluvia** es motivo de gran **alegría** para los niños porque las calles se llenan de agua. Para ellos es muy divertido jugar en los **charcos** y en las grandes lagunas que se forman. Para las mamás no es tan bueno, porque los hijos llegan a casa **empapados** y **embarrados** de **lodo**.

Hay tanta seguridad en Campeche que los niños pueden salir sin **temor** a que les pase nada. Regresan a casa de la escuela, comen, **hacen la tarea**, ayudan en las **labores domésticas** y luego van con los amigos a la calle hasta que **cae la noche**, a la hora de la **merienda**.

¿A qué juegan los niños campechanos? **Futbol, beisbol, escondidillas, torneos de canicas** y a inventar historias **disparatadas**. Por todas partes hay **bicicletas, pelotas, patines, muñecas** y otros **juguetes**, aunque también hay **palos, llantas, piedras, latas, envases** y otros objetos para sus **juegos**. Sin embargo, después de las tormentas, los niños brincan en los charcos hasta que toda su piel queda **arrugada** y el lodo los cubre **por completo.** Muchas mascotas disfrutan también de la **fiesta acuática** y deben recibir un buen baño, igual que sus alegres **dueños.**

Hay una zona que se localiza en la salida de la ciudad hacia Yucatán, otro **estado** del sureste mexicano. Siempre hay muchos tráileres porque los **choferes** suelen detenerse allí para comer y descansar antes de volver a tomar la carretera. Son personas amables que juegan y bromean con los chicos, para luego meterse a sus **cabinas** a dormir porque su trabajo es **agotador**. Algunos cuelgan **hamacas** en los árboles cercanos para **tomar la siesta** a la **sombra**.

Una noche cayó una tormenta tan intensa que esa zona se **inundó** mucho. Los choferes esperaron a que **escampara** y luego partieron a su destino. ¡Qué contentos se pusieron los niños cuando vieron una inmensa **laguna** afuera de sus casas! Comieron **a toda prisa,** hicieron la tarea y salieron para **arrojarse** al agua. Las mamás los vieron tan **emocionados** que los dejaron partir **sin reclamos.**

Por la noche, **muy a su pesar,** los chicos volvieron a casa contando que habían **nadado** en el **arcoíris**. Ninguno de los padres les **creyó** esa historia, aunque se repitió por varios días. "Mamá, papá, ¡nadamos en el arcoíris!", decían los niños, pero los adultos pensaban que eran **fantasías infantiles** y no les **prestaban atención.** Con el intenso calor, la gran laguna se **redujo** y se secó en poco tiempo, para gran **tristeza** de los pequeños.

Luego regresaron los tráileres. Los niños contaron a los choferes las aventuras que **gozaron** en su gran charco. Los choferes se dieron cuenta de que en realidad los chicos habían nadado en agua contaminada por el **diésel** de sus tráileres. Resulta que este líquido, al **derramarse**, brilla con la luz y refleja muchos colores. **Sin embargo**, **nunca** les dijeron la verdad para no **arruinar** su ilusión de haber nadado en el arcoíris.

GLOSSARY	
Sureste	Southeast
Clima	Weather
Cálido	Warm
Invierno	Winter
Tormentas	Storms
Lluvia	Rain
Alegría	Joy
Inundar	To flood
Charcos	Poodles
Empapados	Soaked
Embarrados	Smeared
Lodo	Mud
Temor	Fear
Hacer la tarea	To do homework
Labores domésticas	Domestic chores
Cae la noche	The night falls
Merienda	Supper
Futbol	Football (soccer)

GLOSSARY	
Juegos	Games
Arrugada	Wrinkled
Por completo	Completely
Fiesta acuática	Aquatic party
Dueños	Owners
Estado	State
Choferes	Drivers
Cabinas	Cabins
Agotador	Exhausting
Hamacas	Hammocks
Tomar la siesta	Take a nap
Sombra	Shadow
Escampar	To clear up
Laguna	Lagoon
A toda prisa	At full speed
Arrojarse	Initiative
Emocionados	Excited
Sin reclamos	No claims

GLOSSARY	
Beisbol	Baseball
Escondidillas	Hide-and-seek
Torneos de canicas	Marble tournaments
Disparatadas	Crazy
Bicicletas	Bicycles
Pelotas	Balls
Patines	Skates
Muñecas	Dolls
Juguetes	Toys
Palos	Sticks
Llantas	Tires
Piedras	Stones
Latas	Cans
Envases	Containers

GLOSSARY	
Muy a su pesar	Much to their regret
Nadar	To swim
Arcoíris	Rainbow
Creer	To believe
Fantasías infantiles	Childhood fantasies
Prestar atención	To pay attention
Reducir	To reduce
Tristeza	Sadness
Gozar	To enjoy
Diésel	Diesel
Derramar	To spill
Sin embargo	However
Nunca	Never
Arruinar	To ruin

CHAPTER 17:
LIKES AND DISLIKES
I LIKED APPLES

It would be impossible to get to know other people and allow them to get to know you without learning to express likes and dislikes. They convey our opinions and other key parts of our personality. By using **me gusta** and **no me gusta**, we can finally tell people what we really think!

However, what is learning without some challenge? We are going to take the likes and dislikes a step further and talk about **past** likes and dislikes. **Me gustaba** or **me gustó** and **no me gustaba** or **no me gustó**.

17.1 Constructions With Me Gusta and No Me Gusta

Poema XV

Pablo Neruda

Me gusta cuando callas
Porque estás como ausente,
Y me oyes desde lejos,
Y mi voz no te toca. [...]

"I like it when you're silent / because you're sort of absent / and you hear me from afar / and my voice doesn't touch you."

This is part of a poem by Chilean poet Pablo Neruda (1904-1973), who wrote in various styles, including passionate love poems, and won the Nobel Prize in Literature in 1971.

The verb **gustar** is used in Spanish to express likes and dislikes:

- **Me gusta leer** (*I like to read*)
- **No me gustan los gatos** (*I don't like cats*)

But **gustar** does not literally mean *to like*.

Strictly speaking, *gustar* means *to be pleasing (to someone)*. It needs to be used with an indirect object to make complete sense. This indirect object is whatever it is you're expressing your affection or fondness for.

The indirect object can be a pronoun (me, te, le, nos, os, le) or a person/object/animal preceded by a → a + person/name/object.

For example:

A María le gustó el helado. (*Maria liked the ice-cream.*)

A mí me gustaban los caballos. (*I liked horses.*)

A Juan y Cristina les gustaba la música clásica. (*Juan and Cristina liked classical music.*)

A sentence like, **A Martín le gustó la comida** has two indirect objects: **le** and **a Martin. A Martín** is used to add emphasis or to clarify who or what the indirect object pronoun is (**le** could be a woman, an animal, or almost anything).

Notice, too, that the verb **gustar** must agree with its subject, i.e., the person or thing that is liked, *not* the person who is being described. In the sentences above, we used both **gustaba** and **gustaban** to agree with the different nouns.

A Martín le gustaban los caballos → **gustaban** matches **caballos**, not Martín.

To say that you *don't* like something, you need to add **no** before the indirect object pronoun.

No me gustaron los perros. (*I didn't like dogs.*)

No les gustaron los gatos. (*They didn't like cats.*)

No nos gustaban las motos. (*We didn't like motorcycles.*)

Indirect Object Pronouns

me: for me

te: for you

le: for you, him, her, it

nos: for us

os: for you

les: for you, them

Now check these sentences:

- **A Martín le gustaban los mapas**: *Martin liked maps* (or *Maps were pleasing to Martin.)* In this case, since maps is plural, "gustaban" is in the plural form. **Le** is the indirect object and **A Martin** is used in addition to the indirect object pronoun for clarification or emphasis.
- **A mí me gustó el deporte**: *I liked the sport* (or *The sport was pleasing to me.)* Again, **deporte** agrees with the singular **gustó**. **Me** is the indirect object pronoun and **A mí** is used as emphasis.
- **¿A usted le gustaron las flores?:** *Did you like the flowers?* (*Were the flowers pleasing to you?*) **Las flores** agrees with the plural **gustaron**. **Le** is the indirect object. **A usted** is used for clarification (since **le** can also refer to someone else).
- **A ellos les gustaba el teatro**: *They liked the theatre.* (*The theatre was pleasing to them.*) **El teatro** is singular and agrees with **gustaba.** The indirect object is **les** and **A ellos** is used for emphasis.

Tip: Just as in English, you can combine **like + a verb** (*I like running*). In Spanish, **gustar** is combined with the **infinitive** of the verb (not the gerund, like in English): **gustar + verbo en infinitivo.**

Examples:

Te gustaba correr. (*You liked running.*)

Me gustaba ver televisión. (*I liked watching TV.*)

Les gustó cocinar. (*They liked cooking.*)

X Do not say: Me gustaba corriendo

✓ Say: Me gustaba correr

Don't forget; context is the main difference between using the imperfect and the preterit when it comes to likes and dislikes. For example, if you say **Me gustó el pollo** you are usually referring to a specific chicken that you ate at a specific time. If you say **Me gustaba el pollo** you are speaking broadly to a time in the past when you liked chicken. Your childhood, for example. It's all about context and meaning.

17.1 Practice

A. Write an indirect object pronoun for each subject pronoun.

1. A nosotros __________ gustaba.
2. A vosotros __________ gustó.
3. A ustedes __________ gustaban.
4. A ellos __________ gustaron.
5. A Juan y Matías __________ gustó.
6. A mí __________ gustaban.
7. A ti __________ gustaba.
8. A Juan __________ gustaron.
9. A Elena __________ gustó.

B. Translate the following with the two indirect objects.

Example: She liked the candy from the nearby store. → <u>A ella le gustaban los caramelos de la tienda cercana</u>.

1. I liked the car. ____________________
2. They liked onions. ____________________
3. We didn't like reading. ____________________
4. You (sing.) liked bananas. ____________________
5. You (pl.) liked working. ____________________
6. Marcos liked studying. ____________________
7. Elsa liked tomatoes. ____________________
8. My father liked to eat. ____________________
9. My mother liked fish. ____________________
10. The boys didn't like milk. ____________________
11. Maria liked chicken. ____________________

C. Join the words to make a sentence. Make sure you include two indirect objects (the pronoun + whoever the action is for) and conjugate the verb.

Example: no / las / gustar / le / bananas / a Mirta: A Mirta no le gustaban las bananas.

1. nos / correr / a nosotros / gustar:
   ____
2. no / gustar / las verduras / les / a los niños:
   ____
3. esos zapatos / gustar / a mí / me:
   ____
4. las fiestas / a Luis y Teresa / gustar / les:
   ____
5. tocar piano / a Elena / gustar / le:
   ____
6. gustar / me / a mí / el pescado:
   ____

D. Pick one of the items below and say you liked it. Pick the other one to say you didnt' like it. You can switch the items according to what you liked. You may use an adversative conjunction (**pero, aunque, sin embargo)** or a copulative conjunction (**y**).

Example: **¿comer carne? ¿comer pescado?→ No me gustaba comer carne, pero me gustaba comer pescado.**

1. ¿Leo Messi? ¿Cristiano Ronaldo?
   ____
2. ¿Comer hamburguesas? ¿Comer pastas?
   ____
3. ¿El café? ¿El té?
   ____
4. ¿La actriz Meryl Streep? ¿La actriz Judy Dench?
   ____
5. ¿El tenista Medvedev? ¿El tenista Federer?
   ____
6. ¿Estudiar en la biblioteca? ¿Estudiar en el comedor?
   ____

7. ¿Los perros? ¿Los gatos?
   ____
8. ¿Viajar en tren? ¿Viajar en coche?
   ____

E. Complete the sentences by conjugating **gustar** according to its subject and adding the right pronoun (le/les). This time, pay attention to the sentences to choose if you need the imperfect or the preterit. **Example: A Isabel ________ los niños → A Isabel le gustaron los niños que fueron a su fiesta.**

1. A Sebastián y Nicolás ________ los deportes cuando estaban en la escuela.
2. A vosotros ________ los relojes caros que vimos ayer.
3. A ti ________ las motos antes de tener el accidente.
4. A nosotros ________ aprender español con la profesora la semana pasada.
5. A mí ________ los chocolates, pero ahora soy alérgica.
6. A usted ________ los coches que le mostraron.

F. Complete these questions making **gustar** concur with the subject and adding the appropriate personal pronoun. **Example: ¿(él / gustar) ________ el teatro? → ¿A él le gustaba el teatro?**

1. ¿(nosotros / gustar) ________________ las fiestas?
2. ¿(Teresa / gustar) ________________ su universidad?
3. ¿(ellos / gustar) ________________ recibir gente en su casa?
4. ¿(yo / gustar) ________________ hacer yoga?
5. ¿(tú / gustar) ________________ el pescado?
6. ¿(usted / gustar) ________________ viajar?

G. Complete with a + pronoun + pronoun + verb **gustar**. **Example: ________ (yo) estudiar idiomas→ A mí me gustó estudiar idiomas.**

1. ________________ (nosotros) trabajar en esa empresa
2. ________________ (ustedes) vivir solos cuando estaban en Paraguay.
3. ________________ (vosotros) caminar en el parque los sábados.
4. ________________ (Carolina y Luis) subir montañas el lunes.
5. ________________ (tú) invitar amigos a tu casa.
6. ________________ (ellos) viajar por el mundo.

H. Rewrite these sentences by correcting the mistakes on the Indirect Object Pronouns:

1. A mí nos gustaban los caramelos: ____________________
2. A ti le gustó el pan: ____________________
3. A vosotros me gustaba la leche: ____________________
4. A ti me gustó el café: ____________________
5. A ellos nos gustaban las naranjas: ____________________
6. A él te gustó la carne: ____________________

I. ¿Adónde fuimos en las vacaciones?

The Pérez family each had their own idea of a good vacation and where they preferred to go. Turn the suggested separate elements into a sentence. Remember to include the indirect object that clarifies or adds emphasis. **Example: padre / nadar → Al padre le gustó nadar.**

1. abuelo / cocinar

   ____
2. hermano / hacer surf

   ____
3. tía / leer libros

   ____
4. primos / comprar ropa

   ____
5. padre / comer y beber

   ____
6. hija / buscar caracoles en la orilla

   ____
7. madre / la tranquilidad

   ____
8. sobrinos / correr por la playa

   ____

17.2 Expressing Wants in a Direct and Polite Way

You've learned how to express your likes and dislikes, but what about your wants? How can you tell someone that you want something?"

In Spanish, you use the verb **querer** to express **wants**, e.g. **Yo quiero un café.** (*I want a coffee.*)

How do you say you don't want something? For this, we'll use **no** again.

To say you don't want something, just add a **no** before the verb: **Yo no quiero un café.** (*I don't want a coffee.*)

As with **gustar,** you can also add an infinitive to **querer** when you *want to do something*, e.g. **Quiero aprender alemán.** (*I want to learn German.*)

Sometimes it's not polite to ask directly for something. For example, if you're asking for a map in a hotel lobby, it's more polite to say, **Me gustaría un mapa.** *(I would like a map)* than **Quiero un mapa.** (*I want a map.*)

When you want to express what you would like or wouldn't like, in Spanish you say, **Me gustaría / No me gustaría**.

Of course, **gustaría** is also used when you're wishing or pining for something: **Me gustaría conocer a Luis** (*I would like to meet Luis*). In other words, it's a way of expressing your wants in a less direct way, which is essential for politeness.

With **gustaría** you can also add an infinitive for something you *would like to do*: **Me gustaría subir el Everest**.

17.2 Practice

A. Choose what you would say in each scenario, depending on whether you can be more direct or need to be more polite:

1. You're at a bar and ask the waiter for a glass of water: __________ (quiero / me gustaría) un vaso de agua.
2. You're expressing your need for sleep to a friend __________ (quiero / me gustaría) dormir.
3. You're explaining to a professor that you would like to speak Spanish well. __________(me gustaría / quiero) hablar bien español.
4. You're asking a salesperson at a store to hand you that green dress: __________ (quiero / me gustaría) ese vestido verde.
5. You're telling your friend you want to fix the roof. __________ (quiero / me gustaría) arreglar el techo.

STORY #4 Ramona La Distraída

(Ramona The Absent-Minded)

Ramona es muy **distraída**. ¡Siempre está **con la cabeza en las nubes**! Se mete en algunos problemas, pero **la mayoría de las veces** provoca situaciones muy graciosas. Tiene suerte porque es bonita y agradable, entonces siempre hay algún **caballero** dispuesto a ayudarla. Si no fuera así, Ramona sería un verdadero peligro **para sí misma** y para los demás.

Casi a diario dice que alguien, **por maldad,** le esconde sus cosas. Ramona busca y busca y al final resulta que no recuerda dónde las puso. ¿Quién guarda sus **llaves** en el **refrigerador** o colocar sus **anteojos** debajo de la almohada? Muchas veces **deja plantadas** a sus amigas porque no recuerda que tiene una **cita** con ellas para ir a **tomar un helado** en el **centro comercial. De igual manera,** muchas veces se **enoja** con ellas porque dice que la dejan plantada, cuando la cita fue el día anterior. Cuando se entera de la verdad, la **encantadora** Ramona se ríe de sí misma y **le quita importancia al asunto**, aunque no le gusta que se rían de ella.

Una vez salió de una fiesta con una **bolsa de plástico amarrada** en un pie, porque decidió quitarse los zapatos y perdió uno. Los padres de ella y de sus amigas las **castigaron** por no llegar a la hora permitida, pero es que pasaron muchas horas buscando el zapato perdido, que nunca encontraron. También pasa que **se esfuerza mucho** estudiando para un examen de matemáticas, cuando la prueba es de cualquier otra materia. ¡A veces **ni siquiera** hay examen!

Cierto día, Ramona salió de la **preparatoria** con varias amigas para tomar el autobús que las llevaría a casa, porque todas vivían en **áreas cercanas.** Las chicas platicaban sobre la **jornada** y se hacían bromas unas a otras. Al llegar a la parada del autobús, en una avenida muy grande, Ramona comentó que se sentía **muy cansada** y se sentó en el **cofre de un automóvil.** A continuación colocó su **pesado** bolso junto a ella.

Sus amigas comenzaron a **hacerle señas** y a reír, pero Ramona les platicaba sobre uno de sus **pretendientes** y no les prestó atención. Después, sacó de su bolso un **lápiz labial** y un **espejo** y se pintó los labios. Ella continuaba hablando y admirándose en el espejo, sin darse cuenta de que los autos en la avenida ya habían comenzado a avanzar, porque el **semáforo** ya estaba en luz verde.

Ramona buscaba algo en su bolso. Sacó un **cepillo**, una **agenda**, un **estuche de lápices**, una **libreta** y unas **tijeras**, que fue colocando sobre el cofre del auto. Por fin encontró una **liga para el cabello**, se hizo una **cola de caballo** y siguió platicando, sin darse cuenta de nada.

Entonces, del auto sobre el que Ramona estaba sentada, salió un hombre joven, alto y atractivo, que se acercó a ella. "Señorita, ¿**sería tan amable** de permitirme avanzar?," le dijo. Ramona lo miró sin entender que estaba **sentada** sobre un auto **encendido** y que todas sus cosas estaban sobre el cofre. "Pues **avanza,**" le dijo con una linda sonrisa, al ver que el joven era muy **guapo** y amable. "Sí, pero es que usted está sentada sobre mi auto y el semáforo ya está en verde," explicó el hombre.

Ramona **saltó** como si **de repente** su asiento se hubiera puesto **muy caliente. Apenada,** intentó recoger sus cosas y guardarlas en su bolso. **Divertido,** el joven la ayudó a **cargar** el bolso mientras ella guardaba todo, entre mil **disculpas**.

"Usted puede sentarse sobre mi auto **cuando guste,** señorita," le dijo el muchacho. "**Es un honor** para mí, solo que debo irme." Ramona lo despidió con la mejor de sus sonrisas, muy **ruborizada.** El hombre se subió a su auto y empezó a avanzar, pero el semáforo se puso en rojo otra vez.

Ramona tuvo que aguantar la **vergüenza** todo el tiempo de la luz roja. El muchacho la saludaba desde su **asiento** dentro del auto, y ella respondía con **coquetería.** Cuando por fin el hombre pudo marcharse, Ramona **se volvió hacia** sus amigas y les reclamó, **furiosa:** "¿Por qué no me **avisaron** que había un hombre dentro del auto y que el motor estaba encendido? **¡Qué malas son!** ¡Son **las peores amigas del mundo**!"

Las chicas no pudieron responderle **con claridad** porque reían a carcajadas. "Si te dijimos y, no nos escuchaste," intentaron explicarle. Una de ellas le dijo: **"¿Y perdernos de esto?"**

La mejor **venganza** de Ramona fue que, al día siguiente, el joven **estacionó** su auto en el mismo sitio del día anterior para que Ramona pudiera sentarse. Ahora ya no tenía prisa y pudo platicar con ella **mientras** llegaba el autobús.

GLOSSARY	
Distraída	Distracted
Con la cabeza en las nubes	With the head in the clouds
La mayoría de las veces	Most of the times
Caballero	Gentleman
Para sí misma	For herself
Por maldad	Out of malice
Llaves	Keys
Refrigerador	Fridge
Anteojos	Glasses
Alrededor	Around
Dejar plantadas	Leave them standing up
Cita	Date, appointment
Tomar un helado	Have an ice cream
Jornada	Day
Muy cansada	Very tired
Cofre de un automóvil	Hood of a car
Hacer señas	To beckon
Pretendientes	Suitors
Lápiz labial	Lipstick
Espejo	Mirror

GLOSSARY	
Centro comercial	Mall, shopping center
De igual manera	Likewise
Enojar	To get mad
Encantadora	Charming
Le quita importancia al asunto	Downplays the matter
A veces	Sometimes
Bolsa de plástico	Plastic bag
Amarrada	Tied
Castigar	To punish
Se esfuerza mucho	She works really hard
Ni siquiera	There is not even
Preparatoria	High school
Áreas cercanas	Nearby areas
Muy caliente	Very hot
Apenada	Ashamed
Divertido	Amused
Cargar	To carry
Disculpas	Apologies
Cuando guste	Whenever you want
Es un honor	It's an honor

GLOSSARY	
Semáforo	Traffic light
Cepillo	Brush
Agenda	Agenda
Estuche de lápices	Pencil case
Libreta	Notebook
Tijeras	Scissors
Liga para el cabello	Hair tie
Cola de caballo	Ponytail
¿Sería tan amable?	Would you be so kind?
Sentada	Sitting
Encendido	On
Avanzar	To go on
Guapo	Handsome
Saltar	To jump
De repente	Suddenly

GLOSSARY	
Ruborizada	Blushed
Vergüenza	Shame, embarrassment
Asiento	Seat
Coquetería	Flirtatiousness
Volverse hacia	Turned to
Furiosa	Furious
Avisar	To notify
¡Qué malas son!	How bad you are!
Las peores amigas del mundo	The worst friends in the world
Con claridad	Clearly, with clarity
¿Y perdernos de esto?	And miss out on this?
Venganza	Revenge
Estacionar	To park
Mientras	While

CHAPTER 18:
INDICATIVE MOOD: THE FUTURE
THE SUN WILL COME OUT TOMORROW

The Future

The future tense is probably the easiest tense in Spanish. For regular verbs, you form the future by adding one ending to the infinitive for all conjugations. All endings are the same. Check out how easy it is!

hablar *(to speak)*		**comer** *(to eat)*		**vivir** *(to live)*	
yo	hablar-**é**	yo	comer-**é**	yo	vivir-**é**
tú	hablar-**ás**	tú	comer-**ás**	tú	vivir-**ás**
él, ella	hablar-á	él, ella	comer-**á**	él, ella	vivir-**á**
nosotros/as	hablar-**emos**	usted	comer-**á**	usted	vivir-**á**
vosotros/as	hablar-**éis**	nosotros/as	comer-**emos**	nosotros/as	vivir-**emos**
ellos, ellas	hablar-**án**	vosotros/as	comer-**éis**	vosotros/as	vivir-**éis**
ustedes	hablar-**án**	ellos, ellas	comer-**án**	ellos, ellas	vivir-**án**
		ustedes	comer-**án**	ustedes	vivir-**án**

The endings of the future are:

-é	**-á**	**-éis**
-ás	**-emos**	**-án**

The following verbs add these future endings to irregular stems:

decir:	**dir-**	
venir:	**vendr-**	
hacer	**har-**	
tener:	**tendr-**	-é
salir:	**saldr-**	-ás
poder:	**podr-**	-á
poner:	**pondr-**	-emos
querer:	**querr-**	-éis
saber	**sabr-**	-án

Tip: The future in Spanish can also be expressed with the **verb ir + infinitive**: **Voy a jugar al tenis.** (*I'm going to play tennis.*)

You can see the future in action in this beautiful poem by Spanish Nobel-prize winning poet Juan Ramón Jiménez (1881-1958).

El viaje definitivo	**The Final Trip**
Y yo me **iré**... Y se **quedarán** los pájaros cantando. Y se **quedará** mi huerto, con su verde árbol y con su pozo blanco.	And I **shall leave**... And the birds **shall remain** singing; and my garden, with its green tree and its white well **shall remain**.
Todas las tardes, el cielo **será** azul y plácido; y **tocarán**, como esta tarde están tocando, las campanas del campanario.	Every afternoon, the sky **will be** blue and placid; and the bells in the bell tower **will toll** like they are tolling this afternoon.
Se **morirán** aquellos que me amaron; y el pueblo se **hará** nuevo cada año; y en el rincón aquel de mi huerto florido y encalado, mi espíritu **errará** nostálgico.	Those who loved me **shall die**; and the town **shall renew** itself each year; and in that corner of my florid and blanched orchard, my spirit **shall wander** nostalgic.
Y yo me **iré**; y **estaré** solo, sin hogar, sin árbol verde, sin pozo blanco, sin cielo azul ni plácido... Y se **quedarán** los pájaros cantando.	And I **shall leave**, and **shall be** alone, with no home, no green tree, no white well, no blue and placid sky... And the birds **shall remain** singing.

Glossary:

quedarse: *to remain*	huerto: *orchard*	rincón: *corner*
tocar: *to touch*	pozo: *well*	florido: *full of flowers*
morir: *to die*	plácido: *placid*	encalado: *whitewashed/blanched*
errar: *to wander*	campanario: *bell tower*	nostálgico: *nostalgic*

Practice 18

A. Here is the poem again but this time we've changed the verbs. We hope Juan Ramón Jiménez doesn't turn in his grave! Match the verbs to the subjects in the future form. Remember that this is poetry, so the order of a sentence is not always linear. Sometimes the subject is behind the verb. Another useful thing to remember is that when the verb suggested is reflexive (**irse**), you should put the pronoun before the conjugated verb in the appropriate person: **me voy**.

Y yo ___________[1] **(correr)**.
Y ___________[2] **(permanecer)** los pájaros cantando. — los pájaros: is the subject
Y ___________[3] (**continuar**) mi huerto, con su verde árbol y con su pozo blanco. — mi huerto: is the subject

Todas las tardes, el cielo ___________[4] (**volverse**) azul y plácido;
y ___________[5] (**sonar**), como esta tarde están tocando,
las campanas del campanario.

___________[6] **(irse)** aquellos que me amaron;
y el pueblo ___________[7] (**renovarse**) cada año;
y en el rincón aquel de mi huerto florido
y encalado, mi espíritu ___________[8] (**volar**) nostálgico.

Y yo ___________[9] (**desaparecer**); y ___________[10](**estar**) solo, sin hogar, sin árbol verde, sin pozo blanco,
sin cielo azul ni plácido...
Y ___________[11] **(seguir)** los pájaros cantando.

B. Imagine you win the lottery. What are some of the thing's you'll do or won't do? Complete the sentences with the appropriate form of the verb in the future.

1. ___________ (yo/tener) un presupuesto (*a budget*).
2. ___________ (yo/saber) administrar (*manage*) el dinero.
3. ___________ (yo/poder) comprarme un coche de lujo (*luxury car*).
4. ___________ (yo/salir) todas las noches con mis amigos.
5. ___________ (yo/hacer) compras (*shopping*) todo el año.
6. ___________ (yo/comprar) regalos (*gifts*) para mis amigos.
7. ___________ (yo/querer) viajar mucho.

8. __________ (yo/comprar) una casa grande.
9. __________ (yo/usar) todo mi dinero.
10. __________ (yo/ayudar) a las personas necesitadas (*people in need*).

C. Sylvia's daughter is going on an exchange trip to France. This is what she tells her daughter before she leaves.

1. __________ (tú/practicar) francés.
2. __________ (visitar) los museos y los edificios importantes.
3. __________ (ir) a la Torre Eiffel.
4. __________ (comer) muchas baguettes.
5. __________ (navegar) en un bote sobre el río Sena.
6. __________ (subir) al Arco de Triunfo.

D. Answer the questions in this dialogue, responding to the person addressed in the question.

Example: —¿A qué hora vendrás a comer? —Vendré a comer a las ocho.

1. —¿A qué hora iréis al cine? 8:00 p.m. (nosotros)

   —____

2. —¿A qué hora cenarán Tomás y Malena? (10:00 p.m.)

   —____

3. —¿A qué hora vendrá Martha a mi casa? (mediodía)

   —____

4. —¿A qué hora haremos la reunión? 3:00 p.m. (nosotros)

   —____

5. —¿A qué hora saldréis hacia el aeropuerto? mañana (nosotros)

   —____

6. —¿A qué hora podrán ayudarnos? 7:00 a.m. (ellos)

   —____

E. Think about the world in the year 2080 and give these answers in the future. You can use the following adverbs to help with your answers:

- **probablemente** (*probably*)
- **seguramente** (*certainly*)
- **posiblemente** (*possibly*)

Example: nosotros / ser / tolerantes: Probablemente, todos seremos tolerantes.

1. yo / conducir / coches voladores
 ____
2. vosotros / poder / comunicar con los ojos
 ____
3. Juan y Santiago / saber / cocinar / sin ensuciar
 ____
4. Tú / ser / muy viejo
 ____
5. Nosotros / vivir / en cápsulas espaciales (*space capsules*)
 ____
6. Martín / poder / casarse / con un robot
 ____

F. Answer these questions about yourself 20 years from now. Use the same verb in the first part but conjugated in the first person. Remember this is a give and take: if the question is with **tú**, you should answer with **yo**.

Example: ¿Dónde vivirás? Viviré en Bombay.

1. ¿Qué te gustaría ser? ____________________________
2. ¿Dónde trabajarás? ____________________________
3. ¿Con quién te casarás (*marry*)? ____________________
4. ¿Cuántos hijos tendrás? __________________________
5. ¿Cuánto dinero ganarás? _________________________
6. ¿En qué gastarás tu dinero? _______________________
7. ¿Cuál será tu pasatiempo (*hobby*)? _________________

Vocabulary: finance

English	Spanish	Pronunciation
money	**dinero**	*[dee-neh-roh]*
credit cards	**tarjetas de crédito**	*[tahr-heh-tas deh kreh-dee-toh]*
to ask for a loan	**pedir un préstamo**	*[peh-deer oon prehs-tah-moh]*
to get the paycheck	**cobrar el sueldo**	*[koh-brahr ehl swehl-doh]*
to invest in the stock market	**invertir en la bolsa**	*[een-behr-teer ehn lah bohl-sah]*
to buy stocks	**comprar acciones**	*[kohm-prahr ahk-thyoh-nes]*
to pay cash	**pagar al contado**	*[pah-gahr ahl kohn-tah-doh]*
to adapt oneself to a budget	**adaptarse a un presupuesto**	*[ah-dahp-tahr-seh ah oon preh-soo-pwehs-toh]*
debts	**deudas**	*[deoo-das]*
to borrow	**pedir prestado**	*[peh-deer prehs-tah-doh]*
to lend	**prestar**	*[prehs-tahr]*
savings account	**caja de ahorro**	*[kah-hah deh ah-oh-rroh]*
ATM	**cajero electrónico**	*[kah-heh-roh eh-lehk-troh-nee-koh]*

G. Raúl got his paycheck and these are his thoughts on what to do with the money. Join the clauses to make a sentence in future tense. **Example: Raúl/pagar/ tarjetas de crédito/sus: Raúl pagará sus tarjetas de crédito.**

1. Raúl / invertir / en / la bolsa: ______________________
2. Raúl / no / pedir / ningún / préstamo: ______________
3. Raúl / administrar / bien / su dinero: _______________
4. Raúl / adaptarse / a / su presupuesto: ______________
5. Raúl / usar / parte del dinero / para / invertir en la bolsa:

   ____
6. Raúl / comprar / acciones: ______________________
7. Raúl / prestar / dinero / a un amigo: ________________
8. Raúl / pagar / al contado / sus compras: ____________

H. This is your busy schedule during the week. Say what you'll do tomorrow based on this schedule. Choose 10 activities. **Example**: **A las 6:00 a.m. me levantaré**.

6:00 a.m.: levantarse
7:00 a.m.: preparar el desayuno
7:30 a.m.: salir al trabajo
8:00 a.m.: tomar el tren
8:30 a.m.: llegar a la estación
9:00 a.m.: reunirse con el jefe
9:30 a.m.: preparar un informe
12:00 a.m.: almorzar
3:00 p.m.: ir a clase de yoga
4:00 p.m.: ir a la estación de tren
4:20 p.m.: tomar el tren
5:00 p.m.: llegar a casa
6:00 p.m.: bañarse
8:00 p.m.: mis amigas (venir a mi casa)
9:00 p.m.: salir (nosotros) a tomar algo

I. What will these people say when accused of parking in the wrong spot? Write a sentence conjugating the verb in the future.

Example: Julia dirá que no vio el letrero. (*the sign*)

1. Martín ________________ que no sabía.
2. Pedro y Pablo __________ que estaban apurados. (*They were in a hurry*)
3. Yo ____________________ que tenía una urgencia.
4. Nosotros ______________ que no tenemos auto.
5. Vosotros ______________ que hay lugar para todos.
6. Tú ____________________ que no tienes auto.

J. Choose the right verb and conjugate it in the future:

hacer – poder – poner – querer – saber – salir – tener – venir

1. Fernando y Sofía ______________ esta noche a bailar.
2. (nosotros) ______________________ la comida.
3. Mi tío ___________________________ desde Escocia para visitarnos.
4. Vosotros _______________________ comer temprano.
5. Tú _____________________________ trabajar en tu casa.
6. Ella ____________________________ las flores en el altar.
7. Después de estudiar ingeniería (*engineering*) en la universidad, tú ______________________________ mucho.
8. Vosotros _______________________ un buen viaje.

STORY #5 Los Bromistas Gómez

(The Pranking Gómez)

La familia Gómez es muy **bromista**: se asustan unos a otros, se ponen notitas graciosas en las **mochilas de la escuela**, se esconden cosas hasta que el dueño **enloquece** y muchas **travesuras** más. Los amigos y los **parientes** opinan que los Gómez son muy divertidos y agradables.

La mamá dice que odia las **bromas**, pero se ríe bastante cuando descubre que falta un **calcetín** de todos los **pares** que acaba de lavar.

Una noche, el hijo menor escondió **chícharos congelados** debajo de las **cobijas** en la cama de sus padres. Ellos no se **dieron cuenta** de la broma hasta que se acostaron para dormir. Desde su habitación, el chico escuchó los gritos de sus padres y ahogó sus carcajadas en su **almohada**.

En otra ocasión, el papá llevó a la hija mayor a la escuela. La muchacha estaba muy nerviosa porque tendría un **examen final** muy difícil, así que no notó cuando su papá puso en su bolso una pesada **pinza de metal**, con una nota pegada para desearle buena suerte, con el dibujo de un **conejo** con ojos enloquecidos. La chica cargó el **estorboso** bolso todo el día, hasta que descubrió la broma. ¡Cómo rieron sus amigas con aquel dibujo tan **horrible**! Ella reclamó a su papá Él le respondió: "Eres muy distraída. ¿No habrás guardado esa pinza en tu bolso por error?", le dijo. Ella **fingió disgusto** y le juró **vengarse**.

Pasaron varios días sin bromas en casa, pero la chica convenció a su mamá y a su hermano de ser sus **cómplices** en una broma **magistral** para él. El papá se preparaba para una **junta** muy importante con los directivos de una gran **empresa.** El proyecto le interesaba mucho y deseaba que se lo **aprobaran**. Con ese negocio podría hacer algunos **arreglos en casa** y llevar a su familia de vacaciones a la **playa**.

La noche anterior a la cita, el papá se vistió de **traje y corbata** e hizo la presentación frente a su familia, para escuchar sus recomendaciones. "No tienes que ser tan **serio**, papá. Tú eres más... **simpático,**" opinó su hijo. "Yo creo que así está muy bien," dijo la mamá. "Yo sí aprobaría el proyecto," comentó la hija, "aunque creo que debes usar otra corbata. Esa no **combina** con tu traje." A continuación eligió otra más elegante, que él se puso de inmediato. "¡Perfecto! Ya estás listo para **triunfar,**" le dijo.

Al día siguiente, el papá **pulió** sus zapatos, tomó su **portafolios** y se despidió de su esposa. Ella le aseguró que **confiaba** en su éxito. Al dejar a sus hijos en la escuela, ellos lo **abrazaron** y le desearon suerte en su **reunión de negocios**.

El hombre llegó a la gran empresa, se dirigió a la **sala de juntas** y saludó a los directores. Luego colocó su portafolios sobre la mesa y lo abrió. En el interior encontró una hoja de papel con el dibujo de una **gallina desplumada** que **cacareaba** "¡Queremos vacaciones!" con grandes letras. El señor Gómez rio un poco, pero se controló porque los directores lo miraban. Al tomar los documentos que había preparado para **repartirlos**, descubrió que debajo de ellos había dos grandes rollos de **papel de baño** y varios **gorritos de fiesta**. Incapaz de controlarse, el papá **estalló en carcajadas**.

"¿Qué le sucede, señor Gómez?" preguntó el presidente de la empresa, con mucha curiosidad. El papá **no tuvo más remedio** que mostrar a los directivos la **ridícula** gallina, el papel de baño y los gorritos. Les explicó que su familia es muy bromista y que esa es su manera de demostrarse **cariño**. Todos celebraron la travesura con risas. La broma logró **romper el hielo** y la junta fue exitosa. El proyecto fue aprobado unos días después.

Sin embargo, la mejor broma de la **temporada** fue la de la señora Gómez. Ya en la playa de sus sueños, cuando sus hijos y su esposo le dijeron que tenían mucha **sed**, les ofreció frescas **bebidas de frutas**... ¡En enormes **biberones**! La hija mayor se avergonzó un poco, pero, **a fin de cuentas**, ella pertenece a esa familia tan graciosa.

GLOSSARY	
Bromista	Joking
Mochilas de la escuela	School bags
Enloquecer	To go mad
Travesuras	Rogueries
Parientes	Relatives
Bromas	Pranks
Calcetín	Sock

GLOSSARY	
Junta	Meeting
Empresa	Company
Aprobar	To approve
Arreglos en casa	Home repairs
Playa	Beach
Traje y corbata	Suit and tie
Serio	Serious

GLOSSARY	
Pares	Pairs
Chícharos congelados	Frozen peas
Cobijas	Blankets
Darse cuenta	To realize
Almohada	Pillow
Examen final	Final exam
Pinza de metal	Metal clamp
Conejo	Rabbit
Estorboso	Cumbersome
Horrible	Awful
Fingir	To pretend
Disgusto	Displeasure
Vengarse	To get revenge
Cómplices	Accomplices
Magistral	Masterful
Estallar en carcajadas	To burst out laughing
No tener más remedio	To have no other choice
Ridícula	Ridiculous
Cariño	Affection
Romper el hielo	To break the ice

GLOSSARY	
Simpático	Funny
Combinar	To combine
Triunfar	To succeed
Pulir	To polish
Portafolios	Suitcase
Confiar	To trust
Abrazar	To hug
Reunión de negocios	Business meeting
Sala de juntas	Meeting room
Gallina	Hen
Desplumada	Plucked
Cacarear	To cluck
Repartir	To hand out
Papel de baño	Toilet paper
Gorritos de fiesta	Party hats
Temporada	Season
Sed	Thirst
Bebidas de frutas	Fruit drinks
Biberones	Baby bottles
A fin de cuentas	After all

CHAPTER 19:

THE SUBJUNCTIVE MOOD: REGULAR FORMS

I INSIST THAT WE MEET

19.1 The Subjunctive Mood

We have studied the indicative mood, which is used for stating real objective facts. The subjunctive mood is used, instead, for expressing imagined/subjective states. For example, in the sentence *I wish you were here*, the verb *were* is in the subjunctive mood because it expresses a wish, something not yet real, as opposed to *You are here*, a statement expressing a real situation. Notice that the present subjunctive cannot exist alone. It always depends on another element in the sentence.

You use the subjunctive to express:

Purpose	Example + English Translation
➲ What you want	**Quiero que vengas.** *(I want you to come)*
➲ what you wish for	**Deseo que estés bien.** *(I hope you're alright)*
➲ what you have doubts on	**Dudo de que vaya.** *(I doubt she'll go)*
➲ what you try to get others to do	**Intento que estudie.** *(I'm trying to get him to study)*
➲ what your emotions are	**Tengo miedo de que llueva.** *(I'm afraid that it will rain)*
➲ what your assessment is of an action or situation	**Es importante que trabaje.** *(It's important that he works)*

Expressions to use the present subjunctive

+	Es probable que	(*It's probable that...*)
+	Es bueno que	(*It's good that...)*
+	Es necesario que	(*It's necessary that...)*
+	Es difícil que	(*It's hard that...)*
+	Es fácil que	(*It's easy that...)*
+	Es posible que	(*It's possible that...*)
+	Es una lástima que	(*It's a shame that...*)
+	Espero que	(*I hope that...*)
+	Puede que	(*It's possible that...*)
+	Ojalá que	(*Let's hope that...*)
+	Quizás	(*Maybe*)
+	Tal vez	(*Maybe*)
+	Quiero que	(*I want that...*)
+	Que	(*Let's hope that...*)

Tip: It's very important to know the **yo** form of the indicative mood since the subjunctive comes from that form. For example: **yo pongo** (*poner* / indicative mood) → **yo ponga** (*poner* / subjunctive mood).

19.2 Regular Forms of the Present Subjunctive

hablar *(to speak)*		**comer** *(to eat)*		**vivir** *(to live)*	
yo	habl-**e**	yo	com-**a**	yo	viv-**a**
tú	habl-**es**	tú	com-**as**	tú	viv-**as**
él, ella	habl-**e**	él, ella	com-**a**	él, ella	viv-**a**
ustedes	habl-**e**	usted	com-**a**	usted	viv-**a**
nosotros/as	habl-**emos**	nosotros/as	com-**amos**	nosotros/as	viv-**amos**
vosotros/as	habl-**éis**	vosotros/as	com-**áis**	vosotros/as	viv-**ais**
ellos, ellas	habl-**en**	ellos, ellas	com-**an**	ellos, ellas	viv-**an**
ustedes	habl-**án**	ustedes	com-**an**	ustedes	viv-**an**

Verbs that end in **-car, -gar,** and **-zar** (**buscar, pagar,** and **empezar**) change all the persons of the present subjunctive to keep the **-c-, -g-**, and **-z-** sounds.

Buscar: c → **qu**

Pagar: g → **gu**

Empezar: z → **c**

Present tense subjunctive of buscar, pagar, and empezar

buscar *(to look for)*		**pagar** *(to pay)*		**empezar** *(to start)*	
yo	bus-**que**	yo	pa-**gue**	yo	emp-**iece**
tú	bus-**ques**	tú	pa-**gues**	tú	emp-**ieces**
él, ella	bus-**que**	él, ella	pa-**gue**	él, ella	emp-**iece**
usted	bus-**que**	usted	pa-**gue**	usted	emp-**iece**
nosotros/as	bus-**quemos**	nosotros/as	pa-**guemos**	nosotros/as	emp-**ecemos**
vosotros/as	bus-**quéis**	vosotros/as	pa-**gueis**	vosotros/as	emp-**ecéis**
ellos, ellas	bus-**quen**	ellos, ellas	pa-**guen**	ellos, ellas	emp-**iecen**
ustedes	bus-**quen**	ustedes	pa-**guen**	ustedes	emp-**iecen**

Common Mistake: When you see the verb **querer** in a sentence, you know that there will be a subjunctive in the second part of the sentence:

Quiero que comas la sopa (*I want you to eat the soup).*

Be careful with using the Indicative after **quiero**; always use the subjunctive.

X Quiero que me ayudas.

✓ Quiero que me ayudes.

Practice 19

A. Complete the sentences with the right form of the present subjunctive.

1. María quiere que su madre le __________ (prestar) el coche.
2. Juan desea que sus amigos __________ en su casa (comer).
3. Vosotros deseáis que vuestro jefe os __________ (subir) el sueldo (*salary*).

4. Espero que mi padre no __________ (hablar) con el profesor.
5. Es terrible que __________ (ellos/escribir) en las paredes.
6. Mi tía quiere que yo __________ (trabajar) con ella.
7. Tú esperas que Alejandra te __________ (ayudar).
8. Dudo que Martín y Elena __________ (vivir) en un apartamento.

B. Finish the sentences conjugating the verb in the subjunctive.

1. Quiero que tú __________ (jugar) con Pedro.
2. Quieres que tu profesor __________ (investigar) bien el tema (*the subject*).
3. Quiere que nosotros __________ (empezar) a cocinar.
4. Queremos que ellos __________ (pagar) la comida.
5. Quiero que vosotros __________ (buscar) un buen médico (*doctor*).
6. Quieren que yo __________ (almorzar) con ellos.

C. Finish the sentences conjugating the verbs in the subjunctive:

1. Es bueno que vosotros __________ (rezar) en la iglesia.
2. Es necesario que vosotros __________ (explicar) el problema.
3. Espero que él __________ (entregar) el paquete en su casa.
4. Es fundamental que ustedes __________ (sacar) el coche del estacionamiento (*parking garage*).
5. Es difícil que __________ (él/llegar) temprano.
6. Es posible que __________ (vosotros/tocar) el violín. (*violin*)

D. Tomás is on a diet. Form sentences as if you were a friend and were recommending what he shouldn't eat to lose weight. **Example: (comer/pan) <u>Te recomiendo que no comas pan</u>.**

1. Comer / caramelos ______________________________
2. Comer / pastas ______________________________
3. Comer / chocolates ______________________________
4. Comer / pasteles (*cakes*) ______________________________
5. Beber / alcohol ______________________________
6. Beber / gaseosas con azúcar ______________________________
7. Beber / leche con chocolate ______________________________

E. Complete these sentences with subjunctive forms

1. Quiero que Pablo __________ (trabajar) en el informe.
2. Deseo que Paula me __________ (escribir).
3. Dudo que Mariana __________ (comer) con nosotros.
4. Intento que mi esposo y yo no __________ (mirar) tanta televisión.
5. Es importante que vosotros __________ (leer) mucho.
6. Quiero que __________ (tú/guardar) tus juguetes.
7. Tengo miedo de que los niños no __________ (estudiar) para el examen.
8. Quiero que __________ (nosotros/escribir) un libro juntos.

F. Expressing emotions. Write sentences where the second part depends on the first part and needs a subjunctive. **Example: Tiene miedo. El bebe rompe el celular → <u>Tiene miedo de que el bebé rompa el celular</u>** <u>*(She's afraid the baby will break the cellphone)*</u>.

1. Nos sorprende. Ellos compran tantos alimentos.

   ____

2. Es terrible. Vosotros creéis en supersticiones (*superstitions*).

   ____

3. Es extraño. La luz no prende.

   ____

4. Es emocionante. Sofía visita a su hermana.

   ____

5. Es maravilloso. Pablo trabaja y estudia al mismo tiempo (*at the same time*).

   ____

6. Es increíble. Aquellos escaladores suben el Everest en dos meses.

   ____

7. Es un orgullo. Tomás recibe un premio por su pintura.

   ____

8. Es una pena. (*It's sad*) Vosotros discutís mucho.

   ____

G. Translate to Spanish. **Example: What do you want us to discuss? → <u>Qué quieres que discutamos?</u>**

1. What do you want me to learn? ______________________
2. What do they want you (vosotros) to open? ____________
3. What do you (pl) want me to write? __________________
4. What does the teacher want me to study? _____________
5. What does she want them to buy? ___________________
6. What do you (tú) want us to prepare? _______________
7. What do they want me to pay? _____________________
8. What do we want them to teach? ___________________

H. An office director gives advice to job applicants. Change the infinitives to sentences with the subjunctive. **Example: (leer bien la descripción del trabajo) → <u>Es importante que los candidatos lean bien la descripción del trabajo.</u>**

1. Es importante que los candidatos (estar bien vestidos [*be well-dressed*])

   ____

2. Es importante que los candidatos (prepararse para entrevista)

   ____

3. Es importante que los candidatos (llegar puntualmente a la cita [*on time*])

   ____

4. Es importante que los candidatos (hacer preguntas sobre el trabajo)

   ____

5. Es importante que los candidatos (creer en sí mismos)

   ____

6. Es importante que los candidatos (responder con honestidad)

   ____

7. Es importante que los candidatos (conocer la empresa)

   ____

I. Express your personal feelings. Use one of the following phrases to say how you feel. **Example: entrar en la universidad → <u>Es emocionante que entre en la universidad.</u>**

Es una pena **Es genial** **Es emocionante** **Deseo que**
Me sorprende que **Espero que** **Me encanta (*I love that...*)**

1. Mis amigos no me llamaron para mi cumpleaños:

   ____

2. Me invitan a esquiar:

   ____

3. Me suben el sueldo en el trabajo:

   ____

4. Tu amiga se recupera pronto de su enfermedad (*illness*):

   ____

5. La señora Reta ayuda a una anciana a cruzar la calle:

   ____

6. Lo invitan a jugar al fútbol:

   ____

J. Fill in the missing squares with the right subjunctive form.

Infinitive	sacar	entregar	comenzar	realizar	apagar	pescar *(fish)*
yo		entregue			apague	
tú	saques			realices		
él, ella, usted			comience			pesque
nosotros	saquemos			realicemos		
vosotros			comencéis			pesquéis
ellas, ellos, ustedes		entreguen			apaguen	

STORY #6 El Terremoto de 2017

(The Earthquake of 2017)

Todos estábamos exhaustos. El **terremoto** en México, en septiembre de 2017, había causado grandes **destrozos**, todavía había **brigadas** rescatando víctimas de los **escombros** y muchas **poblaciones** cercanas y lejanas **clamaban donaciones** de ropa, agua, comida y **medicamentos**.

En el **centro de acopio,** muchos **voluntarios** trabajábamos horas **interminables** para prestar toda la ayuda posible. Recibíamos donaciones, las clasificábamos, las organizábamos y las enviábamos a las zonas donde las necesitaban. Fueron días terribles. Trabajábamos tanto que perdíamos la **noción del tiempo** entre el miedo, el hambre, el cansancio, la tristeza y el **dolor**. Nuestras manos sangraban, nuestros músculos ardían y no teníamos muchas **oportunidades** para descansar.

Dicen que los mexicanos nos unimos ante la **desgracia** y esa fue una **prueba** de que es **verdad**. Había médicos atendiendo **heridos** sin cobrar ni un peso; los que tenían cualquier vehículo llevaban donaciones **de un lugar para el otro**. La gente de las casas cercanas nos llevaba **aguas de frutas** y alimentos **hechos en casa**. Los **ancianos** colaboraban clasificando la comida enlatada. Uno de ellos organizó una sección entera de botellas de agua **por tamaños**. Trasladó **botella por botella** hasta que terminó y pudimos **despacharlas** a diferentes sitios. Los niños hacían dibujos y escribían **notitas cariñosas** para otros niños en poblados destrozados.

Una empresa prestó **tráileres** para enviar donaciones a zonas remotas de Oaxaca, muy afectadas por el **sismo**. Nos habían avisado que un tráiler llegaría a nuestro centro de acopio a **medianoche**, así que trabajamos mucho para tener todo listo. Sin embargo, los daños en las **carreteras** y el **tránsito** de ambulancias y maquinaria para remover escombros **retrasaron** mucho su llegada. En la **madrugada** ya habíamos terminado, pero no podíamos marcharnos porque teníamos que **cargar** las donaciones en el tráiler, así que esperamos.

Éramos **más o menos** veinte voluntarios. Habíamos organizado todo por tipo de productos: **comida enlatada, productos higiénicos,** medicamentos, agua, cobijas, ropa, zapatos, **productos de limpieza, palas**, **cubetas**, guantes industriales y **equipos de protección personal,** todo listo para su traslado.

Comimos tacos y bebimos café que nos trajeron los vecinos; luego nos sentamos **en el suelo** para descansar un poco y curarnos las heridas **unos a otros.** Ni siquiera podíamos **platicar**. Además, teníamos mucho miedo: ya se habían registrado muchas **réplicas** del sismo que solo **empeoraban** la situación. Temíamos por nuestros **seres queridos** en una tragedia tan grande.

Poco a poco se hizo el silencio. Algunos **dormitaban** en posturas muy incómodas. De pronto, como si **alucináramos,** escuchamos música en la calle. A continuación un hombre entró al centro de acopio, se sentó en una **butaca desvencijada** y comenzó a tocar **canciones suaves** en una guitarra. Luego empezó a cantar con muy buena voz, **profunda** y triste.

El hombre parecía **tan cansado como nosotros** y estaba cubierto de polvo y lodo. En una de sus piernas tenía un **vendaje** de pedazos de **trapo** y **cojeaba** un poco. Seguro venía de la zona de derrumbes y solo deseaba compañía.

Agradecimos la música **con toda nuestra alma**. Fue como **un baño de agua cálida**, **un abrazo al corazón**, un consuelo para nuestros **espíritus temerosos** y nuestras **heridas sangrantes**. Algunos de nosotros cantamos con él, **muy bajito** para no perder fuerzas.

Eso nos llenó de un **vigor renovado**. Cuando por fin llegó el tráiler, con la débil luz del nuevo día, trabajamos en perfecta organización hasta mandarlo lleno de donaciones a su **destino**. La música de ese **artista anónimo** nos **convenció** de que todo estaría bien.

GLOSSARY	
Terremoto	Earthquake
Destrozos	Destruction
Brigadas	Brigades
Escombros	Debris
Poblaciones	Towns
Clamar	To cry out
Donaciones	Donations
Medicamentos	Medicines

GLOSSARY	
Botella por botella	Bottle by bottle
Despachar	To dispatch
Notitas cariñosas	Loving little notes
Tráiler	Trailer
Sismo	Seism
Medianoche	Midnight
Carreteras	Roads
Tránsito	Traffic

GLOSSARY	
Centro de acopio	Donation center
Voluntarios	Volunteers
Interminables	Endless
Noción del tiempo	Track of time
Dolor	Pain
Oportunidades	Chances
Desgracia	Misfortune
Prueba	Proof
Verdad	True
Heridos	Wounded
De un lado para el otro	From one place to another
Aguas de frutas	Fruit waters
Hechos en casa	Homemade
Ancianos	Elderly
Por tamaños	By size
Réplicas	Aftershocks
Empeorar	To worsen
Seres queridos	Beloved ones
Dormitar	To doze

GLOSSARY	
Retrasar	To delay
Madrugada	Dawn
Cargar	To load
Esperar	To wait
More or less	Más o menos
Trayecto	Journey
Comida enlatada	Canned food
Productos higiénicos	Hygienic products
Productos de limpieza	Cleaning products
Palas	Shovels
Cubetas	Buckets
Equipos de protección personal	Personal safety equipment
En el suelo	On the floor
Unos a otros	Each other
Platicar	To chat
Con toda nuestra alma	With all our soul
Un baño de agua cálida	A shower of warm water
Un abrazo al corazón	A hug to the heart
Espíritus temerosos	Fearful spirits

GLOSSARY	
Alucinar	To hallucinate
Butaca	Armchair
Desvencijada	Rickety
Canciones suaves	Gentle songs
Profunda	Deep
Tan cansado como nosotros	As tired as we were
Vendaje	Bandage
Trapo	Rag
Cojear	To limp

GLOSSARY	
Heridas sangrantes	Bleeding wounds
Muy bajito	Very softly
Vigor	Vigor
Renovado	Renewed
Destino	Destination
Artista	Artist
Anónimo	Anonymous
Convencer	To convince

CHAPTER 20:

THE SUBJUNCTIVE MOOD: IRREGULAR FORMS

I WISH IT WERE FRIDAY

Irregular Forms of the Present Subjunctive

An irregular verb is a verb that doesn't follow the usual rules of grammar. **Hablar**, for example, is a regular verb. The present indicative of **habl-ar** (*to talk*) is **yo habl-o** and the present subjunctive is **yo habl-e**. You can see how the stem is the same in both cases.

But check out **dec-ir** (*to say*): it should say **yo dec-o** in the present indicative, and, instead, it's **digo**, and it should be **dec-e** in the present subjunctive, but it's **diga**. The stem is entirely different! That's what you call irregular.

Below you'll find different forms of irregularity for the subjunctive:

a. Some verbs take the irregularity from the first-person singular indicative and repeat it in all persons in the present subjunctive. Remember the verb **decir**? In the indicative mood it was regular in all persons, except the **first-person singular → yo digo, tú dices, él dice, nosotros decimos, vosotros decís, ellos dicen**.

   Well, the present subjunctive of this verb follows the irregularity of that **first person → yo diga, tú digas, él diga, nosotros digamos, vosotros digáis, ellos digan**.

   Below are some other verbs that follow the same pattern:

Infinitive	first person singular indicative	singular subjunctive form
decir	digo	diga, digas, diga...
tener	tengo	tenga, tengas, tenga...
traer	traigo	traiga, traigas, traiga...
venir	vengo	venga, vengas, venga...
ver	veo	vea, veas, vea...
salir	salgo	salga, salgas, salga...
poner	pongo	ponga, pongas, ponga...

Infinitive	first person singular indicative	singular subjunctive form
oír	oigo	oiga, oigas, oiga...
caer	caigo	caiga, caigas, caiga...
hacer	hago	haga, hagas, haga...

b. Other verbs are irregular but are completely different from the indicative:

infinitive	subjunctive form
dar	dé, des, dé, demos, deis, den
estar	esté, estés, esté, estemos, estéis, estén
ir	vaya, vayas, vaya, vayamos, vayáis, vayan
saber	sepa, sepas, sepa, sepamos, sepáis, sepan
ser	sea, seas, sea, seamos, seáis, sean
haber	haya, hayas, haya, hayamos, hayáis, hayan

c. As for stem-changing verbs in the indicative (see Lesson 16), **-ar** and **-er** stem-changing verbs, like **pensar** (*yo pienso*) and **volver** (*yo vuelvo*), follow the stem-changing pattern of the present indicative:

infinitive	first person singular indicative	singular subjunctive form
pensar	p**ie**nso	p**ie**nse, pienses, piense...
volver	v**ue**lvo	v**ue**lva, vuelvas, vuelva...

-ir stem-changing verbs have two changes:

infinitive	person	first stem-change	second stem-change
dormir	**yo**	duerma	
	tú	duermas	
	él/ella/usted	duerma	
	nosotros/as		durmamos
	vosotros/as		durmáis
	ellos, ellas, ustedes	duerman	

d. Verbs that end in **-gir** and **-guir**:

	Verbos en -gir: **elegir** *(to elect, to choose)*	**Verbos en -guir:** **conseguir** *(to obtain)*
yo	elija	consiga
tú	elijas	consigas
usted	elija	consiga
él, ella	elija	consiga
nosotros/as	elijamos	consigamos
vosotros/as	elijáis	consigáis
ellos, ellas	elijan	consigan

e. Verbs that end in **-iar** *(enviar)* or **-uar** *(continuar)* have an accent mark on the -i or u- of the first, second, third person singular, and the third person plural.

	enviar	**continuar**
yo	envíe	continúe
tú	envíes	continúes
usted	envíe	continúe
él, ella	envíe	continúe
nosotros/as	enviemos	continuemos
vosotros/as	enviéis	continuéis
ellos, ellas	envíen	continúen
ustedes	envíen	continúen

Some verbs ending in -iar are **criar** *(to raise)*, **fotografiar** *(to photograph)*, **enfriar** *(to cool down)*, **guiar** *(to guide)*, **variar** *(to alter)*, **espiar** *(to spy)*, and **ampliar** *(to amplify)*.

And some verbs ending in -uar are **averigua**r *(find out)*, **actuar** *(to act)*, and **evaluar** *(to evaluate)*.

Practice 20

A. Complete the sentences with the same verb that shows up in the first part of the sentence, but conjugated in the subjunctive.

Example: ¿Te darán el trabajo? Espero que me den el trabajo.

1. —¿Dónde está Julio?

   —Puede que __________ en su oficina.
2. —¿Llamaste a tu abuelo?

   —Quizás lo __________ hoy.
3. —¿Ganaron la carrera?

   —Ojalá __________ la carrera.
4. —¿Llegáis al restaurante a las 8:00 de la noche?

   —Tal vez __________. (nosotros)
5. —¿Se suben al tren?

   —Es probable que __________ al tren.
6. —¿Ayuda a sus padres con las compras?

   —Espero que __________ a sus padres con las compras.

B. The García family is going on vacation. What do each of the members want the family to do? **Example: Juan: ir a las montañas → Juan quiere que vayan a las montañas.**

1. Mariana: ir al mar → ______________________________
2. Pedro: hacer un campamento (*camping*) → ______________________
3. La madre: estar en una isla remota → ______________________
4. El padre: ir a una ciudad interesante → ______________________
5. La abuela: dar un paseo (*drive along*) por la costa (*coast*) → ______
6. El abuelo: ir a pescar → ______________________________

C. Juana leads an unhealthy life. Pretend you are a good friend of hers. Read Juana's description of her habits and then use the highlighted verbs to recommend what she should do. You can use **te recomiendo** *(I recommend)* and **te aconsejo** *(my advice is to)*. **Example: Todas las noches me acuesto tarde → te recomiendo que no te acuestes tarde.**

Hola, soy Juana. Esta es mi vida: me **levanto** tarde y no **desayuno**. Luego voy a trabajar y **discuto** mucho con mis colegas del trabajo. Vuelvo a mi casa y **veo** televisión. Jamás **hago** ejercicio. Nunca **cocino**. Por eso **como** comida chatarra (*junk food*). De noche, **salgo** con amigos y me **acuesto** tarde. **Bebo** mucho alcohol y **fumo** mucho.

1. Te recomiendo que ______________________
2. Te aconsejo que ______________________
3. Te recomiendo que no ______________________
4. Te aconsejo que no ______________________
5. Te recomiendo que ______________________
6. Te aconsejo que ______________________
7. Te recomiendo que no ______________________
8. Te aconsejo que no ______________________
9. Te recomiendo que no ______________________
10. Te aconsejo que no ______________________
11. Te recomiendo que no ______________________

D. The Perez family are going to build a treehouse. The father decides what each member should get to make it. **Example: Quiero que vosotros ________ (conseguir) los ladrillos (*bricks*): Quiero que vosotros consigáis los ladrillos.**

1. Quiero que José ________ (conseguir) un serrucho (*saw*).
2. Quiero que Mónica ________ (conseguir) madera.
3. Quiero que David y Elena ________ (conseguir) las ventanas.
4. Quiero que tú (his wife) ________ (conseguir) los muebles (*furniture*)
5. Quiero que nosotros ________ (conseguir) una escalera (*ladder*)
6. Quiero que vosotros (his kids) ________ (conseguir) la puerta.

E. Fill in the blanks with the right subjunctive form of the verbs between parenthesis.

1. Deseo que nosotros ________________ (realizar) el viaje.
2. Ojalá que Mariana ________________ (buscar) las flores.
3. Puede que mañana ________________ (llover)
4. Intenta que su hijo ________________ (estudiar)
5. Tengo miedo de que tú no ____________ (venir)
6. Es necesario que todos ______________ (lavarse) los dientes tres veces (*times*) por día.
7. Tal vez el director ________________ (dirigir) la orquesta este viernes.
8. Quizás vosotros ________________ (sacar) un pez (*fish*) del mar.
9. Es probable que el profesor __________ (explicar) la lección.
10. Me emociona que ________________ (llegar) la primavera.

F. Translate the following sentences.

1. It's good that people eat more vegetables.

   ____

2. Marta is happy that her son is going on a trip.

   ____

3. It's probable that Juan and Ivan are coming for dinner.

   ____

4. I hope you (vosotros) win the election.

   ____

5. They want to be invited to the party.

   ____

6. It's necessary that you (tú) go outside to smoke.

   ____

G. Write an I (for indicative) and an S (for subjunctive) before each verb form.

1. __________ baile
2. __________ buscan
3. __________ busquen
4. __________ coma
5. __________ miramos
6. __________ diga
7. __________ miréis
8. __________ salgas
9. __________ van
10. __________ vuele
11. __________ expliquemos
12. __________ leemos

H. Express what you want (**quiero**) for the following people. Turn the verb in the first sentence to the subjunctive in the second one. If needed, add a ***no***.

Example: A mi hermano le gusta comer helados → Quiero que mi hermano coma helados.

1. El bebé tiene malos sueños → ____________________
2. Mi hermana no hace ejercicio → ____________________
3. Mi padre no me da dinero → ____________________
4. Nuestros tíos no saben esa noticia → ____________________
5. Mi hijo no es responsable → ____________________
6. Vosotros no vais de vacaciones → ____________________
7. No hay flores en mi casa → ____________________
8. Juan está muy solo → ____________________

I. Complete the sentences with the correct form of the present subjunctive of verbs ending in **-iar** or **-uar**. Remember some forms have an accent! **Example: No le gusta que lo __________ (fotografiar) → No le gusta que lo fotografíen.**

1. No quiere que lo __________ (criar) los abuelos.
2. Prefiero que __________ (ellos/continuar) en este colegio.
3. Pedisteis que os __________ (evaluar).
4. No nos gusta que nos __________ (espiar).
5. No creo que __________ (ampliar) el colegio.
6. Es importante que __________ (yo/averiguar) a qué hora sale el ómnibus.
7. Quieren que __________ (ella /actuar) de la Mujer Araña (*Spiderwoman*).
8. Debes esperar que __________ (enfriarse) el pastel.

J. Use the indicative or the subjunctive of the verb in parenthesis.

María __________[1] (querer) ver al doctor Castro porque no __________[2] (dormir) bien. El doctor le aconseja que __________[3] (hacer) un ritual antes de ir a la cama. Insiste en que __________[4] (beber) un vaso de leche tibia y no __________[5] (prender) la televisión. También le dice que no __________[6] (escuchar) música justo antes de ir a dormir. El doctor le sugiere a María que __________[7] (leer) una novela en la cama y __________[8] (bajar) la luz. Por último, le prohíbe que __________[9] (irse) a dormir con el celular cerca.

CHAPTER 21:

THE IMPERATIVE MOOD

FASTEN YOUR SEATBELTS

The Imperative Mood

In Spanish, the Imperative Mood is the special tense used to give commands or make requests to someone else. It's an important aspect of the language that will come in handy in various situations. Whether you need to tell someone to do something quickly, ask for help, or tell your friend to be quiet during a movie – the Imperative Mood will be there to help you. While it may take some practice to master the usage of the Imperative Mood, it's definitely worth it to learn how to communicate your needs and desires clearly in Spanish.

Read the next dialogue between a stewardess and a passenger. Notice the way the stewardess says the safety instructions.

En el avión	
AZAFATA:	Señores y señoras, vamos a despegar. Por favor, **abróchense** los cinturones, **enderecen** el respaldo de sus asientos, **guarden** todas sus pertenencias debajo del asiento delante de ustedes y **apaguen** su teléfono celular.
PASAJERO:	Señorita, yo necesito ir al baño.
AZAFATA:	Señor, ahora no puede ir al baño. No puede caminar en el avión. **Siéntese** y **quédese** en el asiento.
PASAJERO:	Pero tengo mucha urgencia.
AZAFATA:	No se **pare**. Por favor, **abróchese** el cinturón. El avión está a punto de despegar.
PASAJERO:	Pero no puedo esperar.
AZAFATA:	Señor, lo siento. **Permanezca** en su asiento y no se **mueva**. En un rato puede ir al baño.
PASAJERO:	¡En un rato quizás sea demasiado tarde!

Glossary:

abrocharse el cinturón: *fasten one's seatbelt*
vamos a despegar: *we're going to take off*
a punto de: *getting ready to*
respaldo: *seat back*
asiento: *seat*
enderezar: *straighten*
apagar: *turn off*
quieto: *still*
urgencia: *urgency*

21.1 Imperative mood with regular verbs

For the regular verbs, command forms for **usted** (formal singular you) and **ustedes** (formal plural you) are the same as the present subjunctive forms for **usted** and **ustedes**.

Example: Subjunctive = **usted coma** / Imperative = **¡coma usted**!

As you see, in the imperative, the pronoun goes **after** the verb.

The command for **tú** is identical to the third person singular of the present tense.

Indicative: **La niña corre** → Imperative: **¡corre tú!**

Of course, when you give a command to someone informally, you don't need to add the **tú**: **¡Habla!** (*speak!*).

The command for nosotros is formed by changing the letter before **-mos** to either **-e** or **-a,** depending on what the original verb's ending is (-ar, -er, or -ir): indicative.

For example, **nosotros cocinamos** → Imperative: **¡cocinemos nosotros!**

The command for vosotros is formed based on the infinitive, substituting the final -r with an -a: infinitive = secar → command = **¡secad los platos, vosotros!** *(dry the plates, all of you!)*

The command for ellos/ellas is the same as for ustedes: use the form of the present subjunctive for ustedes.

Example: Subjunctive = **ellos coman** / Imperative = ¡**que coman**! (the imperative is many times used with **que**).

hablar *(to speak)*		**comer** *(to eat)*		**vivir** *(to live)*	
tú	habl**a**	tú	com**e**	tú	viv**e**
él/ella		él/ella		él/ella	
usted	habl**e**	usted	com**a**	usted	viv**a**
nosotros/as	habl**emos**	nosotros/as	com**amos**	nosotros/as	viv**amos**
vosotros/as	habl**ad**	vosotros/as	com**ed**	vosotros/as	viv**id**
ellos/ellas		ellos/ellas		ellos/ellas	
ustedes	habl**en**	ustedes	com**an**	ustedes	viv**an**

21.2 The imperative mood in the negative form

Something funny happens with the imperative in the second person singular (tú) and the second person plural (vosotros). It's different!

The same happens with irregular verbs, like pensar, volver, and pedir.

For example, the affirmative imperative of **hablar** for **tú** is **¡Habla tú!** But the negative imperative is **¡No hables tú!** In fact, the negative form is the same as the present subjunctive.

With **pensar,** for example, the affirmative imperative for **tú** is **¡Piensa!** And the negative imperative is **¡No pienses!**

tú	habla/ no hables	piensa/ no pienses
vosotros	hablad/ no habléis	pensad/ no penséis

21.2 Practice

A. Give the command form of the following verbs in the **usted** form:

1. Bailar: ____________
2. Comprar: ____________
3. Hablar: ____________
4. Descansar: ____________
5. Entrar: ____________
6. Regresar: ____________
7. Vender: ____________
8. Abrir: ____________
9. Escribir: ____________
10. Comer: ____________

21.3 Imperative mood with irregular verbs

The imperative mood follows the irregularities of the subjunctive mood.

a. Stem-changing verbs show the same stem change of the present indicative:

infinitive	first person singular indicative	singular subjunctive
pensar	p**ie**nso	p**ie**nse, pienses, piense...
volver	v**ue**lvo	v**ue**lva, vuelvas, vuelva...

-ir stem-changing verbs have two changes: one for four forms, and another for **nosotros** and **vosotros**.

infinitive	person	first stem-change	second stem-change
dormir	**yo**	duerma	
	tú	duermas	
	él/ella/usted	duerma	
	nosotros/as		durmamos (nosotros)
	vosotros/as		durmáis (vosotros)
	ellos, ellas, ustedes	duerman	

b. Verbs ending in **-car, -gar**, and **-zar** have a spelling change: buscar → **busque usted**, pagar → **pague usted**, and empezar → **empiece usted**

c. Commands for verbs that have irregular **yo** forms in the indicative carry that irregularity to commands.

   Conocer → **yo conozco → conozca usted**

   Decir → **yo digo → diga usted**

   Other verbs that follow the pattern of **conocer** and **decir** are **hacer – oír – poner – salir – tener – traer – venir – ver**

d. Commands for irregular present subjunctive forms.

   ser: sé tú, sea él, sea usted...

   estar: está tú, esté él, esté usted...

   ir: ve tú, vaya usted, vayamos nosotros...

   dar: da tú, dé usted, demos nosotros...

   saber: sepa usted, sepamos nosotros, sabed vosotros...

   haber: haya...

e. There are a few affirmative tú commands that differ from the present tense él form of the verb. Learn these seven irregular affirmative tú commands:

Infinitive	Affirmative tú command	English
tener	ten	have
poner	pon	put
salir	sal	leave
venir	ven	come
hacer	haz	make or do
decir	di	say or tell
ser	sé	be
ir	ve	go

21.3 Practice

A. Fill in the blanks with the command form (imperative) according to each case.
   Example: ¡__________ el documento! (usted/traer): ¡Traiga el documento!

   1. ¡__________ temprano! (usted / llegar)
   2. ¡__________ un rato todos los días (tú / leer)
   3. ¡__________ el nombre (vosotros / escribir)
   4. ¡__________ la puerta! (ustedes / abrir)

5. ¡__________ bien! (nosotros / pensar)
6. ¡__________ tranquilos! (ustedes / estar)
7. ¡__________ las sillas! (nosotros / traer)
8. ¡__________ el pasado! (tú / olvidar)

B. Professor Lando is giving his students (*ustedes*) advice on how to have a productive year.

__________ (levantarse) [1] temprano y __________ (tomar)[2] un buen desayuno. __________ (llegar)[3] al colegio puntualmente *(on time)* y __________ (sentarse)[4] en su banco *(desk).* __________ (organizar)[5] todos los útiles (*school materials*) que necesiten. __________ (empezar)[6] a trabajar en seguida, sin perder tiempo. No __________ (perder)[7] tiempo. __________ (usar)[8] la cabeza. Cuando termine la hora, __________ (cerrar)[9] las carpetas *(folders)* y __________ (ir) [10] a su casa.

In Spanish, the imperative for **ir** has a different affirmative and negative form. Check it out below.

ir (*to go*)			
ve	tú	**vamos**	nosotros
		id	vosotros
vaya	usted él ella	**vayan**	ustedes ellos ellas

ir (*to go - negative*)			
no vayas	tú	**no vayamos**	nosotros
		no vayáis	vosotros
no vaya	usted él ella	**no vayan**	ustedes ellos ellas

C. Your friend Teresa is planning a trip to France. Give her advice on where she should go or not go. Check the verb **ir** (*to go*) to help you out.

1. No ____________ a la Torre Eiffel.
2. ______________ al museo de Louvre.
3. ______________ a los jardines de Luxemburgo.
4. No ____________ al barrio La Défense.
5. No ____________ a los restaurantes caros.
6. ______________ al museo d'Orsay para ver a los impresionistas.
7. ______________ a Montmartre.
8. ______________ a la plaza Vendôme.

D. Teresa is asking for directions. We'll put the following sentences into commands. The relationship between the agent and Teresa is formal (usted).

Example: Debe seguir por esta avenida → <u>Siga por esta avenida.</u>

1. Debe doblar a la derecha → ____________________________
2. Debe avanzar hasta el semáforo → ____________________
3. Debe seguir hacia el norte → __________________________
4. Debe llegar a una rotonda → ___________________________
5. Debe continuar por la misma calle → ___________________
6. Debe girar a la derecha → _____________________________

E. Reply to these people who are complaining about different things (vosotros). Some verbs you can use are: **comer – beber – pedir – trabajar – descansar – hablar – buscar.** Other words that might come in handy are: **pedir ayuda** *(ask for help)* – **hacer amigos** *(make friends)*. **Example: Tenemos sueño: <u>Dormid</u>.**

1. Tenemos hambre ______________________________________
2. Tenemos sed ____
3. Estamos solos ____
4. No entendemos el ejercicio ______________________________
5. Estamos cansados _____________________________________
6. Necesitamos más dinero ________________________________
7. Nuestros padres quieren hablar con nosotros ____________
8. No encontramos nuestras mochilas (*backpack*) __________

F. What commands would you give to the following people (formal relationship: usted/ustedes)? You can use these verbs and nouns:

gobernar – cocinar – tener paciencia – nadar – jugar al tenis - estudiar – correr – cantar – rezar

1. El presidente: ______________________________
2. Miley Cyrus: ______________________________
3. El chef Joël Robuchon: ______________________________
4. Usain Bolt: ______________________________
5. El Papa Francisco: ______________________________
6. Roger Federer: ______________________________
7. Michael Phelps: ______________________________
8. Los estudiantes: ______________________________
9. Las madres: ______________________________

G. Martín is out of a job. As a counselor, offer advice to him (formal relationship: **usted**) in the form of affirmative or negative commands. Verbs and nouns you can use:

hacer una capacitación *(do a training)*
hacer un test vocacional (*do a vocational test*)
incluirlo en el CV *(include in the résumé)*
trabajar al aire libre *(work in the outdoors)*
empleos disponibles (*available jobs*)
tener confianza en sí mismo (*have confidence in yourself*)
buscar un trabajo
trabajar en una oficina
averiguar (*find out*)
ser valiente (*to be brave*)
preparar un CV (*prepare a résumé*)

1. No tengo trabajo: ______________________________
2. No me gusta trabajar en una oficina: ______________
3. Tengo miedo de buscar trabajo: __________________
4. No estudié nada: ______________________________
5. No sé cuáles son los empleos disponibles: __________
6. No sé cuáles son mis habilidades: ________________
7. No me gusta trabajar al aire libre (*outdoors*): ________
8. Soy inseguro: ______________________________
9. No tengo un CV: ______________________________
10. Tengo experiencia laboral (*job experience*): _________

H. Translate these commands to Spanish.

1. *Look* (tú): ______
2. *Pay* (vosotros): ______
3. *Pay* (ustedes): ______
4. *Start* (nosotros): ______
5. *Look* (vosotros): ______
6. *Look* (ustedes):______
7. *Start* (tú): ______
8. *Pay* (nosotros): ______

I. This is part of the dialogue at the beginning of the lesson, where a man was asking the flight attendant if he could go to the bathroom. The airplane is now in the air, and the flight attendant turns her negative commands into affirmative ones. Change the verbs highlighted in the text to an affirmative command. Notice that the reflexive pronoun that goes before the verb in the negative command moves behind it in the affirmative version.

Example: ¡No se mueva! → ¡Muévase!

PASAJERO: Señorita, yo necesito ir al baño.
AZAFATA: Señor, ahora no puede ir al baño. No puede caminar en el avión. Siéntese y quédese en el asiento.
PASAJERO: Pero tengo mucha urgencia.
AZAFATA: No se pare. Por favor, abróchese el cinturón. El avión está a punto de despegar.
PASAJERO: Pero no puedo esperar.
AZAFATA: Señor, lo siento. Permanezca en su asiento y no se mueva. En un rato puede ir al baño.

1. ______
2. ______
3. ______
4. ______
5. ______
6. ______
7. ______
8. ______
9. ______

J. Complete with an affirmative or negative command according to the situation. Remember that for tú and vosotros, the negative and the affirmative are different. **Example: ¡(tú/comer)__________ tu comida, Daniel!: ¡Come tu comida, Daniel!** and **¡(tú/no/comer)__________ tu comida: ¡No comas tu comida, Daniel!**

1. (tú/no/gritar) __________. Puedo escuchar bien.
2. (vosotros/practicar) __________ el violín y seréis grandes músicos.
3. (nosotros/pagar) __________ la comida y (irse) __________.
4. (ustedes/abrócharse) __________ los cinturones. El avión aterrizará pronto.
5. (usted/tocar) __________ el timbre (*doorbell*) de la casa.
6. (vosotros/no/hablar fuerte) __________ en la iglesia.
7. (tú/no/cruzar) __________ la calle cuando el semáforo está rojo.
8. (ustedes/escuchar) __________ la clase del profesor.

CHAPTER 22:
THE CONDITIONAL MOOD
I'D LIKE TO...

How to Form the Conditional Mood

If you're thinking, 'Oh, no, not another mood!', relax! The conditional mood is *as* easy to learn as the future. Plus, you hardly have any irregular verbs in the conditional! As for its use, the conditional mood is used for hypothetical or conditional situations.

Remember that for other moods you had to remove the ending of the infinitive to add other endings (e.g.: **habl-ar→ habl-ó**)? Well, in the conditional you just have to add endings to the infinitive as it is. For example, **hablar→ hablaría** (*I would speak*), **hablar-ías** (*you would speak*), **hablar-ía** (*he/she/you would speak*), and so on. By the way, the ending for the conditional is the SAME ending you use for **-er** and **-ir** verbs in the imperfect.

Reading Comprehension

Si ganara la lotería...

Si ganara la lotería, **ayudaría** a mis amigos. Le **pagaría** los estudios a Roberto, a Elena le **regalaría** un apartamento y a José lo **ayudaría** a comprar un coche para su trabajo. **Iría** a un hospital y **daría** regalos a los niños enfermos. **Contrataría** una orquesta de músicos para dar un concierto y alegrarles la vida a los niños. **Construiría** un edificio para albergar a las personas de la calle. Les **ofrecería** una habitación hermosa y comida rica. Todo esto **haría** con el dinero de la lotería.

Glossary:

si ganara: *if I won...*
estudios: *studies*
contratar: *hire*
dar un concierto: *give a concert*
construir: *build*
ofrecer: *to offer*
lotería: *lottery*
enfermos: *sick*
orquesta: *orchestra*
alegrar: *cheer up*
albergar: *give shelter*
personas de la calle: *homeless people*

The conditional mood is used to express what you would do in a situation if something were to happen. It is also used to express wishes, with verbs like **desear, querer, preferir, gustar,** and **estar interesado**.

In English, the conditional is formed by adding an extra word to the infinitive (*would*)→ *I would go*. In Spanish, you just use one word, and that word comes from adding endings to the infinitive of the verb: **-ía, -ías, -ía, -íamos, -íais, -ían**. For example: **comer → yo comer-ía** (*I would eat*). As you see, you don't need auxiliary words.

So far, not too complicated. Except for the fact that some verbs form the conditional on irregular stems.

Remember how there were some verbs in the future that were formed on irregular stems? Well, those verbs use the same stem to form the conditional:

decir:	**dir-**	
venir	**vendr-**	
hacer	**har-**	
tener:	**tendr-**	-ía
salir:	**saldr-**	-ías
poder:	**podr-**	-ía
poner:	**pondr-**	-íamos
querer:	**querr-**	-íais
saber	**sabr-**	-ían

Practice 22

A. Answer the following questions based on the reading at the beginning of the lesson.

1. ¿A quién le regalaría un apartamento el autor del texto?

   ____

2. ¿Para qué le compraría un coche a José?

   ____

3. ¿Qué le daría a los niños enfermos?

   ____

4. ¿Qué haría para alegrar la vida a los niños?

   ____

5. ¿Cómo albergaría a las personas de la calle?

____

6. ¿Qué ofrecería a las personas de la calle?

____

B. Susana dreams about going to Argentina. Turn the verbs into the conditional mood to help her express her wishes:

Me __________[1] (encantar) ir a Argentina. Allí __________[2] (visitar) la Patagonia y los glaciares. __________[3] (conocer) Bariloche, la tierra de los lagos y las montañas. __________[4] (volar) a las Cataratas del Iguazú, una de las siete maravillas naturales del mundo. __________[5] (probar) la carne argentina. Dicen que es deliciosa. También __________[6] (beber) vino, uno de los atractivos de este país. __________[7] (recorrer) la capital, Buenos Aires, y __________[8] (ver) un show de tango. ¡Cómo me __________[9] (gustar) ir a Argentina!

C. Fill in the missing squares with the appropriate conditional form:

Infinitive form of verb	hablar	comer	vivir
yo		comería	
tú	hablarías		
él/ella/usted			viviría
nosotros	hablaríamos		
vosotros			viviríais
ellas/ellos/ustedes		comerían	

D. What would you do? Follow the example, asking and answering according to the example. Remember that in Spanish, questions have a sign at the beginning and at the end of the sentence: ¿...? **Example: mentir** *(tell lies)* **/ decir la verdad → <u>¿Mentirías? No, diría la verdad.</u>**

1. Venir bailar / ir a tomar algo (*have a drink*)

____

2. Hacer yoga / hacer pilates

____

3. Tener un perro /tener un gato

____

4. Salir de noche / salir de día

 ____

5. Poder preparar lasagna / poder preparar pollo al horno

 ____

6. Poner el dinero en el banco / poner el dinero en una compañía de inversiones

 ____

7. Querer aprender japonés / querer aprender chino

 ____

8. Aprender a conducir una lancha *(boat)* / aprender a remar un bote

 ____

E. Pick one of the two options in each situation, and write it in the conditional. Notice the pronouns that go behind the infinitive are switched to the front of the verb when you conjugate it. **Example: Usted está en la calle y una señora se cae** (*falls down*). **¿Qué haría? a. Dejarla en el suelo. b. Ayudarla a levantarse** (*get up*)**: La ayudaría a levantarse**.

1. Usted sale del cine y olvida su cartera en el asiento (*seat*). ¿Qué haría?
   a. Hablar con la dependienta
   b. Ir a buscar la cartera al asiento
2. Usted está en su casa y se corta la luz *(there's a power outage*). ¿Qué haría?
   a. Llamar a la compañía eléctrica (*electric company*)
   b. Prender muchas velas (*candles*)
3. Usted quiere ir al parque y empieza a llover. ¿Qué haría?
   a. Ir al parque de todos modos (*anyway*)
   b. Quedarse en casa a ver una película (*movie*)
4. Usted está preparando un pastel y este se quema (*it gets burned*). ¿Qué haría?
   a. Comerlo de todos modos
   b. Tirarlo a la basura (*trash*)
5. Estamos en un ascensor (*elevator*) y deja de funcionar (*it stops working*). ¿Qué haría?
   a. Llamar a alguien por mi celular
   b. Gritar para que me oigan (*to be heard*)

6. Su hijo no quiere comer. ¿Qué haría?
    a. Dejarlo sin comer
    b. Darle otra cosa para comer
7. El señor Pérez está en la fila (*line*) del banco y aparece una anciana. ¿Qué haría?
    a. Dejarla esperar en la fila
    b. Dejarla pasar primero
8. Vuestra mejor amiga sube de peso. ¿Qué haríais?
    a. Decirle que está gorda
    b. No decir nada

F. On Sunday you and your friends are having a picnic if it's a nice day. Complete the sentences with the conditional verb. **Example: Catalina __________ (comprar) el jamón y el queso → <u>Catalina compraría el jamón y el queso.</u>**

1. Patricio ________________ (traer) sandwiches de pollo.
2. María y yo ______________ (venir) con el postre (*dessert*).
3. José ___________________ (comprar) las bebidas.
4. Sonia __________________ (hacer) un pastel.
5. Tomás _________________ (ocuparse) de los platos y las servilletas.
6. Luis ____________________ (poner) una sombrilla (*umbrella*)
7. Pablo y Sergio __________ (querer) beber agua.
8. Luisa __________________ (poder) traer hielo (*ice*).

G. *I'd like to...* Use these verbs to express what the person wants/prefers/ is interested in in each case. **Example: Mi amiga __________ (querer) ser abogada (*lawyer*) →** Mi amiga <u>querría</u> ser abogada.

1. Me ______________________ (gustar) viajar a África.
2. Mis padres _____________ (preferir) quedarse en casa.
3. Mi esposa ______________ (querer) aprender español.
4. Mi amigo _______________ (estar) interesado en comprar ese libro.
5. Mis hermanos __________ (querer) ir a la fiesta también.
6. Nuestros hijos __________ (preferir) ir al parque.
7. Mis colegas ____________ (estar) interesados en conocer ese producto (*product*).
8. Nosotros _______________ (preferir) beber agua.

H. Complete this phone dialogue with the conditional mood of the verb suggested.

Javier: ¿Hola?

Roberto: Hola, Javier. Soy Roberto. ¿__________[1](tú/estar) interesado en venir a un concierto con tu hermano Juan?

Javier: Hola, Roberto. Claro que __________[2](nosotros/estar) interesados. ¡Nos encantan los conciertos! ¿Cuándo __________[3](ser) el evento (*event*)?

Roberto: __________[4](ser) este sábado. ¿__________[5](nosotros/poder) ir en tu coche? Mi coche está en el mecánico (*repair shop*).

Javier: Por supuesto (*of course*). ¿__________[6](nosotros/ir) solo nosotros?

Roberto: También __________[7](venir) mi hermana, Luisa.

Javier: Qué bien. Creo que __________[8](nosotros/caber) todos en mi coche.

Roberto: Genial. Nos vemos el sábado. Adiós.

Javier: ¡Adiós y muchas gracias!

I. Review conditional forms. Turn the present forms to the conditional mood, according to the person: **Example: miro → <u>miraría</u>**

1. ponemos __________
2. dices __________
3. somos __________
4. hacéis __________
5. pueden __________
6. vengo __________
7. tenemos __________
8. salgo __________
9. quiere __________
10. saben __________
11. sé __________
12. bajan __________

J. Some people have a job they like, but sometimes wish they were something different. Turn the first sentence into a conditional one.

Example: Os gusta ser enfermeros → <u>os gustaría ser médicos.</u>

1. Me gusta ser enfermera → Me __________ ser chef.
2. A Juan le gusta ser profesor → Le __________ ser piloto de avión (*plane pilot*).
3. A Teresa y Pedro les gusta ser violinistas → Les __________ ser pianistas.
4. A nosotros nos gusta ser abogadas → Nos __________ ser ingenieras.
5. A ellos les gusta ser arquitectos → Les __________ ser diseñadores.
6. A mí me gusta ser escritora → Me __________ ser actriz (*actress*).
7. A ti te gusta ser programador (*computer programmer*) → Te __________ ser analista (*analyst*).
8. A vosotros os gusta cantar → Os __________ bailar.

CHAPTER 23:

SUPERLATIVES

THE MOST BEAUTIFUL OF THEM ALL

Superlatives

Superlatives are a way of expressing the extreme quality of a thing or a group of things. Sometimes you're not just happy, but **very happy.** Sometimes you might even feel like **the most happy** person.

In the story of "Goldilocks and the Three Bears," we encounter various examples of superlatives. When Goldilocks enters the house in the forest, she finds three bowls of soup on the table. The first bowl is the hottest, the second is colder, and the third is just right. Similarly, when she tries the beds, the first is the hardest, the second is the softest, and the third is the most comfortable.

However, the story takes a turn when Goldilocks encounters the bears. She wakes up to find them and, upon seeing them, experiences the worst scare of her life. She quickly flees from the bears' house and runs back home.

Ricitos de Oro (Goldilocks)

Había una vez una niña que fue al bosque y vio la casa **más preciosa del mundo.** Entró y vio sobre la mesa tres platos de sopa. El primer plato era **el más caliente de todos**, el segundo estaba más frío y el tercero estaba perfecto. Luego vio tres camas. La primera era **la cama más dura de todas**. La segunda era **la cama más suave de todas** y la tercera era **la cama más cómoda de todas**. Ricitos de Oro se quedó dormida. De pronto, llegaron los osos. La niña se despertó y saltó de la cama. Al ver a los osos, tuvo **el peor susto de** su vida. Salió de la casa de los osos y corrió hasta su casa.

In Spanish, there are two groups of superlatives: **absolute superlatives** (not to be compared with anything else) and **relative superlatives** (compared with something else).

23.1 Absolute Superlatives

Absolute superlatives point to a noun's qualities that don't compare to anything else. This is the way to form them:

- adjective or adverb + the ending **ísimo, ísima, ísimos, ísimas**.
  - When the adjective ends in a vowel, remove the vowel and replace with **ísimo, ísima, ísimos, ísimas**: **niños buen-os → niños buen-ísimos**.
  - When the adjective ends in **-io** or **-ia**, remove both vowels and replace with **ísimo, ísima, ísimos, ísima**: **cocina suc-ia → cocina sucísima.**
  - When the adjective ends in **-ue, uo, or -ua**, or **ía and ío,** remove the last vowel and add **ísimo, ísima, ísimos, ísimas**: **día frí-o → día friísimo.**
  - When an adjective ends in a consonant **l** or **r**, just add the endings **ísimo, ísima, ísimos, ísimas**: **examen fácil → examen facilísimo.**
  - When an adjective ends in **-or** or **-n**, add **-c** + **ísimo, ísima, ísimos, ísimas**: **señor mayor → señor mayorcísimo** or **profesor jovencísimo**.
  - When an adjective ends in **-z**, change the **-z** for **-c** and add **ísimo, ísima, ísimos, ísimas**: **corredora veloz → corredora velocísima.**
  - Some adjectives don't have a superlative form: **estupendo, genial** and **fatal**.
  - Adjectives that end in **-ble**, replace this syllable for **-bílisimo, -bílisima, -bílisimos, -bilísimas**: **vendedora amabilísima** or **músico sensiblísimo**.
  - Adjectives that end in **-co, -ca, -go**, and **-ga**, replace these with **-quísimo**: **comida rica → comida riquísima** or piernas largas **→ piernas larguísimas.**
- Other irregular superlatives:
  - **mueble antiguo → mueble antiquísimo** (*very antique piece of furniture*)
  - **mujer amable → mujer amabilísima** (*very kind woman*)
  - **plato caliente → plato calientísimo** (*very hot plate*)
  - **perro fiel → perro fidelísimo** *(very loyal dog)*
  - **tormenta fuerte → tormenta fortísima** (*very strong storm*)

21.2 Relative Superlatives

Relative superlatives point to a noun quality's greater or lesser degree but within a larger group. For example: That building is the tallest in the city: **Ese edificio es el más alto de la ciudad**.

In English you just add **-est** to an adjective or use expressions such as **the most** and **the least.** In Spanish, the superlative is the same as the comparative but you need to add a definite article: **el más fuerte.** And if you want to say it's the most of something, you add **de... + el mundo, la tierra**, or any other reference.

Examples:

Nueva York es la ciudad más bella de los Estados Unidos.	*New York is the most beautiful city in the United States.*
Ese hombre es el más anciano de la sala.	*That man is the oldest in the room.*
Este es el coche menos caro de la tienda.	*This is the least expensive car in the store.*
Esta es la casa menos bonita del pueblo.	*This is the least pretty house in town.*
Martín es el más alto de la clase.	*Martín is the tallest in the class.*
Este es el país más frío de Europa.	*This is the coldest country in Europe.*
Elisa es la deportista más rápida de la clase.	*Elisa is the fastest athlete in the class.*

Vocabulary: More Adjectives

amplio	*[ahm-plyoh]*	wide
estrecho	*[ehs-treh-choh]*	narrow
cómodo	*[koh-moh-doh]*	comfortable
incómodo	*[eeng-koh-moh-doh]*	uncomfortable
agrio	*[ah-gryoh]*	sour
popular	*[poh-poo-lahr]*	popular
burlón	*[boor-lohn]*	mocking
mayor	*[mah-yohr]*	older, bigger
vacío	*[bah-thee-oh]*	empty

lleno	*[yeh-noh]*	full
frío	*[free-oh]*	cold
caliente	*[kah-lyehn-teh]*	hot
especial	*[ehs-peh-thyahl]*	special
feroz	*[feh-rohth]*	vicious
ágil	*[ah-heel]*	agile
veloz	*[beh-lohth]*	fast
lento	*[lehn-toh]*	slow

Bueno *(good)* and malo *(bad)* have two absolute superlatives and one relative superlative:

Adjective	Absolute Superlatives		Relative Superlative
bueno	buenísimo	óptimo	el mejor de
malo	malísimo	pésimo	el peor de

Examples:

Son los **mejores actores de** Hollywood. (*They're the best actors in Hollywood.*)

Es **el peor libro de** la biblioteca. (*It's the worst book in the library.*)

Es el hombre **más rico del** mundo. (*He's the richest man on earth.*)

Practice 23

A. Answer these questions on the Goldilocks story above:

1. ¿Cómo era la casa que vio la niña en el bosque?

   ____

2. ¿Cómo era el primer plato?

   ____

3. ¿Cómo era la primera cama?

   ____

4. ¿Cómo era la segunda cama?

   ____

5. ¿Cuál era la cama más cómoda de todas?

   ____

6. ¿Cómo fue el susto que tuvo Ricitos de Oro al ver a los osos?

   ____

B. Complete these sentences with the right absolute superlative.

For example: niña → linda: **niña lindísima**

1. persona baja: ______________________
2. perros y gatos cariñosos: ______________________
3. buen profesor: ______________________
4. actor guapo: ______________________
5. buen periódico: ______________________
6. ejercicio difícil: ______________________
7. amigos simpáticos: ______________________

C. Write the absolute superlative of these adjectives:

1. La Antártida es un continente ______________ (frío)
2. Ese actor es ______________ (guapo)
3. Tienes un pantalón ______________ (corto)
4. Su brazo es ______________ (largo)
5. Este restaurante es ______________ (popular)
6. Mis estudiantes son ______________ (joven)
7. Fueron días ______________ (feliz)
8. Esos coches son ______________ (veloz)
9. Los tigres son animales ______________ (feroz)
10. La doctora es ______________ (amable)

D. You meet a friend and she asks you about your family holidays at the beach. You're so excited you exaggerate your responses using the superlative. **Example: ¿Cómo fue tu vacación? (buena): Fue buenísima.**

1. ¿Cómo estuvo el viaje? ______________ (lindo)
2. ¿Cómo estaba el mar? ______________ (frío)
3. ¿Cómo estuvo la comida? ______________ (sabroso)
4. ¿Cómo estuvieron tus hijos? ______________ (contento)
5. ¿Cómo fue hacer esquí acuático (*water ski*)? ______________ (difícil)
6. ¿Cómo eran los paisajes (*landscapes*)? ______________ (hermoso)
7. ¿Cómo eran los precios (*prices*)? ______________ (baratos)

E. Answer these questions freely with your own words:

1. ¿Quién es la persona más guapa del mundo? ___________
2. ¿Cuál es el postre más rico del mundo? ___________
3. ¿Cuál es el mejor restaurante de tu ciudad? ___________
4. ¿Cuál es la canción más bonita del año? ___________
5. ¿Quién es el deportista más popular del mundo? ___________
6. ¿Cuál es el animal más lento de todos? ___________

F. Now give an absolute superlative to describe the following:

1. Alaska es ___________
2. El monte Everest es ___________
3. El río Amazonas es ___________
4. Rusia es ___________
5. La comida francesa es ___________
6. El perro rottweiler es ___________
7. Las tortugas son ___________

G. Write sentences following the cues. **Example: periódico / bueno / de México: <u>Es el mejor periódico de México.</u>**

1. sofá / incómodo / sala ___________
2. cantante / popular / América Latina ___________
3. animal / ágil / todos ___________
4. día / especial / año ___________
5. cama / incómoda / apartamento ___________
6. calle / estrecha / ciudad ___________

H. Use the adjectives suggested to complete the sentences.

Example: George Clooney es el actor ___________ del mundo → George Clooney es el actor más guapo del mundo.

veloz – popular – cariñosos – alto – rico – difíciles – guapo – discretas *(discreet)*

1. Sofía Vergara es la actriz ___________
2. Jeff Bezos es el hombre ___________
3. Los suizos son las personas ___________
4. Los perros son los animales ___________
5. Los exámenes para entrar en Harvard son ___________

6. Tacko Fall es el jugador de baloncesto ________________
7. El Ferrari es el coche ______________________________

I. Now write sentences according to the model. **Example: Ese coche es muy amplio (tienda) → <u>Ese coche es el más amplio de la tienda.</u>**

1. El metro de Berlín es muy rápido (mundo) →

   ____

2. El niño es muy burlón (clase) →

   ____

3. Es un árbol muy pequeño (bosque) →

   ____

4. Es un hombre muy viejo (orquesta) →

   ____

5. Mónica y Luisa son empleadas muy trabajadoras (oficina) →

   ____

6. La señora Gómez es una profesora sensible (colegio) →

   ____

J. Write the absolute superlatives for these adjectives.

Example: piano antiguo → <u>piano antiquísimo</u>.

1. Dependiente amable → ____________________________
2. Plato caliente → ________________________________
3. Perro fiel → ____________________________________
4. Tormenta fuerte → _______________________________
5. Músico sensible → _______________________________
6. Comida rica → __________________________________
7. Camino largo → _________________________________

BOOK III & IV: ESSENTIAL WORDS AND PHRASES

Are you ready to take your Spanish fluency to the next level and engage in longer, more meaningful conversations with native speakers? Are you excited to expand your verbal repertoire and express yourself more vividly in the enchanting Spanish language? If so, you're in the right place!

This section of the book is tailored specifically for you. The Spanish-speaking world eagerly awaits your newfound ability to communicate confidently in Spanish. As you journey through these pages, you'll discover that conversational Spanish becomes second nature, thanks to the wealth of vocabulary and common expressions at your fingertips.

Don't hesitate to embrace the challenge! We assure you, most Spanish speakers are incredibly friendly and supportive, eager to assist you in your language learning journey. Plus, you'll likely forge numerous friendships along the way. Remember, the more you practice, the more comfortable Spanish will feel, fueling your motivation to further develop your skills.

And one day, seemingly out of nowhere, you'll catch yourself thinking in Spanish. That's the ultimate sign that true learning is taking place! How amazing is that? Get ready to embark on this exciting journey—it's the best and fastest way to learn! ¿Comenzamos? Shall we begin?

BE DESCRIPTIVE

Enrich Your Conversations

You can be as descriptive in Spanish as you are in English. Perhaps more! Descriptions enrich your conversation and help you express your ideas more accurately. They also invite the other party to listen to you attentively and to participate in a fluid conversation. Here are some more adjectives that you can add to your regular speech:

People

English	Spanish	Pronunciation
That man is very intelligent.	**Ese hombre es muy inteligente.**	*[Eh-seh om-breh es mooeeh een-teh-lee-hen-teh]*
That woman is a great leader.	**Esa mujer es una gran líder.**	*[Eh-sah moo-her es oonah gran leeh-der]*
My work team is really enthusiastic.	**Mi equipo de trabajo es realmente entusiasta.**	*[Mee eh-kee-poh deh trah-ba-hoh es real-men-teh en-too-see-as-tah]*
Children are always noisy.	**Los niños siempre son ruidosos.**	*[Los neeh-nyos seeh-em-preh son rueeh-doh-sos]*
People should be more polite.	**La gente debería ser más educada.**	*[Lah hen-teh deh-beh-reeah ser mas eh-dooh-kah-dah]*
A lady is always elegant.	**Una dama siempre es elegante.**	*[Oonah dah-mah see-em-preh es eh-leh-gan-teh]*
These people are very hardworking.	**Esas personas son muy trabajadoras.**	*[Eh-sas per-soh-nas son mooeeh trah-bah-hah-doh-ras]*
I like honest people.	**Me agrada la gente honesta.**	*[Meh ah-grah-dah lah hen-teh oh-nes-tah]*

Places

English	Spanish	Pronunciation
This place is beautiful.	**Este lugar es hermoso.**	*[Es-teh looh-gar es er-moh-soh]*
Lima is a polluted city.	**Lima es una ciudad contaminada.**	*[Leeh-mah es oonah seeh-ooh-dad kon-tah-meeh-nah-dah]*
Patagonia is a remote region.	**La Patagonia es una región remota.**	*[Lah Pah-tah-go-neeah es oonah reh-heeon reh-moh-tah]*
The streets in my neighborhood are always clean.	**Las calles en mi vecindario siempre están limpias.**	*[Las ka-yes en meeh beh-sin-dah-reeoh seeh-em-preh es-tan leem-peeas]*
Tokyo is ranked as the most modern city in the world.	**Tokio está calificada como la ciudad más moderna del mundo.**	*[To-kee-oh es-ta kah-lee-fee-kah-da ko-moh lah see-oo-dad mas mo-der-nah del moon-doh]*
Traveling to Europe is inspiring.	**Viajar a Europa es inspirador.**	*[Beeah-har ah Eooh-roh-pah es eens-peeh-rah-dor]*
The country is calming.	**El campo es tranquilizante.**	*[El kam-poh es tran-keeh-leeh-san-teh]*
The sea is mysterious and powerful.	**El mar es misterioso y poderoso.**	*[El mar es mees-teh-reeoh-soh eeh poh-deh-roh-soh]*

Arts

English	Spanish	Pronunciation
That painting is colorful.	**Esa pintura es colorida.**	*[Eh-sah peen-tooh-rah es koh-loh-reeh-dah]*
I like romantic music.	**Me gusta la música romántica.**	*[Meh goos-tah lah mooh-seeh-kah roh-man-teeh-kah]*
The David is an impressive sculpture.	**El David es una escultura impresionante.**	*[El Dah-beed es oonah es-kool-tooh-rah eem-preh-seeoh-nan-teh]*
Some theater plays are boring.	**Algunas obras de teatro son aburridas.**	*[Al-goonas oh-bras deh teh-ah-tro son abooh-rreeh-das]*

English	Spanish	Pronunciation
Dance is a demanding discipline.	**La danza es una disciplina exigente.**	*[Lah dan-sah es oo-na dee-see-pleeh-na ek-see-hen-teh]*
Not all poetry is artistic.	**No toda la poesía es artística.**	*[Noh toh-dah lah poeh-seeah es ar-tees-teeh-kah]*
Some books are highly valuable.	**Algunos libros son muy valiosos.**	*[Al-gooh-nos leeh-bros son mooeeh bah-leeoh-sos]*
Mayan buildings are intriguing.	**Las construcciones mayas son intrigantes.**	*[Las kons-trook-seeon-es mah-yas son een-tree-gan-tes]*

Food

English	Spanish	Pronunciation
Mexican food is delicious.	**La comida mexicana es deliciosa.**	*[Lah koh-meeh-dah meh-heeh-kah-nah es deh-leeh-seeoh-sah]*
Anchovies are very salty.	**Las anchoas son muy saladas.**	*[Las an-choh-as son mooeeh sah-lah-das]*
Donuts are too greasy.	**Las donas son demasiado grasosas.**	*[Las doh-nas son deh-mah-seeah-doh grah-soh-sas]*
The taste of this sauce is subtle.	**El sabor de esta salsa es sutil.**	*[El sah-bor deh es-tah sal-sah es sooh-teel]*
Asian people eat exotic food.	**Los asiáticos comen comida exótica.**	*[Los aseeah-teeh-kos koh-men koh-meeh-dah eksoh-teeh-kah]*
This wine is poetic.	**Este vino es poético.**	*[Es-teh beeh-no es poeh-teeh-koh]*
If you like bitter tastes, try some black olives.	**Si te gustan los sabores amargos, prueba algunas aceitunas negras.**	*[Seeh teh goos-tan los sah-boh-res ah-mar-gos, prooeh-bah al-gooh-nas ah-se-eeh-tooh-nas neh-gras]*
I had never tasted something so sweet.	**Nunca había probado algo tan dulce.**	*[Noon-kah ah-beeah proh-bah-doh al-goh tan dool-seh]*

Comparisons Are Inevitable

We use comparisons when we need to establish the differences and similarities between items. Sometimes we take an item as reference to describe something else, and here's how you can do that in Spanish too. We dare you to think of some examples for the following comparative adjectives in Spanish.

English	Spanish	Pronunciation
Big	**Grande**	*[Gran-deh]*
Bigger than ________	**Más grande que ________**	*[Mas gran-deh keh ________]*
The biggest	**El más grande** **La más grande** **Lo más grande**	*[El mas gran-deh]* *[Lah mas gran-deh]* *[Loh mas gran-deh]*
As big as ________	**Tan grande como ________**	*[Tan gran-deh koh-moh ________]*
Not as big as ________	**No tan grande como ________**	*[Noh tan gran-deh koh-moh ________]*
Very big	**Muy grande**	*[Mooeeh gran-deh]*
Very big	**Grandísimo**	*[Gran-deeh-seeh-mo]*
Small	**Pequeño** **Pequeña**	*[Peh-keh-nyoh]* *[Peh-keh-nyah]*
Smaller than ________	**Más pequeño que ________** **Más pequeña que ________**	*[Mas peh-keh-nyoh keh ________]* *[Mas peh-keh-nyah keh ________]*
The smallest	**El más pequeño** **La más pequeña** **Lo más pequeño**	*[El mas peh-keh-nyoh]* *[Lah mas peh-keh-nyah]* *[Loh mas peh-keh-nyoh]*
As small as ________	**Tan pequeño como ________** **Tan pequeña como ________**	*[Tan peh-keh-nyoh koh-moh ________]* *[Tan peh-keh-nyah koh-moh ________]*

English	Spanish	Pronunciation
Not as small as ________	**No tan pequeño como ________** **No tan pequeña como ________**	*[Noh tan peh-keh-nyoh koh-moh ________]* *[Noh tan peh-keh-nyah koh-moh ________]*
Very small	**Muy pequeño** **Muy pequeña**	*[Mooeeh peh-keh-nyoh]* *[Mooeeh peh-keh-nyah]*
Very small	**Pequeñísimo** **Pequeñísima**	*[Peh-keh-nyeeh-seeh-moh]* *[Peh-keh-nyeeh-seeh-mah]*
Tall	**Alto** **Alta**	*[Al-toh]* *[Al-tah]*
Taller than ________	**Más alto que ________** **Más alta que ________**	*[Mas al-toh keh ________]* *[Mas al-tah keh ________]*
The tallest	**El más alto** **La más alta** **Lo más alto**	*[El mas al-toh]* *[Lah mas al-tah]* *[Loh mas al-toh]*
As tall as ________	**Tan alto como ________** **Tan alta como ________**	*[Tan al-toh koh-moh ________]* *[Tan al-tah koh-moh ________]*
Not as tall as ________	**No tan alto como ________** **No tan alta como ________**	*[No tan al-toh koh-moh ________]* *[No tan al-tah koh-moh ________]*
Very tall	**Muy alto** **Muy alta**	*[Mooeeh al-toh]* *[Mooeeh al-tah]*
Very tall	**Altísimo** **Altísima**	*[Al-teeh-seeh-moh]* *[Al-teeh-seeh-mah]*
Good	**Bueno** **Buena**	*[Booeh-noh]* *[Booeh-nah]*
Better than ________	**Mejor que ________**	*[Me-hor que ________]*

English	Spanish	Pronunciation
The best	**El mejor** **La mejor** **Lo mejor**	*[El meh-hor]* *[Lah meh-hor]* *[Loh meh-hor]*
As good as ________	**Tan bueno como ________** **Tan buena como ________**	*[Tan booeh-noh koh-moh ________]* *[Tan booeh-nah koh-moh ________]*
Not as good as ________	**No tan bueno como ________** **No tan buena como ________**	*[Noh tan booeh-noh koh-moh ________]* *[Noh tan booeh-nah koh-moh ________]*
Very good	**Muy bueno** **Muy buena**	*[Mooeeh booeh-noh]* *[Mooeeh booeh-nah]*
Very good	**Buenísimo** **Buenísima**	*[Booeh-neeh-seeh-moh]* *[Booeh-neeh-seeh-ma]*
Bad	**Malo** **Mala**	*[Mah-loh]* *[Mah-lah]*
Worse than ________	**Peor que ________**	*[Peh-or keh ________]*
The worst	**El peor** **La peor** **Lo peor**	*[El peh-or]* *[Lah peh-or]* *[Loh peh-or]*
As bad as ________	**Tan malo como ________** **Tan mala como ________**	*[Tan mah-loh koh-moh ________]* *[Tan mah-lah koh-moh ________]*
Not as bad as ________	**No tan malo como ________** **No tan mala como ________**	*[Noh tan mah-loh koh-moh ________]* *[Noh tan mah-lah koh-moh ________]*
Very bad	**Muy malo** **Muy mala**	*[Mooeeh mah-loh]* *[Mooeeh mah-lah]*
Very bad	**Malísimo** **Malísima**	*[Mah-leeh-seeh-moh]* *[Mah-leeh-seeh-mah]*

English	Spanish	Pronunciation
Low	**Bajo** **Baja**	*[Bah-hoh]* *[Bah-hah]*
Lower than ________	**Más bajo que ________** **Más baja que ________**	*[Mas bah-hoh keh ________]* *[Mas bah-hah keh ________]*
Lowest	**El más bajo** **La más baja** **Lo más bajo**	*[El mas bah-hoh]* *[Lah mas bah-hah]* *[Loh mas bah-hoh]*
As low as ________	**Tan bajo como ________** **Tan baja como ________**	*[Tan bah-hoh koh-moh ________]* *[Tan bah-hah koh-moh ________]*
Not as low as ________	**No tan bajo como ________** **No tan baja como ________**	*[Noh tan bah-hoh koh-moh ________]* *[Noh tan bah-hah koh-moh ________]*
Very low	**Muy bajo** **Muy baja**	*[Mooeeh bah-hoh]* *[Mooeeh ba-hah]*
Very low	**Bajísimo** **Bajísima**	*[Ba-heeh-seeh-moh]* *[Bah-heeh-seeh-mah]*
High	**Elevado** **Elevada**	*[Eh-leh-bah-doh]* *[Eh-leh-bah-dah]*
Higher than ________	**Más elevado que ________** **Más elevada que ________**	*[Mas eh-leh-bah-doh keh ________]* *[Mas eh-leh-bah-dah keh ________]*
Highest	**El más elevado** **La más elevada** **Lo más elevado**	*[El mas eh-leh-bah-doh]* *[Lah mas eh-leh-bah-dah]* *[Loh mas eh-leh-bah-doh]*

English	Spanish	Pronunciation
As high as ______	**Tan elevado como ______** **Tan elevada como ______**	*[Tan eh-leh-bah-doh koh-moh ______]* *[Tan eh-leh-bah-dah koh-moh ______]*
Not as high as ______	**No tan elevado como ______** **No tan elevada como ______**	*[Noh tan eh-leh-bah-doh koh-moh ______]* *[Noh tan eh-leh-bah-dah koh-moh ______]*
Very high	**Muy elevado** **Muy elevada**	*[Mooeeh eh-leh-bah-doh]* *[Mooeeh eh-le-bah-dah]*
Very high	**Elevadísimo** **Elevadísima**	*[Eh-leh-bah-deeh-seeh-moh]* *[Eh-leh-ba-deeh-seeh-mah]*
Hot	**Caliente**	*[Kah-lee-en-teh]*
Hotter than ______	**Más caliente que ______**	*[Mas kah-lee-en-teh keh ______]*
Hottest	**El más caliente** **La más caliente** **Lo más caliente**	*[El mas kah-lee-en-teh]* *[Lah mas kah-lee-en-teh]* *[Loh mas kah-lee-en-teh]*
As hot as ______	**Tan caliente como ______**	*[Tan kah-lee-en-te koh-moh ______]*
Not as hot as ______	**No tan caliente como ______**	*[Noh tan kah-lee-en-teh koh-moh ______]*
Very hot	**Muy caliente**	*[Mooeeh kah-lee-en-teh]*
Very hot	**Calientísimo** **Calientísima**	*[Kah-lee-en-teeh-seeh-moh]* *[Kah-lee-en-teeh-seeh-mah]*
Cold	**Frío** **Fría**	*[Freeoh]* *[Freeah]*

English	Spanish	Pronunciation
Colder than ______	**Más frío que ______** **Más fría que ______**	*[Mas freeoh keh ______]* *[Mas freeah keh ______]*
Coldest	**El más frío** **La más fría** **Lo más frío**	*[El mas freeoh]* *[Lah mas freeah]* *[Loh mas freeoh]*
As cold as ______	**Tan frío como** ______ **Tan fría como** ______	*[Tan freeoh koh-moh ______]* *[Tan freeah koh-moh ______]*
Not as cold as ______	**No tan frío como** ______ **No tan fría como** ______	*[Noh tan freeoh koh-moh ______]* *[Noh tan freeah koh-moh ______]*
Very cold	**Muy frío** **Muy fría**	*[Mooeeh freeoh]* *[Mooeeh freeah]*
Very cold	**Friísimo** **Friísima**	*[Freeh-eeh-seeh-moh]* *[Freeh-eeh-seeh-mah]*
Soft	**Suave**	*[Sooah-beh]*
Softer than ______	**Más suave que** ______	*[Mas sooah-beh keh ______]*
Softest	**El más suave** **La más suave** **Lo más suave**	*[El mas sooah-beh]* *[Lah mas sooah-beh]* *[Loh mas sooah-beh]*
As soft as ______	**Tan suave como** ______	*[Tan sooah-beh koh-moh ______]*
Not as soft as ______	**No tan suave como** ______	*[Noh tan sooah-beh koh-moh ______]*
Very soft	**Muy suave**	*[Mooeeh sooah-beh]*
Very soft	**Suavísimo** **Suavísima**	*[Sooah-beeh-seeh-moh]* *[Sooah-beeh-seeh-mah]*

English	Spanish	Pronunciation
Hard	**Duro** **Dura**	*[Dooh-roh]* *[Dooh-rah]*
Harder than ________	**Más duro que ________** **Más dura que ________**	*[Mas dooh-roh keh ________]* *[Mas dooh-rah keh ________]*
Hardest	**El más duro** **La más dura** **Lo más duro**	*[El mas dooh-roh]* *[Lah mas dooh-rah]* *[Loh mas dooh-roh]*
As hard as ________	**Tan duro como ________** **Tan dura como ________**	*[Tan dooh-roh koh-moh ________]* *[Tan dooh-rah koh-moh ________]*
Not as hard as ________	**No tan duro como ________** **No tan dura como ________**	*[Noh tan dooh-roh koh-moh ________]* *[Noh tan dooh-rah koh-moh ________]*
Very hard	**Muy duro** **Muy dura**	*[Mooeeh dooh-roh]* *[Mooeeh doo-rah]*
Very hard	**Durísimo** **Durísima**	*[Dooh-reeh-seeh-moh]* *[Doo-reeh-seeh-mah]*
Nice	**Agradable**	*[Ah-grah-dah-bleh]*
Nicer than ________	**Más agradable que ________**	*[Mas ah-grah-dah-bleh keh ________]*
The nicest	**El más agradable** **La más agradable** **Lo más agradable**	*[El mas ah-grah-dah-bleh]* *[Lah mas ah-grah-dah-bleh]* *[Loh mas ah-grah-dah-bleh]*
As nice as ________	**Tan agradable como ________**	*[Tan ah-gra-da-bleh ko-moh _]*
Not as nice as ________	**No tan agradable como ________**	*[Noh tan ah-grah-dah-bleh koh-moh ________]*

English	Spanish	Pronunciation
Very nice	**Muy agradable**	*[Mooeh ah-grah-dah-bleh]*
Very nice	**Agradabilísimo** **Agradabilísima**	*[Ah-grah-dah-beeh-leeh-seeh-moh]* *[Ah-grah-dah-beeh-leeh-seeh-mah]*
Disgusting	**Desagradable**	*[Des-ah-grah-dah-bleh]*
More disgusting than ________	**Más desagradable que ________**	*[Mas des-ah-grah-dah-bleh keh ________]*
The most disgusting	**El más desagradable** **La más desagradable** **Lo más desagradable**	*[El mas des-ah-gra-da-bleh]* *[Lah mas des-ah-gra-da-bleh]* *[Loh mas des-ah-gra-da-bleh]*
As disgusting as ________	**Tan desagradable como ________**	*[Tan des-ah-grah-dah-bleh koh-moh ________]*
Not as disgusting as ________	**No tan desagradable como ________**	*[Noh tan des-ah-grah-dah-bleh koh-moh ________]*
Very disgusting	**Muy desagradable**	*[Mooeeh des-ah-grah-dah-ble]*
Very disgusting	**Desagradabilísimo** **Desagradabilísima**	*[Des-ah-gra-dah-beeh-leeh-seeh-moh]* *[Des-ah-grah-dah-beeh-leeh-seeh-mah]*
More ________ than	**Más ________ que**	*[Mas ________ keh]*
Less ________ than	**Menos ________ que**	*[Meh-nos ________ keh]*
The most ________ of ________	**El más ________ de ________** **La más ________ de ________** **Lo más ________ de ________**	*[El mas ________ deh ________]* *[Lah mas ________ deh ________]* *[Loh mas ________ deh ________]*

English	Spanish	Pronunciation
The least ________ of ________	**El menos ________ de ________** **La menos ________ de ________** **Lo menos ________ de ________**	*[El meh-nos ________ deh ________]* *[Lah meh-nos ________ deh ________]* *[Loh meh-nos ________ deh ________]*
As ________ as ________	**Tan ________ como ________**	*[Tan ________ koh-moh ________]*
Not as ________ as ________	**No tan ________ como ________**	*[Noh ________ koh-moh ________]*

EXPRESS YOURSELF

Talking About Yourself

Sometimes we do not feel confident to express our opinions and feelings in other languages, and we prefer to remain silent. Not anymore! Your opinions and feelings are important. These options will help you express yourself as well as native Spanish speakers.

English	Spanish	Pronunciation
In my opinion...	**En mi opinión...**	*[Enh meeh oh-peeh-neeh-on...]*
I think that...	**Yo opino que...** **Yo creo que...**	*[Eeoh oh-peeh-noh keh...]* *[Eeoh kreh-oh keh...]*
I agree with you.	**Estoy de acuerdo contigo.**	*[Es-toeeh deh ah-kwer-doh kon-teeh-goh]*
I don't agree with you.	**No estoy de acuerdo contigo.**	*[Noh es-toeeh deh ah-kwer-doh kon-teeh-goh]*
I disagree with you.	**Estoy en desacuerdo contigo.**	*[Es-toeeh en des-ah-kwer-doh kon-teeh-goh]*
I would prefer...	**Yo preferiría...**	*[Eeoh preh-feh-reeh-reeah...]*
I'd rather...	**Yo preferiría...**	*[Eeoh preh-feh-reeh-reeah...]*
I prefer...	**Yo prefiero...**	*[Eeoh preh-fee-eh-roh...]*
I feel...	**Me siento...**	*[Meh seeh-en-toh...]*
As I see it...	**Como yo lo veo...**	*[Koh-moh eeoh loh beoh...]*
From my perspective...	**Desde mi perspectiva...**	*[Des-deh meeh pers-pek-teeh-bah...]*
From my point of view...	**Desde mi punto de vista...**	*[Des-deh meeh poon-toh deh bees-tah...]*

The following phrases will help you express how you feel at certain moments, and also to understand how your counterparts feel as well. Keep in mind that Spanish words are very specific about genders.

English	Spanish	Pronunciation
I'm tired.	**Estoy cansado.** **Estoy cansada.**	*[Es-toeeh kan-sah-doh]* *[Es-toeeh kan-sah-dah]*
I'm exhausted.	**Estoy exhausto.** **Estoy exhausta.**	*[Es-toeeh eks-aoos-toh]* *[Es-toeeh eks-aoos-tah]*
I'm hungry.	**Tengo hambre.**	*[Ten-goh am-breh]*
I'm happy.	**Estoy contento.** **Estoy contenta.**	*[Es-toeeh kon-ten-toh]* *[Es-toeeh kon-ten-tah]*
I feel sick.	**Me siento mal.**	*[Me seeh-en-toh mal]*
I'm comfortable.	**Estoy cómodo.** **Estoy cómoda.**	*[Es-toeeh koh-moh-doh]* *[Es-toeeh koh-moh-dah]*
I'm uncomfortable.	**Estoy incómodo.** **Estoy incómoda.**	*[Es-toeeh een-koh-moh-doh] [Es-toeeh een-koh-moh-dah]*
I'm sad.	**Estoy triste.**	*[Es-toeeh trees-teh]*
I'm angry.	**Estoy enojado.** **Estoy enojada.**	*[Es-toeeh eh-noh-hah-doh]* *[Es-toeeh eh-noh-hah-dah]*
I'm sleepy.	**Tengo sueño.**	*[Ten-goh sooeh-nyoh]*
I like this.	**Esto me gusta.**	*[Es-toh meh goos-tah]*
I love this.	**Esto me encanta.**	*[Es-toh meh en-kan-tah]*
I'm in love.	**Estoy enamorado.** **Estoy enamorada.**	*[Es-toeeh eh-na-mo-ra-doh]* *[Es-toeeh eh-na-mo-rah-dah]*
I don't like this.	**Esto no me gusta.**	*[Es-toh noh meh-goos-tah]*
I hate this.	**Odio esto.**	*[Oh-deeoh es-toh]*
I'm worried.	**Estoy preocupado.** **Estoy preocupada.**	*[Es-toeeh preoh-kooh-pah-doh] [Es-toeeh preoh-kooh-pah-dah]*

English	Spanish	Pronunciation
I'm excited.	**Estoy emocionado.** **Estoy emocionada.**	*[Es-toeeh eh-mo-seeo-na-doh]* *[Es-toeeh eh-mo-seeo-na-dah]*
I'm in a hurry.	**Tengo prisa.**	*[Ten-goh preeh-sah]*
I'm fascinated.	**Estoy fascinado.** **Estoy fascinada.**	*[Es-toeeh fah-seeh-nah-doh]* *[Es-toeeh fah-seeh-nah-dah]*
I'm confused.	**Estoy confundido.** **Estoy confundida.**	*[Es-toeeh kon-foon-deeh-doh] [Es-toeeh kon-foon-deeh-dah]*
I'm disappointed.	**Estoy decepcionado.** **Estoy decepcionada.**	*[Es-toeeh de-sep-seeo-na-doh]* *[Es-toeeh de-sep-seeo-na-dah]*
I'm scared.	**Estoy asustado.** **Estoy asustada.**	*[Es-toeeh ah-soos-tah-doh]* *[Es-toeeh ah-soos-tah-dah]*

Reciprocating

If you want to be attentive and find out how another person thinks or feels, you can use these questions. Remember: attitude is everything; that is, your words must match your behavior towards the other person.

English	Spanish	Pronunciation
What is your opinion about this?	**¿Cuál es tu opinión sobre esto?**	*[Kwal es tooh o-peeh-neeh-on so-breh es-toh?]*
What do you think?	**¿Qué opinas?**	*[Keh opeeh-nas?]*
Do you agree?	**¿Estás de acuerdo?**	*[Es-tas deh ah-kwerh-doh?]*
Don't you agree?	**¿No estás de acuerdo?**	*[Noh es-tas deh ah-kwerh-doh?]*
What do you prefer?	**¿Qué prefieres?**	*[Keh preh-fee-eh-res?]*
How do you feel?	**¿Cómo te sientes?**	*[Koh-moh te see-en-tes?]*

English	Spanish	Pronunciation
Are you tired?	**¿Estás cansado?** **¿Estás cansada?**	*[Es-tas kan-sah-doh?]* *[Es-tas kan-sah-dah?]*
Are you exhausted?	**¿Estás exhausto?** **¿Estás exhausta?**	*[Es-tas eks-aoos-toh?]* *[Es-tas eks-aoos-tah?]*
Are you hungry?	**¿Tienes hambre?**	*[Teeh-eh-nes am-breh?]*
Are you happy?	**¿Estás contento?** **¿Estás contenta?**	*[Es-tas kon-ten-toh?]* *[Es-tas kon-ten-tah?]*
Do you feel sick?	**¿Te sientes mal?**	*[Teh seeh-en-tes mal?]*
Are you comfortable?	**¿Estás cómodo?** **¿Estás cómoda?**	*[Es-tas koh-moh-doh?]* *[Es-tas koh-moh-dah?]*
Are you uncomfortable?	**¿Estás incómodo?** **¿Estás incómoda?**	*[Es-tas een-koh-moh-doh?]* *[Es-tas een-koh-moh-dah?]*
Are you sad?	**¿Estás triste?**	*[Es-tas trees-teh?]*
Are you angry?	**¿Estás enojado?** **¿Estás enojada?**	*[Es-tas eh-noh-hah-doh?]* *[Es-tas eh-noh-hah-dah?]*
Are you sleepy?	**¿Tienes sueño?**	*[Teeh-eh-nes sueh-nyoh?]*
Do you like this?	**¿Te gusta esto?**	*[Te goos-tah es-toh?]*
Do you love this?	**¿Te encanta esto?**	*[Teh en-can-tah es-toh?]*
Are you in love?	**¿Estás enamorado?** **¿Estás enamorada?**	*[Es-tas eh-nah-moh-rah-doh?]* *[Es-tas eh-nah-moh-rah-dah?]*
Don't you like this?	**¿No te gusta esto?**	*[Noh teh goos-tah es-toh?]*
Do you hate this?	**¿Odias esto?**	*[Oh-dee-as es-toh?]*
Are you worried?	**¿Estás preocupado?** **¿Estás preocupada?**	*[Es-tas preoh-kooh-pah-doh?]* *[Es-tas preoh-kooh-pah-dah?]*
Are you excited?	**¿Estás emocionado?** **¿Estás emocionada?**	*[Es-tas eh-mo-seeoh-na-doh?]* *[Es-tas eh-mo-seeoh-na-dah?]*
Are you in a hurry?	**¿Tienes prisa?**	*[Teeh-eh-nes preeh-sah?]*

English	Spanish	Pronunciation
Are you fascinated?	**¿Estás fascinado?** **¿Estás fascinada?**	*[Es-tas fah-seeh-nah-doh?]* *[Es-tas fah-seeh-nah-dah?]*
Are you confused?	**¿Estás confundido?** **¿Estás confundida?**	*[Es-tas kon-foon-deeh-doh?]* *[Es-tas kon-foon-deeh-dah?]*
Are you disappointed?	**¿Estás decepcionado?** **¿Estás decepcionada?**	*[Es-tas de-sep-seeoh-na-do?]* *[Es-tas de-sep-seeoh-na-da?]*
Are you scared?	**¿Estás asustado?** **¿Estás asustada?**	*[Es-tas ah-soos-tah-doh?]* *[Es-tas ah-soos-tah-dah?]*

Politeness and Help

Spanish speaking people are usually very polite and eager to help others. If you want to behave like them in a natural way, you can use these phrases.

English	Spanish	Pronunciation
Are you OK?	**¿Estás bien?**	*[Es-tas beeh-en?]*
What can I do for you?	**¿Qué puedo hacer por ti?**	*[Keh pooeh-doh ah-ser por teeh?]*
Can I help you?	**¿Puedo ayudarte?**	*[Pooeh-doh ayooh-dar-teh?*
How can I help you?	**¿Cómo puedo ayudarte?**	*[Koh-moh pooeh-doh ayooh-dar-teh?]*
How do I help you?	**¿Cómo te ayudo?**	*[Koh-moh teh ayooh-doh?]*
What can I do to make you feel better?	**¿Qué puedo hacer para que te sientas mejor?**	*[Keh pooeh-doh ah-ser pah-rah keh teh seeh-en-tas meh-hor?*
Do you need help?	**¿Necesitas ayuda?**	*[Neh-seh-seeh-tas ayooh-dah?]*
Let me know if I can help you with that.	**Avísame si puedo ayudarte con eso.**	*[Ah-beeh-sah-meh seeh pooeh-doh ayooh-dar-teh kon eh-soh]*

English	Spanish	Pronunciation
Tell me what happens.	**Cuéntame lo que pasa.**	*[Kwen-tah-me loh keh pah-sah]*
Why don't you tell me what happens?	**¿Por qué no me cuentas lo que pasa?**	*[Por keh noh meh kwen-tas loh keh pah-sah?]*
Tell me more about that.	**Cuéntame más sobre eso.**	*[Kwen-tah-meh mas soh-bre eh-soh]*
Do you want us to talk about this?	**¿Quieres que platiquemos sobre esto?**	*[Keeh-eh-res keh pla-teeh-keh-mos soh-bre es-toh?*
And then?	**¿Y entonces?**	*[Eeh en-ton-ses?]*
I hope you feel better.	**Espero que te sientas mejor.**	*[Es-peh-roh keh teh seeh-en-tas meh-hor]*
Everything will be fine.	**Todo estará bien.**	*[Toh-doh es-tah-rah beeh-en]*
I'm sure you'll figure it out.	**Estoy seguro de que lo resolverás.** **Estoy segura de que lo resolverás.**	*[Es-toeeh seh-gooh-roh deh keh loh re-sol-beh-ras]* *[Es-toeeh seh-gooh-rah deh keh loh re-sol-beh-ras]*
I'm happy for you.	**Me alegro por ti.**	*[Meh ah-leh-groh por teeh]*
I'm really sorry.	**Lo lamento mucho.**	*[Loh lah-men-toh mooh-choh]*

Phrases About Feelings and Behaviors

Spanish is a very rich language and Spanish-speaking people are very imaginative when transforming feelings and behaviors into metaphors. Here are some more common expressions that you will hear frequently and how to use them.

Scenario	Metaphor (Translation)	Pronunciation
When someone blushed a lot	**Se puso como un tomate.** (He/she turned like a tomato)	*[Seh pooh-soh koh-moh oon toh-mah-teh]*

Scenario	Metaphor (Translation)	Pronunciation
When someone behaved like crazy	**Se puso como una cabra.** (He/she turned like a goat)	*[Seh poo-so koh-moh oohnah kah-brah]*
When someone ignores something bad	**Ojos que no ven, corazón que no siente.** (Eyes that don't see, heart that doesn't feel)	*[Oh-hos keh noh ben, koh-rah-son keh noh seeh-en-teh]*
When someone is really angry	**Está echando chispas.** (He/she is sparking)	*[Es-tah eh-chan-doh chees-pas]*
When someone is in a very bad mood	**Está de un humor de perros.** (He/she is in dogs' mood)	*[Es-tah deh oon ooh-mor deh peh-rros]*
When someone was furious	**Se puso como fiera.** (He/she turned like a wild beast)	*[Seh pooh-soh koh-moh feeh-eh-rah]*
When someone is annoyed by something	**Está hasta las narices.** (He/she is up to the noses)	*[Es-tah as-tah las nah-reeh-ses]*
When someone is in love	**Está flechado** (He is arrowed) **Está flechada** (She is arrowed)	*[Es-tah fleh-chah-do]* *[Es-tah fleh-chah-dah]*
When someone was in shock	**Se quedó de piedra.** (He/she stayed like a stone)	*[Seh keh-doh deh peeh-eh-drah]*
When someone is bored	**Aburrido como una ostra. Aburrida como una ostra.** (Bored like an oyster)	*[Ah-booh-rreeh-doh koh-moh oonah os-trah]* *[Ah-booh-rreeh-dah koh-moh oonah os-trah]*

Scenario	Metaphor (Translation)	Pronunciation
When someone is absolutely happy	**Como niño con zapatos nuevos.** (Like a child with new shoes)	*[Koh-moh neeh-nyoh kon sah-pah-tos nooeh-bos]*
When someone is not well-intentioned	**Es mala leche.** (He/she is bad milk)	*[Es mah-lah leh-cheh]*
When someone is a very good person	**Es bueno como el pan.** (He is as good as bread) **Es buena como el pan.** (She is as good as bread)	*[Es booeh-noh koh-moh el pan]* *[Es booeh-nah koh-moh el pan]*
When someone cried a lot	**Lloró como una Magdalena.** (He/she cried like a Magdalena)	*[Yoh-roh koh-moh oo-nah Mag-dah-leh-nah]*
When I don't have a good feeling about somebody or something	**No me da buena espina.** (It does not give me a good thorn)	*[Noh meh dah booeh-nah es-peeh-nah]*
When someone sleeps very soundly	**Duerme como un lirón** (He/she sleeps like a dormouse)	*[Dooh-er-meh koh-moh oon leeh-ron]*
When a situation needs to be changed	**Hay que darle la vuelta a la tortilla** (The tortilla needs to be flipped)	*[Aeeh keh dar-leh lah booel-tah ah lah tor-teeh-yah]*
When someone is distracted	**Está con la cabeza en las nubes** (He/she is with the head in the clouds)	*[Es-tah kon lah kah-beh-sah en las nooh-bes]*
When someone tries to ignore me	**Me saca la vuelta** (He/she takes the turn out of me)	*[Meh sah-kah lah booel-tah]*

Scenario	Metaphor (Translation)	Pronunciation
When someone is obsessed with something	**Está enganchado con eso** (He is hooked with that) **Está enganchada con eso** (She is hooked with that)	*[Es-tah en-gan-chah-do kon eh-so]* *[Es-tah en-gan-chah-dah kon eh-so]*
When someone is very talkative	**Habla como un perico** (He/she speaks like a parrot)	*[Ah-blah koh-mo oon peh-ree-koh]*
When a person or a place is very silent	**Es callado como una tumba** (He is quiet like a grave) **Es callada como una tumba** (She is quiet like a grave)	*[Es kah-yah-doh koh-moh oonah tom-bah]* *[Es kah-yah-dah koh-moh oona toom-bah]*
When someone deceives me	**Me vio la cara** (He/she saw my face)	*[Meh beeoh lah kah-rah]*
When someone is very stubborn	**Es terco como una mula** (He is stubborn like a mule) **Es terca como una mula** (She is stubborn like a mule)	*[Es ter-koh koh-moh oonah mooh-lah]* *[Es ter-kah koh-moh oonah mooh-lah]*

COMMUNICATE

Communicate Yourself to the (Spanish) World

In simple words, "to communicate" means to let others know something about you and to know something about others in a continuous exchange. We all know that good communication strengthens bonds amongst people. Here are some ways to express your perspective on things.

English	Spanish	Pronunciation
I like this book I'm reading because...	**Me gusta el libro que estoy leyendo porque...**	*[Meh goos-tah el lee-bro keh es-toeeh le-yen-do por-keh...]*
I don't like this book I'm reading because...	**No me gusta el libro que estoy leyendo porque...**	*[No meh goos-tah el lee-bro keh es-toeeh le-yen-do por-keh...]*
I'm interested in watching that movie because...	**Me interesa ver esa película porque...**	*[Meh een-teh-reh-sah ber esah peh-leeh-kooh-lah por-keh...]*
I'm not interested in watching that movie because...	**No me interesa ver esa película porque...**	*[Noh meh een-teh-reh-sah ber esah peh-leeh-kooh-lah por-keh...]*
I'd love to visit that place because...	**Me encantaría visitar ese lugar porque...**	*[Meh en-kan-tah-reeah beeh-seeh-tar eh-seh looh-gar por-keh...]*
I wouldn't love to visit that place because...	**No me encantaría visitar ese lugar porque...**	*[Noh meh en-kan-tah-reeah beeh-seeh-tar eh-seh looh-gar por-keh...]*

English	Spanish	Pronunciation
I enjoyed my vacation there because...	**Disfruté mis vacaciones allá porque...**	*[Dees-frooh-teh mees bah-kah-seeoh-nes ah-yah por-keh...]*
I did not enjoy my vacation there because...	**No disfruté mis vacaciones allá porque...**	*[Noh dees-frooh-teh mees bah-kah-seeoh-nes ah-yah por-keh...]*
I am a huge ________ fan because...	**Soy muy aficionado a ________ porque...** **Soy muy aficionada a ________ porque...**	*[Soeeh mooeeh a-fee-seeoh-na-doh ah ________ por-keh...]* *[Soeeh mooeeh ah-feeh-seeoh-nah-dah ah ________ por-keh...]*
I am not a huge ________ fan because...	**No soy muy aficionado a ________ porque...** **No soy muy aficionada a ________ porque...**	*[Noh soeeh mooeeh ah-feeh-seeoh-nah-doh ah ________ por-keh...]* *[Noh soeeh mooeeh ah-feeh-seeoh-nah-dah ah ________ por-keh...]*
I admire ________ people.	**Admiro a las personas ________.**	*[Ad-meeh-roh ah las per-soh-nas ________]*
I remember when...	**Recuerdo cuando...**	*[Reh-kwer-doh kwan-doh...]*
Seeing this makes me...	**Ver esto me hace...**	*[Ber es-toh meh ah-seh...]*
Hearing this makes me...	**Escuchar esto me hace...**	*[Es-kooh-char es-toh meh ah-seh...]*
Smelling this makes me...	**Oler esto me hace...**	*[Oh-ler es-toh meh ah-seh...]*
Tasting this makes me...	**Saborear esto me hace...**	*[Sa-bo-re-ar es-toh meh ah-se...]*
Touching this makes me...	**Tocar esto me hace...**	*[Toh-kar es-toh meh ah-seh...]*
Remembering that makes me...	**Recordar eso me hace...**	*[Re-kor-dar e-soh meh a-seh...]*

English	Spanish	Pronunciation
Thinking about that makes me...	**Pensar en eso me hace...**	*[Pen-sar en e-soh meh ah-seh...]*
Talking about this makes me...	**Hablar sobre esto me hace...**	*[Ah-blar soh-breh es-toh meh ah-seh...]*
Arguing about this makes me...	**Discutir sobre esto me hace...**	*[Dees-kooh-teer soh-bre es-toh meh ah-seh...]*

Get Your Counterpart Involved

You can also invite the other person to share their perspective on things. Here is how you can do that.

English	Spanish	Pronunciation
Do you like ____________?	**¿Te gusta____________?**	*[Teh goos-tah ____________?]*
Did you like ____________?	**¿Te gustó ____________?**	*[Teh goos-toh ____________?]*
Would you like to ____________?	**¿Te gustaría ____________?**	*[The goos-tah-reeah ____________?]*
Are you interested in____________?	**¿Te interesa ____________?**	*[The een-teh-reh-sah ____________?]*
Do you enjoy ____________?	**¿Disfrutas ____________?**	*[Dees-froo-tas ____________?*
Are you a ____________ fan?	**¿Eres fan de ____________?**	*[Eh-res fan deh ____________?]*
What do you think about ____________?	**¿Qué piensas de ____________?**	*[Keh peeh-en-sas deh ____________?]*
What do you remember about ____________?	**¿Qué recuerdas de ____________?**	*[Keh reh-kwer-das deh ____________?]*
How does this make you feel?	**¿Cómo te hace sentir esto?**	*[Koh-moh teh ah-seh sen-teer es-toh?]*

English	Spanish	Pronunciation
What would you like to ________?	**¿Qué te gustaría ________?**	*[Keh teh goos-ta-reeah ________?]*
I'd like to know what you think.	**Me gustaría saber qué piensas.**	*[Meh goos-tah-reeah sah-ber keh peeh-en-sas]*
What makes you feel ________?	**¿Qué te hace sentir ________?**	*[Keh teh ah-seh sen-teer ________?]*

That Awkward Silence

Sometimes you need some words or phrases to break impasses in the conversation or to encourage the other person to keep talking. Here is how you can do it in Spanish.

English	Spanish	Pronunciation
That is awesome!	**¡Eso es asombroso!**	*[Eh-soh es ah-som-bro-soh!]*
That sounds great!	**¡Eso suena genial!**	*[Eh-soh sooeh-nah heh-neeal!]*
Tell me more about that.	**Cuéntame más sobre eso.**	*[Kwen-tah-meh mas soh-breh eh-soh]*
It's unbelievable!	**¡Es increíble!**	*[Es een-kre-eeh-bleh!]*
What else?	**¿Y qué más?**	*[Eeh keh mas?]*
Of course!	**¡Claro!**	*[Klah-roh!]*
Of course not!	**¡Claro que no!**	*[Klah-roh keh noh!]*
What happened then?	**¿Y qué pasó después?**	*[Eeh keh pah-soh des-pooes?]*
What did you do when________?	**¿Qué hiciste cuando ________?**	*[Keh eeh-sees-teh kwan-doh ________?*
What did you feel when________?	**¿Qué sentiste cuando ________?**	*[Keh sen-tees-teh kwan-doh ________?*
What did you think when________?	**¿Qué pensaste cuando ________?**	*[Keh pen-sas-teh kwan-doh ________?*
When did that happen?	**¿Cuándo pasó eso?**	*[Kwan-doh pah-soh eh-soh?]*
Where did that happen?	**¿Dónde pasó eso?**	*[Don-deh pah-soh eh-soh?]*

You are kidding, right?	**Es broma, ¿verdad?**	*[Es broh-mah, ber-dad?]*
What did he say when__________?	**¿Qué dijo él cuando __________?**	*[Keh deeh-hoh el kwan-doh __________?*
What did she say when__________?	**¿Qué dijo ella cuando __________?**	*[Keh deeh-hoh eh-yah kwan-doh __________?*
Who is that person you mentioned?	**¿Quién es esa persona que mencionaste?**	*[Keeh-en es eh-sah per-soh-nah keh men-seeoh-nas-teh?]*
Really?	**¿En serio?**	*[En seh-reeoh?]*
But what happened with the other person / thing?	**Pero, ¿qué pasó con la otra persona / cosa?**	*[Peh-roh, keh pah-soh kon lah oh-trah per-soh-nah / ko-sah?]*
I see that you are __________ about this.	**Veo que estás __________ por esto.**	*[Beoh keh es-tas __________ por es-toh]*
That is awful!	**¡Eso es horrible!**	*[Eh-soh es oh-rreeh-bleh!]*
I can imagine that.	**Puedo imaginar eso.**	*[Pooeh-doh eeh-mah-heeh-nar eh-soh]*
How could you do that?	**¿Cómo pudiste hacer eso?**	*[Koh-moh poo-dees-teh ah-ser eh-soh?]*
How could he/ she do that?	**¿Cómo pudo hacer eso?**	*[Koh-moh pooh-do ah-ser eh-so?]*
How did you feel when that happened?	**¿Cómo te sentías cuando eso pasó?**	*[Koh-moh teh sen-teeh-as kwan-doh e-soh pah-soh?]*
I'm surprised you are so __________	**Me sorprende que seas tan __________.**	*[Meh sor-pren-deh keh seh-as tan __________]*
When did you start __________?	**¿Cuándo empezaste a __________?**	*[Kwan-doh em-peh-sas-teh ah __________]*
Explain that to me, step by step.	**Explícamelo paso a paso.**	*[Eks-pleeh-kah-meh-loh pah-soh ah pah-soh]*
What are you planning to do with this?	**¿Qué planeas hacer con esto?**	*[Keh plah-neh-as ah-ser kon es-toh?]*
I want to hear the rest of your story.	**Quiero escuchar el resto de tu historia.**	*[Kee-eh-roh es-koo-char el res-toh deh tooh ees-toh-reeah]*

I don't want to hear the rest of your story.	**No quiero escuchar el resto de tu historia.**	*[Noh kee-eh-roh es-koo-char el res-toh deh tooh ees-toh-reeah]*
I want to hear how your story ends.	**Quiero escuchar cómo termina tu historia.**	*[Kee-eh-roh es-koo-char coh-moh ter-meeh-nah tooh ees-toh-reea]*
I don't want to hear how your story ends.	**No quiero escuchar cómo termina tu historia.**	*[Noh kee-eh-roh es-koo-char coh-moh ter-meeh-nah tooh ees-toh-reea]*
I can imagine how this story ends.	**Puedo imaginar cómo termina esta historia.**	*[Pweh-doh eeh-mah-heeh-nar koh-moh ter-meeh-nah es-tah ees-toh-reeah]*
I can't imagine how this story ends.	**No puedo imaginar cómo termina esta historia.**	*[Noh pweh-doh eeh-mah-heeh-nar koh-moh ter-meeh-nah es-tah ees-toh-reeah]*
What do you think now about that?	**¿Qué opinas ahora de eso?**	*[Keh oh-peeh-nas aoh-rah deh eh-soh?]*

ASKING AND RECEIVING

There is a clear difference between giving an order and asking for a favor. Orders are given when something needs to be done at a specific moment in time by a specific individual. Favors, on the other hand, are acts of kindness that one person requests from another.

The same difference applies in Spanish. Let's check some examples below.

Orders (Verb First)

These are direct orders that the receiver must obey. The tone of the speaker's voice indicates how serious the command is.

English	Spanish	Pronunciation
Call me when you get there.	**Llámame cuando llegues.**	*[Yah-mah-me kwan-doh yeh-gues]*
Tell her to pick up the kids at 2:00 p.m.	**Dile que recoja a los niños a las 2:00 de la tarde.**	*[Deeh-leh keh reh-koh-hah ah los neeh-nyos ah las dos deh lah tar-deh]*
Turn off the lights when you leave.	**Apaguen las luces cuando salgan.**	*[Ah-pah-guen las looh-ses kwan-doh sal-gan]*
Don't forget to bring the cake.	**No olvides traer el pastel.**	*[Noh ol-beeh-des trah-er el pas-tel]*
Clean your room before supper.	**Limpia tu habitación antes de la cena.**	*[Leem-peeh-ah tooh ah-beeh-tah-seeon an-tes deh lah seh-nah]*
Don't waste water.	**No desperdicien el agua.**	*[Noh des-per-deeh-seeh-en el ah-gooah]*
Give me a big hug.	**Dame un gran abrazo.**	*[Dah-meh oon gran ah-brah-soh]*
Close the door every time you go out.	**Cierren la puerta cada vez que salgan.**	*[Seeh-eh-rren lah pooh-er-tah kah-dah bes keh sal-gan]*

English	Spanish	Pronunciation
Ask him if he received the package.	**Pregúntale si recibió el paquete.**	*[Preh-goon-tah-leh seeh reh-seeh-beeoh el pah-keh-teh]*
Help me choose a dress for my niece.	**Ayúdame a elegir un vestido para mi sobrina.**	*[Ah-yooh-dah-meh ah eh-leh-heer oon bes-teeh-doh pah-rah meeh soh-breeh-nah]*
Put the groceries in the bags.	**Pon los víveres en las bolsas.**	*[Pon los beeh-beh-res en las bol-sas]*
Do not fall asleep on the bus.	**No se duerman en el autobús.**	*[Noh seh dooer-man en el aooh-toh-boos]*

Orders as Statements

These orders are unquestionable. No rebuttal allowed.

You will call me when you get there.	**Me llamarás cuando llegues.**	*[Me yah-mah-ras kwan-doh yeh-gues]*
You will tell her to pick up the kids at 2:00 p.m.	**Le dirás que recoja a los niños a las 2:00 de la tarde.**	*[Leh deeh-ras keh reh-koh-hah ah los neeh-nyos ah las dos deh lah tar-deh]*
You are going to turn off the lights when you leave.	**Van a apagar las luces cuando salgan.**	*[Ban ah ah-pah-gar las looh-ses kwan-doh sal-gan]*
You will not forget to bring the cake.	**No olvidarás traer el pastel.**	*[Noh ol-beeh-dah-ras trah-er el pas-tel]*
You will clean your room before supper.	**Limpiarás tu habitación antes de la cena.**	*[Leem-peeh-ah-ras tooh ah-beeh-tah-seeon an-tes deh lah seh-nah]*
You will not waste water.	**No desperdiciarán el agua.**	*[Noh des-per-deeh-seeh-ah-ran el ah-gooah]*
You will give me a big hug.	**Me darás un gran abrazo.**	*[Meh dah-ras oon gran ah-brah-soh]*

You are going to close the door every time you go out.	**Van a cerrar la puerta cada vez que salgan.**	*[Ban ah-seh-rrar lah pooh-er-tah kah-dah bes keh sal-gan]*
You will ask him if he received the package.	**Le preguntarás si recibió el paquete.**	*[Leh preh-goon-tah-ras seeh reh-seeh-beeoh el pah-keh-teh]*
You are going to help me choose a dress for my niece.	**Vas a ayudarme a elegir un vestido para mi sobrina.**	*[Bas ah ah-yooh-dar-meh ah eh-leh-heer oon bes-teeh-doh pah-rah meeh soh-breeh-nah]*
You will put the groceries in the bags.	**Pondrás los víveres en las bolsas.**	*[Pon-dras los beeh-beh-res en las bol-sas]*
You are not going to fall asleep on the bus.	**No van a dormirse en el autobús.**	*[Noh ban ah dor-meer-seh en el aooh-toh-boos]*

Orders (with "I Want")

These orders are expressed as wishes; however, the receptors are expected to understand that there is an action to be executed and that they are supposed to perform it.

English	Spanish	Pronunciation
I want you to call me when you get there.	**Quiero que me llames cuando llegues.**	*[Keeh-eh-roh keh meh yah-mes kwan-doh yeh-gues]*
I want you to tell her to pick up the kids at 2:00 p.m.	**Quiero que le digas que recoja a los niños a las 2:00 de la tarde.**	*[Keeh-eh-roh keh leh deeh-gas keh reh-koh-hah ah los neeh-nyos ah las dos deh lah tar-deh]*
I want you to turn off the lights when you leave.	**Quiero que apaguen las luces cuando salgan.**	*[Keeh-eh-roh keh ah-pah-guen las looh-ses kwan-doh sal-gan]*
I don't want you to forget to bring the cake.	**No quiero que olvides traer el pastel.**	*[Noh keeh-eh-roh keh ol-beeh-des trah-er el pas-tel]*
I want you to clean your room before supper.	**Quiero que limpies tu habitación antes de la cena.**	*[Keeh-eh-roh keh leem-peeh-es tooh ah-beeh-tah-seeon an-tes deh lah seh-nah]*

English	Spanish	Pronunciation
I don't want you to waste water.	**No quiero que desperdicien el agua.**	*[Noh keeh-eh-roh keh des-per-deeh-seeh-en el ah-gooah]*
I want you to give me a big hug.	**Quiero que me des un gran abrazo.**	*[Keeh-eh-roh keh meh des oon gran ah-brah-soh]*
I want you to close the door every time you go out.	**Quiero que cierren la puerta cada vez que salgan.**	*[Keeh-eh-roh keh seeh-eh-rren lah pooh-er-tah kah-dah bes keh sal-gan]*
I want you to ask him if he received the package.	**Quiero que le preguntes si recibió el paquete.**	*[Keeh-eh-roh keh leh preh-goon-tes seeh reh-seeh-beeoh el pah-keh-teh]*
I want you to help me choose a dress for my niece.	**Quiero que me ayudes a elegir un vestido para mi sobrina.**	*[Keeh-eh-roh keh meh ah-yooh-des ah eh-leh-heer oon bes-teeh-doh pah-rah meeh soh-breeh-nah]*
I want you to put the groceries in the bags.	**Quiero que pongas los víveres en las bolsas.**	*[Keeh-eh-roh keh pon-gas los beeh-beh-res en las bol-sas]*
I don't want you to fall asleep on the bus.	**No quiero que se duerman en el autobús.**	*[Noh keeh-eh-roh keh seh dooer-man en el aooh-toh-boos]*

Orders (with "I Need")

In this verbal structure, the speaker expresses needs that are supposed to be satisfied by those people receiving the message. As you can see, real intentions are not that different in English and in Spanish.

English	Spanish	Pronunciation
I need you to call me when you get there.	**Necesito que me llames cuando llegues.**	*[Neh-seh-seeh-toh keh meh yah-mes kwan-doh yeh-gues]*
I need you to tell her to pick up the kids at 2:00 p.m.	**Necesito que le digas que recoja a los niños a las 2:00 de la tarde.**	*[Neh-seh-seeh-toh keh leh deeh-gas keh reh-koh-hah ah los neeh-nyos ah las dos deh lah tar-deh]*

English	Spanish	Pronunciation
I need you to turn off the lights when you leave.	**Necesito que apaguen las luces cuando salgan.**	*[Neh-seh-seeh-toh keh ah-pah-guen las looh-ses kwan-doh sal-gan]*
I need you not to forget to bring the cake.	**Necesito que no olvides traer el pastel.**	*[Neh-seh-seeh-toh keh noh ol-beeh-des trah-er el pas-tel]*
I need you to clean your room before supper.	**Necesito que limpies tu habitación antes de la cena.**	*[Neh-seh-seeh-toh keh leem-peeh-es tooh ah-beeh-tah-seeon an-tes deh lah seh-nah]*
I need you not to waste water.	**Necesito que no desperdicien el agua.**	*[Neh-seh-seeh-toh keh noh des-per-deeh-seeh-en el ah-gooah]*
I need you to give me a big hug.	**Necesito que me des un gran abrazo.**	*[Neh-seh-seeh-toh keh meh des oon gran ah-brah-soh]*
I need you to close the door every time you go out.	**Necesito que cierren la puerta cada vez que salgan.**	*[Neh-seh-seeh-toh keh seeh-eh-rren lah pooh-er-tah kah-dah bes keh sal-gan]*
I need you to ask him if he received the package.	**Necesito que le preguntes si recibió el paquete.**	*[Neh-seh-seeh-toh keh leh preh-goon-tes seeh reh-seeh-beeoh el pah-keh-teh]*
I need you to help me choose a dress for my niece.	**Necesito que me ayudes a elegir un vestido para mi sobrina.**	*[Neh-seh-seeh-toh keh meh ah-yooh-des ah eh-leh-heer oon bes-teeh-doh pah-rah meeh soh-breeh-nah]*
I need you to put the groceries in the bags.	**Necesito que pongas los víveres en las bolsas.**	*[Neh-seh-seeh-toh keh pon-gas los beeh-beh-res en las bol-sas]*
I need you not to fall asleep on the bus.	**Necesito que no se duerman en el autobús.**	*[Neh-seh-seeh-toh keh noh seh dooer-man en el aooh-toh-boos]*

Orders (with "You Must")

This verbal structure expresses an obligation. The speaker adopts an authority stance and the listener must obey.

English	Spanish	Pronunciation
You must call me when you get there.	**Debes llamarme cuando llegues.**	*[Deh-bes yah-mar-meh kwan-doh yeh-gues]*
You must tell her to pick up the kids at 2:00 p.m.	**Debes decirle que recoja a los niños a las 2:00 de la tarde.**	*[De-hes deh-seer-leh keh reh-koh-hah ah los neeh-nyos ah las dos deh lah tar-deh]*
You must turn off the lights when you leave.	**Deben apagar las luces cuando salgan.**	*[Deh-ben ah-pah-gar las looh-ses kwan-doh sal-gan]*
You must not forget to bring the cake.	**No debes olvidar traer el pastel.**	*[Noh deh-bes ol-beeh-dar trah-er el pas-tel]*
You must clean your room before supper.	**Debes limpiar tu habitación antes de la cena.**	*[Deh-bes leem-peear tooh ah-beeh-tah-seeon an-tes deh lah seh-nah]*
You must not waste water.	**No deben desperdiciar el agua.**	*[Noh deh-beh des-per-deeh-seear el ah-gooah]*
You must give me a big hug.	**Debes darme un gran abrazo.**	*[Deh-des dar-meh oon gran ah-brah-soh]*
You must close the door every time you go out.	**Deben cerrar la puerta cada vez que salgan.**	*[Deh-ben seh-rrar lah pooh-er-tah kah-dah bes keh sal-gan]*
You must ask him if he received the package.	**Debes preguntarle si recibió el paquete.**	*[Deh-bes pre-goon-tar-leh seeh reh-seeh-beeoh el pah-keh-teh]*
You must help me choose a dress for my niece.	**Debes ayudarme a elegir un vestido para mi sobrina.**	*[Deh-bes ah-yooh-dar-meh ah eh-leh-heer oon bes-teeh-doh pah-rah meeh soh-breeh-nah]*
You must put the groceries in the bags.	**Debes poner los víveres en las bolsas.**	*[Deh-bes poh-ner los beeh-beh-res en las bol-sas]*
You must not fall asleep on the bus.	**No deben dormirse en el autobús.**	*[Noh deh-ben dor-meer-seh en el aooh-toh-boos]*

Orders (with "You Have To")

This structure is similar to the previous one, where the listener must do what the speaker says.

English	Spanish	Pronunciation
You have to call me when you get there.	**Tienes que llamarme cuando llegues.**	*[Teeh-eh-nes keh yah-mar-meh kwan-doh yeh-gues]*
You have to tell her to pick up the kids at 2:00 p.m.	**Tienes que decirle que recoja a los niños a las 2:00 de la tarde.**	*[Teeh-eh-nes keh deh-seer-leh keh reh-koh-hah ah los neeh-nyos ah las dos deh lah tar-deh]*
You have to turn off the lights when you leave.	**Tienen que apagar las luces cuando salgan.**	*[Teeh-eh-nen keh ah-pah-gar las looh-ses kwan-doh sal-gan]*
You have to not forget to bring the cake.	**No tienes que olvidar traer el pastel.**	*[Teeh-eh-nes keh noh ol-beeh-dar trah-er el pas-tel]*
You have to clean your room before supper.	**Tienes que limpiar tu habitación antes de la cena.**	*[Teeh-eh-nes keh leem-peear tooh ah-beeh-tah-seeon an-tes deh lah seh-nah]*
You have to not waste water.	**No tienen que desperdiciar el agua.**	*[Teeh-eh-nen keh noh des-per-deeh-seear el ah-gooah]*
You have to give me a big hug.	**Tienes que darme un gran abrazo.**	*[Teeh-eh-nes keh dar-meh oon gran ah-brah-soh]*
You have to close the door every time you go out.	**Tienen que cerrar la puerta cada vez que salgan.**	*[Teeh-eh-nen keh seh-rrar lah pooh-er-tah kah-dah bes keh sal-gan]*
You have to ask him if he received the package.	**Tienes que preguntarle si recibió el paquete.**	*[Teeh-eh-nes keh pre-goon-tar-leh seeh reh-seeh-beeoh el pah-keh-teh]*
You have to help me choose a dress for my niece.	**Tienes que ayudarme a elegir un vestido para mi sobrina.**	*[Teeh-eh-nes keh ah-yooh-dar-meh ah eh-leh-heer oon bes-teeh-doh pah-rah meeh soh-breeh-nah]*

English	Spanish	Pronunciation
You have to put the groceries in the bags.	**Tienes que poner los víveres en las bolsas.**	*[Teeh-eh-nes keh poh-ner los beeh-beh-res en las bol-sas]*
You have to not fall asleep on the bus.	**No tienen que dormirse en el autobús.**	*[Teeh-eh-nen keh noh dor-meer-seh en el aooh-toh-boos]*

Orders (with "I Ask You")

These are direct requests where there is no doubt that the listeners are compelled to perform a specific action.

English	Spanish	Pronunciation
I ask you to call me when you get there.	**Te pido que me llames cuando llegues.**	*[Teh peeh-doh keh meh yah-mes kwan-doh yeh-gues]*
I ask you to tell her to pick up the kids at 2:00 p.m.	**Te pido que le digas que recoja a los niños a las 2:00 de la tarde.**	*[Teh peeh-doh keh leh deeh-gas keh reh-koh-hah ah los neeh-nyos ah las dos deh lah tar-deh]*
I ask you to turn off the lights when you leave.	**Les pido que apaguen las luces cuando salgan.**	*[Les peeh-doh keh ah-pah-guen las looh-ses kwan-doh sal-gan]*
I ask you not to forget to bring the cake.	**Te pido que no olvides traer el pastel.**	*[Teh pee-doh keh noh ol-beeh-des trah-er el pas-tel]*
I ask you to clean your room before supper.	**Te pido que limpies tu habitación antes de la cena.**	*[Teh peeh-doh keh leem-peeh-es tooh ah-beeh-tah-seeon an-tes deh lah seh-nah]*
I ask you not to waste water.	**Les pido que no desperdicien el agua.**	*[Les peeh-doh keh noh des-per-deeh-seeh-en el ah-gooah]*
I ask you to give me a big hug.	**Te pido que me des un gran abrazo.**	*[The peeh-doh keh meh des oon gran ah-brah-soh]*

English	Spanish	Pronunciation
I ask you to close the door every time you go out.	**Les pido que cierren la puerta cada vez que salgan.**	*[Les peeh-doh keh seeh-eh-rren lah pooh-er-tah kah-dah bes keh sal-gan]*
I ask you to ask him if he received the package.	**Te pido que le preguntes si recibió el paquete.**	*[Teh pee-doh keh leh preh-goon-tes seeh reh-seeh-beeoh el pah-keh-teh]*
I ask you to help me choose a dress for my niece.	**Te pido que me ayudes a elegir un vestido para mi sobrina.**	*[Teh peeh-doh keh meh ah-yooh-des ah eh-leh-heer oon bes-teeh-doh pah-rah meeh soh-breeh-nah]*
I ask you to put the groceries in the bags.	**Te pido que pongas los víveres en las bolsas.**	*[Teh peeh-doh keh pon-gas los beeh-beh-res en las bol-sas]*
I ask you not to fall asleep on the bus.	**Les pido que no se duerman en el autobús.**	*[Les peeh-doh keh noh seh dooer-man en el aooh-toh-boos]*

Orders (as Questions)

It is safe to say that transforming an order into a question softens the tone a little bit. It's still an order, though. Spanish speaking people also get the hint.

English	Spanish	Pronunciation
Can you call me when you get there?	**¿Puedes llamarme cuando llegues?**	*[Pooeh-des yah-mar-meh kwan-doh yeh-gues?]*
Would you tell her to pick up the kids at 2:00 p.m.?	**¿Le dirías que recoja a los niños a las 2:00 de la tarde?**	*[Leh deeh-reeh-as keh reh-koh-hah ah los neeh-nyos ah las dos deh lah tar-deh?]*
Will you turn off the lights when you leave?	**¿Apagarán las luces cuando salgan?**	*[Ah-pah-gah-ran las looh-ses kwan-doh sal-gan?]*
You won't forget to bring the cake,right?	**No olvidarás traer el pastel, ¿verdad?**	*[Noh ol-beeh-dah-ras trah-er el pas-tel, ber-dad?]*
Can you clean your room before supper?	**¿Puedes limpiar tu habitación antes de la cena?**	*[Pooeh-des leem-peeh-ar tooh ah-beeh-tah-seeon an-tes deh lah seh-nah?]*

English	Spanish	Pronunciation
You will not waste water, right?	**No desperdiciarán el agua, ¿cierto?**	*[Noh des-per-deeh-seeh-ah-ran el ah-gooah, seeh-er-toh?]*
Will you give me a big hug?	**¿Me darás un gran abrazo?**	*[Meh dah-ras oon gran ah-brah-soh?]*
Can you close the door every time you go out?	**¿Pueden cerrar la puerta cada vez que salgan?**	*[Pooeh-den seh-rrar lah pooh-er-tah kah-dah bes keh sal-gan?]*
Would you ask him if he received the package?	**¿Le preguntarías si recibió el paquete?**	*[Leh preh-goon-tah-reeh-as seeh reh-seeh-beeoh el pah-keh-teh?]*
Will you help me choose a dress for my niece?	**¿Me ayudarás a elegir un vestido para mi sobrina?**	*[Meh ah-yooh-dah-ras ah eh-leh-heer oon bes-teeh-doh pah-rah meeh soh-breeh-nah?]*
Would you put the groceries in the bags?	**¿Pondrías los víveres en las bolsas?**	*[Pon-dreeh-as los beeh-beh-res en las bol-sas?]*
You are not going to fall asleep on the bus, right?	**No van a dormirse en el autobús, ¿verdad?**	*[Noh ban ah dor-meer-seh en el aooh-toh-boos. ¿Ber-dad?]*

Favors

Here's a piece of advice for you: Spanish-speaking people are quite a bit sensitive to orders, particularly Latin Americans. They find orders somehow imperative and sometimes even offensive. The trick here is to transform orders into favors. In other words, try not to give orders and ask for favors instead. Spanish speakers will always be more than willing to help you!

This is how you can do it:

English	Spanish	Pronunciation
Can you please call me when you get there?	**¿Puedes llamarme cuando llegues, por favor?**	*[Pooeh-des yah-mar-meh kwan-doh yeh-gues, por fah-bor?]*

English	Spanish	Pronunciation
Would you be so kind as to tell her to pick up the kids at 2:00 p.m.?	**¿Serías tan amable de decirle que recoja a los niños a las 2:00 de la tarde?**	*[Seh-reeh-as tan ah-mah-ble deh deh-seer-leh keh reh-koh-hah ah los neeh-nyos ah las dos deh lah tar-deh?]*
Please, turn off the lights when you leave.	**Por favor, apaguen las luces cuando salgan.**	*[Por fah-bor, ah-pah-guen las looh-ses kwan-doh sal-gan]*
I'll thank you for not forgetting to bring the cake.	**Te agradeceré no olvidar traer el pastel.**	*[Teh ah-grah-deh-seh-reh noh ol-beeh-dar trah-er el pas-tel]*
I would appreciate it if you clean your room before supper.	**Apreciaría que limpies tu habitación antes de la cena.**	*[Ah-preh-seeah-reeah keh leem-peeh-es tooh ah-beeh-tah-seeon an-tes deh lah seh-nah]*
Don't waste water, please.	**No desperdicien el agua, por favor.**	*[Noh des-per-deeh-seeh-en el ah-gooah, por fah-bor]*
I would love for you to give me a big hug.	**Me encantaría que me dieras un gran abrazo.**	*[Meh en-kan-tah-reeah keh meh deeh-eh-ras oon gran ah-brah-soh]*
You would help me a lot if you close the door every time you go out.	**Me ayudarían mucho si cierran la puerta cada vez que salgan.**	*[Meh ah-yooh-dah-reean mooh-choh seeh seeh-eh-rran lah pooh-er-tah kah-dah bes keh sal-gan]*
Please ask him if he received the package.	**Por favor pregúntale si recibió el paquete.**	*[Por fah-bor preh-goon-tah-leh seeh reh-seeh-beeoh el pah-keh-teh]*
Would you please help me choose a dress for my niece?	**¿Me ayudarías, por favor, a elegir un vestido para mi sobrina?**	*[Meh ah-yooh-dah-reeas por fah-bor ah eh-leh-heer oon bes-teeh-doh pah-rah meeh soh-breeh-nah?]*
Would you be so kind as to put the groceries in the bags?	**¿Serías tan amable de poner los víveres en las bolsas?**	*[Seh-reeas tan ah-mah-bleh deh poh-ner los beeh-beh-res en las bol-sas?]*
Do me a favor: do not fall asleep on the bus.	**Háganme un favor: no se duerman en el autobús.**	*[Ah-gan-me oon fah-bor: noh seh dooer-man en el aooh-toh-boos]*

How To Respond to Orders and Favor Requests

People usually expect a confirmation for their orders and favor requests. You will hear expressions like the following, and you can certainly use them as well.

You should know that Spanish-speaking people almost never say plain "no". They will always try to explain why they will not obey your orders or do you a favor. Moreover, they will try to apologize for not being helpful to you. Here you will also find some examples of this.

English	Spanish	Pronunciation
Sure.	**Claro.**	*[Clah-roh]*
Sure.	**Seguro.**	*[Seh-gooh-roh]*
Absolutely.	**Absolutamente.**	*[Ab-so-looh-tah-men-teh]*
Right now.	**Ahora mismo.**	*[Aoh-rah mees-mo]*
Right away.	**Ya mismo.**	*[Yah mees-moh]*
No doubt.	**Sin duda.**	*[Seen dooh-dah]*
Immediately.	**De inmediato.**	*[Deh een-meh-deeah-toh]*
Of course.	**Por supuesto.**	*[Por sooh-pooh-es-toh]*
Of course.	**Claro que sí.**	*[Clah-roh keh seeh]*
Certainly.	**Desde luego.**	*[Des-deh looeh-goh]*
Yes.	**Sí.**	*[Seeh]*
Count on that.	**Cuenta con eso.**	*[Kwen-tah kon eh-soh]*
You can count on that.	**Puedes contar con eso.**	*[Pooeh-des kon-tar kon eh-soh]*
Consider it done.	**Considéralo hecho.**	*[Kon-seeh-deh-rah-loh eh-choh]*
Done.	**Hecho.**	*[Eh-choh]*
I'll take care of that.	**Me encargaré de eso.**	*[Meh en-kar-gah-reh deh eh-so]*
I'll do it.	**Yo lo haré.**	*[Eeoh loh ah-reh]*
Don't worry.	**No te preocupes.**	*[Noh teh preh-oh-kooh-pes]*
I'm on it.	**Estoy en eso.**	*[Es-toeeh en eh-so]*
I can't, because...	**No puedo, porque...**	*[Noh pooeh-doh por-keh...]*

English	Spanish	Pronunciation
I'd love to, but...	**Me encantaría, pero...**	*[Meh en-kan-tah-reeah, peh-roh...]*
I'm sorry, I can't help you because...	**Lo lamento, no puedo ayudarte porque...** **Lo siento, no puedo ayudarte porque...**	*[Loh lah-men-toh, noh pooeh-doh ayooh-dar-teh por-keh...]* *[Loh seeh-en-toh, noh pooeh-doh ayooh-dar-teh por-keh...]*
Yes, but later because...	**Sí, pero más tarde porque...**	*[Seeh, peh-roh mas tar-deh por-keh...]*
I can't. Sorry.	**No puedo. Perdón.**	*[Noh pooeh-doh. Per-don]*
I can't, but let me ask ________ if he/she can help you.	**Yo no puedo, pero déjame preguntarle a ________ si puede ayudarte.**	*[Eeoh noh pooeh-doh, peh-roh deh-ha-meh pre-goon-tar-leh ah ________ seeh pooeh-deh ah-yooh-dar-teh]*
I'm too busy now. Can I do it later?	**Estoy muy ocupado ahora. ¿Puedo hacerlo después?** **Estoy muy ocupada ahora. ¿Puedo hacerlo después?**	*[Es-toeeh mooeeh oh-kooh-pah-doh aoh-rah. Pooeh-doh ah-ser-loh des-pooes?]* *[Es-toeeh mooeeh oh-kooh-pah-dah aoh-rah. Pooeh-doh ah-ser-loh des-pooes?]*
I wish I could help you, but...	**Desearía poder ayudarte, pero...**	*[Deh-seah-reeah poh-der ayooh-dar-teh, peh-roh...]*
I'd like to help you, but...	**Me gustaría ayudarte, pero...**	*[Meh goos-tah-reeah ayooh-dar-teh, peh-roh...]*
Maybe some other time.	**Tal vez en otra ocasión.**	*[Tal bes en oh-trah oh-kah-seeon]*
Let me see what I can do.	**Déjame ver qué puedo hacer.**	*[Deh-hah-meh ber keh pooeh-doh ah-ser]*

Gratitude

If you want to be a champion in Spanish-speaking regions, show your gratitude every time another person obeys your orders or does something for you. Here you have a few ways to do it. Some are more expressive and heart-felt than others, so gauge your gratitude according to the situation at hand.

English	Spanish	Pronunciation
Thank you.	**Gracias.**	*[Gra-seeas]*
Thank you very much.	**Muchas gracias.**	*[Mooh-chas gra-seeas]*
I appreciate it.	**Lo aprecio.**	*[Lo ah-pre-seeoh]*
I appreciate it a lot.	**Te lo agradezco mucho.**	*[Teh loh ah-grah-des-koh mooh-choh]*
I really appreciate it.	**En verdad lo aprecio.**	*[En ber-dad loh ah-preh-seeoh]*
I'm very grateful for this. I am very thankful for this.	**Estoy muy agradecido por esto.** **Estoy muy agradecida por esto.**	*[Es-toeeh mooeeh ah-grah-deh-seeh-doh por es-toh]* *[Es-toeeh mooeeh ah-grah-deh-seeh-dah por es-toh]*
You have helped me a lot.	**Me has ayudado mucho.**	*[Meh as ah-yooh-dah-doh moo-choh]*
Thanks for your help.	**Gracias por tu ayuda.**	*[Grah-seeas por tooh ah-yooh-da]*
Thank you for helping me with this.	**Gracias por ayudarme con esto.**	*[Grah-seeas por ah-yooh-dar-meh kon es-toh]*
I appreciate your help.	**Aprecio tu ayuda.**	*[Ah-preh-seeoh tooh ah-yooh-dah]*
I cannot thank you enough.	**No puedo agradecerte lo suficiente.**	*[Noh pooeh-doh ah-grah-deh-ser-teh loh sooh-feeh-seeh-en-teh]*
I couldn't have done it without you.	**No hubiera podido hacerlo sin ti.**	*[Noh ooh-beeh-eh-rah poh-deeh-doh ah-ser-loh seen teeh]*

English	Spanish	Pronunciation
I'm full of gratitude to you.	**Estoy lleno de agradecimiento hacia ti.** **Estoy llena de agradecimiento hacia ti.**	*[Es-toeeh yeh-noh deh ah-grah-deh-seeh-meeh-en-toh ah-seeah teeh]* *[Es-toeeh yeh-nah deh ah-grah-deh-seeh-meeh-en-toh ah-seeah teeh]*
Thanks for your support.	**Gracias por tu apoyo.**	*[Grah-seeas por tooh ah-poh-yoh]*
Your help is really important for me.	**Tu ayuda es muy importante para mí.**	*[Tooh ah-yooh-dah es mooeeh eem-por-tan-teh pah-rah meeh]*
I'll never forget what you did for me.	**Nunca olvidaré lo que hiciste por mí.**	*[Noon-kah ol-beeh-dah-reh loh keh eeh-sees-teh pormeeh]*
I value your help.	**Valoro tu ayuda.**	*[Bah-loh-roh tooh ah-yooh-dah]*
Thanks and sorry for the inconvenience.	**Gracias y perdón por la molestia.**	*[Grah-seeas eeh per-don por lah moh-les-teeah]*
I owe you one.	**Te debo una.**	*[Teh deh-boh oonah]*
Your help means a lot to me.	**Tu ayuda significa mucho para mí.**	*[Tooh ah-yooh-dah seeg-neeh-feeh-kah mooh-choh pah-rah meeh]*
Thanks a million.	**Un millón de gracias.**	*[Oon meeh-yon deh gra-seeas]*

How To Respond to Gratitude

The asking-giving-receiving cycle ends when one receives someone else's gratitude with an appropriate expression like these below:

English	Spanish	Pronunciation
You are welcome.	**De nada.** **Por nada.**	*[Deh nah-dah]* *[Por nah-dah]*
It was a pleasure.	**Fue un placer.**	*[Fooeh oon plah-ser]*
It was my pleasure.	**Fue un placer para mí.**	*[Fooeh ooh plah-ser pah-rah meeh]*
With pleasure.	**Con gusto.**	*[Kon goos-toh]*
Happy to!	**¡Con gusto!**	*[Kon goos-toh!]*
Happy to help!	**¡Feliz de ayudar!**	*[Fe-lees deh ayooh-dar!]*
It's an honor	**Es un honor.**	*[Es oon oh-nor]*
Anything for you.	**Lo que sea por ti.**	*[Loh keh seah por teeh]*
No problem.	**No hay problema.**	*[Noh aeeh proh-bleh-ma]*
I'm at your service.	**Estoy para servirte.**	*[Es-toeeh pah-rah ser-bir-teh]*
At your service.	**A tu servicio.**	*[Ah tooh ser-beeh-seeoh]*
I'm at your command.	**Estoy a tus órdenes.**	*[Es-toeeh ah toos or-deh-nes]*
At your command.	**A tus órdenes.**	*[Ah toos or-deh-nes]*
Glad to be of service.	**Encantado de servirte.** **Encantada de servirte.**	*[En-kan-tah-doh deh ser-beer-teh]* *[En-kan-tah-dah deh ser-beer-teh]*
Glad to be helpful.	**Encantado de serte útil.** **Encantada de serte útil.**	*[En-kan-tah-doh deh ser-teh ooh-teel]* *[En-kan-tah-dah deh ser-teh ooh-teel]*
Glad to help you.	**Encantado de ayudarte.** **Encantada de ayudarte.**	*[En-kan-tah-doh deh ayooh-dar-teh]* *[En-kan-tah-dah deh ayooh-dar-teh]*

English	Spanish	Pronunciation
Glad I could help.	**Encantado de poder ayudarte.** **Encantada de poder ayudarte.**	*[En-kan-tah-doh deh poh-der ayooh-dar-teh]* *[En-kan-tah-dah deh poh-der ayooh-dar-teh]*
Sure.	**Claro.**	*[Klah-roh]*
Don't mention it.	**Ni lo menciones.**	*[Neeh loh men-seeoh-nes]*
Whenever you want.	**Cuando gustes.**	*[Kwan-doh goos-tes]*
Not at all.	**Para nada.**	*[Pah-rah nah-dah]*
It's no bother.	**No es molestia.**	*[Noh es moh-les-teeah]*
It's all right.	**Está bien.**	*[Es-tah beeh-en]*
It's nothing.	**No fue nada.**	*[Noh fooeh nah-dah]*
Sure thing.	**Por supuesto.**	*[Por sooh-pooes-toh]*
You don't need to thank me.	**No necesitas agradecérmelo.**	*[Noh neh-seh-see-taas ah-grah-deh-ser-meh-loh]*

Instructions

As you know, instructions are used to explain how something should be done with the aim of completing a process or achieving a goal. The structure is similar to orders in a step-by-step sequence.

Check this example about painting a wall in a "washed-up" style, very popular in some Latin American towns.

English	Spanish	Pronunciation
Remove the old paint completely.	**Retira por completo la pintura vieja.**	*[Reh-teeh-rah po kom-pleh-toh lah peen-tooh-rah beeh-eh-ha]*
Wash the wall with water and soap.	**Lava la pared con agua y jabón.**	*[Lah-bah lah pah-red kon ah-gooah eeh hah-bon]*
Correct the defects and holes in the wall with cement.	**Corrige los defectos y agujeros en la pared con cemento.**	*[Koh-rreeh-heh los deh-fek-tos eeh ah-gooh-he-ros en lah pah-red kon seh-men-toh]*

English	Spanish	Pronunciation
Let the wall dry completely.	**Deja secar la pared por completo.**	*[Deh-ha seh-kar lah pah-red por kom-pleh-toh]*
Measure the wall and calculate how much paint you will need.	**Mide la pared y calcula cuánta pintura necesitarás.**	*[Meeh-deh lah pah-red eeh kal-kooh-lah kwan-tah peen-tooh-rah neh-seh-seeh-tah-ras]*
Buy: ➲ white paint ➲ one or two colors of your choice ➲ one brush for each color. You can buy a roller for white paint. ➲ comber noil or cotton waste ➲ gloves	**Compra:** ➲ **pintura blanca** ➲ **uno o dos colores a tu elección** ➲ **una brocha para cada color. Puedes comprar un rodillo para la pintura blanca** ➲ **estopa o desecho de algodón** ➲ **guantes**	*[Kom-prah:* ➲ *Peen-tooh-rah blan-kah* ➲ *Oono oh dos koh-loh-res mas ah tooh eh-lek-seeh-on* ➲ *Ooh-nah broh-chah pah-rah kah-dah koh-lor. Pooeh-des kom-prar oon roh-deeh-yoh pah-rah lah peen-tooh-rah blan-kah* ➲ *Es-toh-pah oh deh-seh-choh deh al-goh-don* ➲ *Gwan-tes]*
Cover the wall with one coat of white paint.	**Cubre la pared con una capa de pintura blanca.**	*[Kooh-breh lah pah-red kon oonah kah-pah deh peen-tooh-rah blan-kah]*
Let the wall dry.	**Deja secar la pared.**	*[Deh-hah seh-kar lah pah-red]*
Apply a second coat of white paint, if necessary.	**Aplica una segunda capa de pintura blanca, si es necesario.**	*[Ah-pleeh-kah oonah seh-goon-dah kah-pah deh peen-tooh-rah blan-kah, seeh es neh-seh-sah-reeo]*
If you want another color to be the base, cover the wall with one or two coats.	**Si quieres que otro color sea la base, cubre la pared con una o dos capas.**	*[Seeh keeh-eh-res keh oh-troh koh-lor seh-ah lah bah-seh, kooh-breh lah pah-red kon oonah oh dos kah-pas]*

English	Spanish	Pronunciation
Put on your gloves, if you have not done it already.	**Ponte los guantes, si aún no lo has hecho.**	*[Pon-teh los gwan-tes, seeh ah-oon noh loh as eh-choh]*
Take one piece of comber noil and dip it in the color of your choice.	**Toma un pedazo de estopa y sumérgelo en el color de tu elección.**	*[Toh-mah oon peh-da-soh deh es-toh-pah eeh sooh-mer-heh-loh en el koh-lor deh tooh eh-lek-seeh-on]*
Be brave: draw horizontal or vertical spirals on the wall with the wet comber noil.	**Sé valiente: traza espirales horizontales o verticales en la pared con la estopa húmeda.**	*[Seh bah-leeh-en-teh: trah-sah es-peeh-rah-les oh-reeh-son-tah-les oh ber-teeh-kah-les en la pah-red kon lah es-toh-pah ooh-meh-dah]*
It's up to you how intense you want this color to be and how wide the spirals will be.	**Tú decides cuán intenso quieres que sea ese color y cuán amplios serán los espirales.**	*[Tooh deh-seeh-des kwan een-ten-soh keeh-eh-res keh seh-ah eh-seh koh-lor eeh kwan am-pleeh-os seh-ran los es-peeh-rah-les]*
If you want to add another color, repeat the process above.	**Si quieres agregar otro color, repite el proceso anterior.**	*[Seeh keeh-eh-res ah-greh-gar oh-troh koh-lor, reh-peeh-teh el pro-seh-soh an-teh-reeh-or]*
Look at the wall from different distances and angles.	**Mira la pared desde diferentes distancias y ángulos.**	*[Meeh-rah lah pah-red des-deh deeh-feh-ren-tes dees-tan-seeas eeh an-gooh-los]*
Add the final touches.	**Agrega los toques finales.**	*[Ah-greh-gah los toh-kes feeh-nah-les]*
Enjoy your gorgeous washed-up wall!	**¡Disfruta tu preciosa pared deslavada!**	*[Dees-frooh-tah tooh preh-seeoh-sah pah-red des-lah-bah-da!]*

Suggestions and Advice

The slight differences between suggestions and advice are that the first are usually offered despite the other party not requesting them, while advice is given when requested. On the other hand, it is generally considered that advice is given by experienced people, while suggestions can come from anyone.

In any case, both are expressions of ideas or plans aimed at solving a problem or improving a rather complicated situation.

English	Spanish	Pronunciation
Maybe you should... Perhaps you should...	**Tal vez deberías...**	*[Tal bes deh-beh-reeas...]*
I think the best thing you can do is...	**Creo que lo mejor que puedes hacer es...**	*[Kreoh keh loh meh-hor keh pooeh-des ah-ser es...]*
What I would do is...	**Lo que yo haría es...**	*[Loh keh eeoh areeh-ah es...]*
What I would do in your place is...	**Lo que yo haría en tu lugar es...**	*[Loh keh eeoh areeh-ah en tooh looh-gar es...]*
What would happen if you...?	**¿Y qué pasaría si tú...?**	*[Keh pah-sah-reeah seeh tooh...?]*
What if...?	**¿Y qué tal si...?**	*[Eeh keh tal seeh...?]*
Maybe you should consider...	**Tal vez deberías considerar...**	*[Tal bes de-beh-reeas kon-seeh-deh-rar...]*
Why don't you...?	**¿Por qué no...?**	*[Por keh noh...?]*
The way I see it, you might want to...	**Como yo lo veo, quizá quieras...**	*[Koh-moh eeoh loh beoh, keeh-sah keeh-eh-ras...]*
I think the most convenient thing is...	**Creo que lo más conveniente es...**	*[Kreh-oh keh loh mas kon-beh-neeh-en-teh es...]*
The most convenient thing is...	**Lo más conveniente es...**	*[Loh mas kon-beh-neeh-en-teh es...]*
What has worked for me is...	**Lo que a mí me ha funcionado es...**	*[Loh keh ah meeh meh ah foon-seeoh-na-doh es...]*

English	Spanish	Pronunciation
Based on my experience...	**Con base en mi experiencia...**	*[Kon bah-seh en meeh eks-peh-reeh-en-seeah...]*
I think the best option is...	**Creo que la mejor opción es...**	*[Kreh-oh keh lah meh-hor op-seeon es...]*
What you must do is...	**Lo que debes hacer es...**	*[Loh keh deh-bes ah-ser es...]*
What you must not do is...	**Lo que no debes hacer es...**	*[Loh keh noh deh-bes ah-ser es...]*
Do this...	**Haz esto...**	*[As es-toh]*
Don't do this...	**No hagas esto...**	*[Noh ah-gas es-toh...]*
You must...	**Tú debes...**	*[Tooh deh-bes...]*
You must not...	**Tú no debes...**	*[Tooh noh deh-bes...]*
You have to...	**Tienes que...**	*[Teeh-eh-nes keh...]*

BOOK V: SHORT STORIES

We hope you had fun diving into each of the six stories we came across in chapter 14 to 19. The reason why we scattered them across the chapters was to help drive the concepts home as we covered them while also breaking the monotony of the grammar lessons (we know they can be a lot!)

In case you want to reread the stories during leisure time, it might be a good idea to check out the glossary for each story again. It'll help you understand the language better and pick up on some new words. Plus, it's like having a cheat sheet right there to help you along the way!

Here's a recap of what each story contains so you'll be reminded of what to expect:

In "Cristina y El Gato Poeta," you'll follow Cristina's brave journey to rescue a scaredy-cat named Poeta. It's all about empathy, bravery, and the special bond between humans and animals. Along the way, you'll pick up some vocabulary related to animals, emotions, and actions, so you'll be learning while you enjoy the story.

"El Éxito de Alberto" tells the tale of Alberto's job-hunting struggles and his eventual success through some creative thinking. It's all about perseverance, thinking outside the box, and selling yourself. You'll learn words related to jobs, interviews, and people skills – stuff you can use in the real world.

In "Nadando en El Arcoíris," you'll join the kids of Campeche as they splash around in puddles after a rainstorm. It's all about childhood fun and imagination, with a bit of a twist. You'll learn words related to weather, activities, and feelings – all in everyday situations.

"Ramona La Distraída" is a funny one about Ramona, who's always getting into silly situations because she's so forgetful. It's all about laughs and family ties. You'll pick up words related to daily life, relationships, and different personalities.

In "Los Bromistas Gómez," you'll meet the Gomez family, who love playing pranks on each other. It's all about humor and family bonds. You'll learn words related to jokes, relationships, and everyday stuff; all while having a good laugh.

Finally, "El Terremoto de 2017" takes you to the aftermath of the 2017 earthquake in Mexico, where volunteers come together to help those in need. It's all about solidarity, resilience, and community support. You'll learn words related to disasters, emotions, and acts of kindness; and maybe gain some cultural insight along the way.

Overall, each story in this bundle provides you with a rich and varied learning experience, combining language acquisition with cultural insights and engaging storytelling. Whether you are a beginner or intermediate learner, these narratives offer valuable opportunities to practice Spanish language skills while enjoying captivating tales.

CONCLUSION

Wow! Talk about coming a long way! It seems incredible that we've already gone through 21 lessons and numerous Spanish stories, words and phrases! And don't you feel a sense of accomplishment? By now, you probably have mastered quite a bit of Spanish and gained confidence to move on to the next step. Even if your Spanish still has a way to go, even if you have to constantly check the information because sometimes it seems to slip your mind, you are starting to grasp how the language works. The key has been delivering micro-lessons to keep you from feeling overwhelmed.

As promised, lessons have been bite-sized and manageable. We've offered just the right amount of information to avoid cluttering your brain. The approach has been building gradual, cumulative learning, in which each new class builds on the previous ones to integrate what you already know with further information.

And all this time, we've kept you at the center of your learning journey, giving you soft nudges to keep you going. By using short, to-the-point grammar explanations and lots of practice, you've discovered it's possible to engage in intellectual tasks while you enjoy yourself. At the same time, you've been free to pace yourself without the stress of committing to long boring lessons. Our most important strategy has been allowing you to practice, practice, and practice. Putting grammar rules in use, after all, is the secret to success in any language.

In these lessons, we provided you with an incredible amount of vocabulary related to the most common and everyday situations: a home, a family, the street, a community, and commonplace objects. You should start speaking Spanish immediately and have enough vocabulary to get by in daily situations.

We promised baby steps, and look how far we've come! We know this language course may have seemed more like cheetah strides, as we covered a great deal of material in a pretty short time. Don't expect perfection at this stage. Like going up a mountain, at the beginning of your climb, you see rapid progress, but as you climb higher up, you stop seeing visible progress and feel you've reached a standstill. This doesn't mean that you're not making progress. It means you're at a more complex stage, where you need more time and sophisticated cognition processes to understand and remember higher-level content. But don't despair! You're still making progress even if you don't see it.

The key from now on is to keep practicing what you already know and take in new content in a slow, progressive way, just like you've been doing.

One good piece of advice is to try to get your hands on any Spanish-language material: songs, movies, podcasts, or Spanish Instagram accounts, you name it. Even Spanish ads are worth reading and trying to understand. The more you're exposed to the language, the faster you'll feel at home and comfortable speaking and hearing it.

Finally, we're proud of you. We know this has been an incredible journey, and we've had to deal with your expectations and reality. But we know you're satisfied and proud of your work. All we can say is keep going! And while we know there is a fair amount of work and persistence involved, it's all about feeling the excitement of learning a language and discovering a whole new world. Best of luck on your journey!

ANSWER KEY

CHAPTER 1: SUBJECT PRONOUNS, NOUNS AND ARTICLES

PRACTICE 1.1

A. 1. yo | 2. nosotros | 3. vosotros | 4. ustedes | 5. ellos | 6. tú

B. 1. usted | 2. tú | 3. usted | 4. usted | 5. tú | 6. usted | 7. usted | 8. tú | 9. tú | 10. usted

PRACTICE 1.2

A. 1. la | 2. el | 3. la | 4. la | 5. el | 6. la | 7. la | 8. el | 9. el | 10. el | 11. el | 12. el | 13. el | 14. el | 15. el | 16.la | 17. el | 18. | la | 19. la | 20. el

B. 1. los hombres | 2. las amigas | 3. las conversaciones | 4. los animales | 5. los sistemas | 6. los niños | 7. las casas | 8. los trenes | 9. las ciudades | 10. los doctores

C. 1. la verdad | 2. la televisión | 3. la mano | 4. la perra | 5. el lápiz | 6. la niña | 7. la radio | 8. la comida

PRACTICE 1.3

A. 1. unos abuelos | 2. unas conversaciones | 3. unos perros | 4. unas mujeres | 5. unos estudiantes | 6.unos doctores | 7. unos hoteles | 8. unos trenes | 9. unos lápices | 10. unas ciudades

B. 1. la | 2. una | 3. la / un | 4. una | 5. unas | 6. el | 7. un | 8. las

C. 1. una | 2. la | 3. la | 4. la | 5. el | 6. una | 7. las | 8. un

CHAPTER 2: VERBS IN THE PRESENT TENSE

PRACTICE 2.1

A. 1. Es de plástico o de vidrio | 2. Es de madera o de plástico | 3. Es de ladrillos | 4. Son de cuero | 5. Son de vidrio | 6. Es de madera | 7. Es de metal | 8. Es de papel

B. 1. es | 2. soy | 3. somos | 4. es | 5. son | 6. eres | 7. sois | 8. es | 9. sois/son

C. 1. La mesa y las sillas están sucias. | 2. Él es abogado. | 3. Nosotros estamos cansados. | 4. Es importante estudiar. | 5. Vosotros estáis en la universidad. | 6. Martín y Luis son inteligentes. | 7. El café es para la mujer. | 8. La ciudad es hermosa. | 9. Tú eres una turista. | 10. Yo soy de Guatemala. | 11. La lección es fácil. | 12. El niño está en el colegio. | 13. Ustedes están contentos. | 14. Nosotros somos italianos. | 15. Sara está triste.

PRACTICE 2.2

A. 1. tengo | 2. tenemos | 3. tiene | 4. tienes | 5. tenéis | 6. tiene | 7. tienen | 8. tiene | 9. tiene

B. 1. tienen | 2. tengo | 3. tienes | 4. tenemos | 5. tenéis | 6. tiene | 7. tiene | 8. Tienen

PRACTICE 2.3

1. hacemos | 2. hacen | 3. hago | 4. hacen | 5. hace | 6. hace | 7. haces | 8. hacéis | 9. hace

PRACTICE 2.4

A. 1. trabaja | 2. miran | 3. buscáis | 4. enseña | 5. compro | 6. viajan | 7. explicamos | 8. arregla

B. 1. comprende | 2. prenden | 3. corre | 4. vendemos | 5. coméis | 6. bebemos | 7. leo | 8. aprendes

C.

Infinitive	comer	vender	creer	apender
yo	como	vendo	creo	aprendo
tú	comes	vendes	crees	aprendes
él/ ella/ usted	come	vende	cree	aprende
nosotros	comemos	vendemos	creemos	aprendemos
vosotros	coméis	vendéis	creéis	aprendéis
ellas/ ellos/ ustedes	comen	venden	creen	aprenden

D. 1. comparten | 2. suben | 3. vive, vive | 4. abro | 5. recibes | 6. escribís | 7. discutimos | 8. decides

E.

Infinitive	escribir	recibir	abrir	subir
yo	escribo	recibo	abro	subo
tú	escribes	recibes	abres	subes
él/ella/ usted	escribe	recibe	abre	sube
nosotros	escribimos	recibimos	abrimos	subimos
vosotros	escribís	recibís	abrís	subís
ellas/ellos/ ustedes	escriben	reciben	abren	suben

CHAPTER 3: SABER AND CONOCER

PRACTICE 3.1

1. sabemos | 2. sabes | 3. sabéis | 4. sabe | 5. sé | 6. sabe | 7. saben | 8. sabe

PRACTICE 3.2

A. 1. conocen | 2. conoce | 3. conocéis | 4. conocemos | 5. conozco | 6. conoce | 7. conoces | 8. conoce

B. 1. conoce | 2. sabéis | 3. saben | 4. sabe | 5. conoce | 6. conoces | 7. sé | 8. conocen/conocéis

C. 1. Conozco | 2. sabemos | 3. Conocéis | 4. conoce | 5. Sabes | 6. saben | 7. Conozco | 8. Conoce | 9.saben

D. 1. X | 2. a | 3. X | 4. X | 5. a | 6. a | 7. a

PRACTICE 3.3

A. 1. Novak Djokovic sabe jugar al tenis. | 2. LeBron James sabe jugar al baloncesto. | 3. Tiger Woods sabe jugar al golf. | 4. J. K. Rowling sabe escribir novelas. | 5. Lionel Messi y Cristiano Ronaldo saben jugar al fútbol. | 6. Taylor Swift sabe cantar. | 7. Michael Phelps sabe nadar. | 8. Shakira sabe bailar. | 9.Meryl Streep sabe actuar. | 10. Simone Biles sabe hacer gimnasia artística.

B. 1. Sherlock Holmes conoce a Watson. | 2. Ashton Kutcher conoce a Mila Kunis. | 3. Rhett Butler conoce a Scarlett O'Hara. | 4. Chris Martin conoce a Dakota Johnson. | 5. David Beckham conoce a Victoria Beckham. | 6. Adán conoce a Eva. | 7. Justin Bieber conoce a Hailey Bieber.

C. 1. Yo conozco al profesor Blanco. | 2. Mi hermana y yo conocemos a la madre de Juan. | 3. María y Luis conocen a Sergio. | 4. Vosotros conocéis al director del área comercial. | 5. Tú conoces a la tía Julia.| 6. Carlos conoce a la tía Julia. | 7. Martín y Elena conocen a la tía Julia.

D. 1. Yo sé la verdad. | 2. Ella conoce a María. | 3. Ellos saben nadar. | 4. Pedro y Elena conocen Nueva York. | 5. Conocemos/Sabemos la respuesta. | 6. Conocemos al estudiante. | 7. Tú sabes/conoces mi nombre. | 8. Él conoce/sabe la verdad. | 9. El perro conoce a Juan. | 10. Sé tocar el piano. | 11.Conocemos la universidad.

E. 1. sabe | 2. conozco | 3. Conoces | 4. Saben | 5. conoce

CHAPTER 4: NUMBERS

PRACTICE 4.1

1. un | 2. un | 3. una | 4. Uno | 5. Un | 6. Una

PRACTICE 4.2

A. 1. X Hay una alfombra en la casa. | 2. X Hay tigres en el zoológico. | 3. ✓ | 4. ✓ | 5. X Hay oficinas en el edificio. | 6. ✓ | 7. X Hay turistas en la ciudad. | 8. X Hay personas en el cine.

B. 1. Are there flowers in the garden? | 2. Are there chairs in the office? | 3. Are there cats in the street? | 4. Are there hotels in the city? | 5. Is there a television in the house? | 6. Are there doctors in the hospital? | 7. Is there a dog in the car? | 8. Is there a radio in the car? | 9. Are there two women in the fish store? | 10. Are there tables in a restaurant?

C. 1. No hay animales en el zoológico. | 2. No hay muchos niños en el parque. | 3. No hay un teléfono público en la calle. | 4. No hay mucha gente en el restaurante. | 5. No hay un buen hotel en la ciudad. | 6. No hay muchos planetas en el cielo.

D. 1. está | 2. hay | 3. está | 4. está | 5. Hay | 6. hay | 7. Hay | 8. está | 9. está | 10. Hay

PRACTICE 4.3

A. 1. Cuántos | 2. Cuánta | 3. Cuántos | 4. Cuántas | 5. Cuántos | 6. Cuánto

B. 1. Hay siete días en una semana. | 2. Hay cuatro semanas en un mes. | 3. Hay 365 días en un año. | 4. Hay dos días en un fin de semana. | 5. Hay veintiocho días en el mes de febrero. | 6. Hay cinco dedos en mi mano. | 7. Hay dos (number varies) hospitales en mi ciudad. | 8. Hay una (number varies) televisión en mi casa. | 9. Hay tres (number varies) árboles en mi jardín. | 10. Hay veinte (number varies) sillas en mi casa.

C. 1. Hay dos universidades en la ciudad. | 2. Hay veinte manzanas en la canasta. | 3. Hay doce meses en el año. | 4. Hay una estatua de la Libertad en Nueva York. | 5. Hay dos ojos en la cara. | 6. Hay muchos edificios en la ciudad.

PRACTICE 4.4

A. 1. Cuarenta y seis | 2. Noventa y dos | 3. Ciento sesenta | 4. Ochocientos trece | 5. Cinco mil doscientos nueve | 6. Setenta mil doscientos treinta y siete | 7. Ochocientos cinco mil seiscientos veinticuatro | 8. Un millón novecientos sesenta y dos mil cuatrocientos setenta y siete | 9. Treinta y cuatro millones ochocientos cincuenta y siete mil noventa

B. 1. Ciento cuatro | 2. Cuarenta y siete | 3. Setecientos cincuenta y seis | 4. Veinticuatro mil ciento noventa y nueve | 5. Ciento sesenta y tres mil cuatrocientos cincuenta y tres | 6. Trescientos noventa y seis | 7. Cuatrocientos noventa y cinco

CHAPTER 5: PREPOSITIONS AND CONJUNCTIONS

PRACTICE 5.1

A. 1. en | 2. con | 3. de | 4. de | 5. con | 6. en | 7. de | 8. con | 9. en | 10. de, de | 11. con | 12. de | 13. en | 14. con | 15. con

B. 1. para | 2. sin | 3. a | 4. para | 5. a | 6. sin | 7. a | 8. sin

C. 1. por | 2. para | 3. según | 4. hasta/por | 5. por | 6. contra | 7. hasta | 8. para | 9. según

PRACTICE 5.2

A. 1. María e Inés son amigas desde la niñez. | 2. Hay diez u once niños en la tienda. | 3. Toma la llave e intenta abrir la puerta. | 4. Él nos llama e invita a su fiesta. | 5. Ve algo u oye un ruido. | 6. (Ella) Sabe leer y escribir muy bien.

B. 1. y | 2. o | 3. pero | 4. o | 5. y | 6. pero | 7. o | 8. pero

C. 1. pero | 2. sino | 3. pero | 4. sin embargo | 5. aunque | 6. Aunque

D. 1. porque (I walk everyday because it's good for my health) | 2. pero (They eat in a restaurant everyday but we eat at home) | 3. aunque (Teresa is learning German even though she doesn't need it) | 4. Ni... ni (Neither Elena nor Cristián drink wine) | 5. e (Elena and Hilario are lawyers) | 6. Tanto... como (Both Pedro and Sofía are French) | 7. y (We buy and sell used clothes) | 8. sin embargo (She studies a lot but doesn't learn a lot)

PRACTICE 5.3

A. 1. Pedro y Luis no saben si sus amigos regresan hoy. | 2. Mirta pregunta si hay examen mañana. | 3.José decide si sube el Monte Fitz Roy. | 4. Vosotros no sabéis si Paula necesita algo para la fiesta. | 5. Usted pregunta si los empleados trabajan bien. | 6. Tú decides si bebes café o té.

B. 1. Ella sabe que vivimos en la calle Oro. | 2. Juan piensa que viajamos todo el año. | 3. Yo creo que el señor Ortiz arregla hornos. | 4. Juana dice que a José le gusta comer. | 5. La profesora nos dice que es tarde. | 6. La madre dice que los niños necesitan lápices nuevos.

C. 1. Me gusta que mis hijos ordenan solos. | 2. Trabajo mucho pero gano poco. | 3. Aunque hace frío, hay sol. | 4. Martín cree que está demasiado ventoso para correr. | 5. El verdulero me explica que los tomates están verdes. | 6. Llegas temprano porque sales temprano.

PRACTICE 5.4

A. 1. Muchas | 2. tantos | 3. mismo | 4. otra | 5. Algunas | 6. Cada | 7. otras | 8. toda

B. 1. She has many dogs and cats in her house. | 2. Maria has several daughters, but she has no sons, she wants to have one soon. | 3. Both Luis and Juan have few friends at school. | 4. She/he doesn't read magazines or newspapers. | 5. She/he knows other countries since she/he travels a lot. Her/his favorite is Uruguay. | 6. She/he has the same car as Laura. | 7. She knows every street in Paris, but she doesn't know her own city. | 8. She/he speaks some languages, but she/he doesn't speak English.| 9. It's the same friendship, though we're older. | 10. All languages are useful, even if some are more useful than others.

C. 1. Ningún día es hermoso. | 2. Tengo muchas tristezas. | 3. Hay tan pocas cosas lindas en la vida. | 4.Tengo pocos amigos. | 5. Todos los días son malos. | 6. Toda tarea es imposible.

CHAPTER 6: POSSESSIVE ADJECTIVES

PRACTICE 6

A. 1. abuelo | 2. prima | 3. tía | 4. sobrino | 5. madre/mamá | 6. nieta

B. 1. Es la madre de mi madre o padre. | 2. Es la hija de mis tíos. | 3. Es el hermano de mi madre o mi padre. | 4. Es el hijo del hijo o hija de mi abuela. | 5. Es otro hijo de mis padres.

C. 1. elegante, largo, impresionante, precioso, antiguo | 2. prestigioso, elegante, tranquilo, generoso | 3.antiguos, impresionantes | 4. tranquilo | 5. larga y ancha | 6. variado, elegante.

D. 1. Mi tía es delgada. | 2. Su padre es deportista. | 3. Su abuela es interesante. | 4. Tus sobrinos son solteros. | 5. Vuestro/Su primo es rubio. | 6. Nuestras nietas son pequeñas. | 7. Mi esposo es guapo. | 8. Su hermana es casada. | 9. Tu madre es buena.

E. 1. su | 2. vuestras | 3. sus | 4. su | 5. su | 6. mi | 7. sus | 8. sus | 9. sus | 10. Su

F. 1. Su abuela Marta es anciana. | 2. Su padre Roberto es trabajador. | 3. Sus hermanitos son traviesos.| 4. Su madre Julia es generosa. | 5. Su primo Martín es delgado. | 6. Sus tíos son simpáticos. | 7. Su sobrina Ana es bonita. | 8. Su hermano Pablo es inteligente.

G. 1. Mi abuela Marta es anciana. | 2. Mi padre Roberto es trabajador. | 3. Mis hermanitos son traviesos.| 4. Mi madre Julia es generosa. | 5. Mi primo Martín es delgado. | 6. Mis tíos son simpáticos. | 7. Mi sobrina Ana es bonita. | 8. Mi hermano Pablo es inteligente.

H. 1. Nuestras avenidas son largas. | 2. Nuestros supermercados están completos. | 3. Nuestros teatros son grandes. | 4. Nuestros parques son preciosos. | 5. Nuestras universidades son prestigiosas. | 6.Nuestros museos son interesantes. | 7. Nuestros restaurantes son variados. | 8. Nuestros edificios son elegantes. | 9. Nuestros monumentos son antiguos.

I. 1. Su ciudad es grande. | 2. Su casa es elegante. | 3. Sus coches son negros. | 4. Su gata es blanca. | 5. Sus zapatos son viejos.

J. 1. Nuestras avenidas son largas. | 2. Nuestros edificios son altos. | 3. Mi oficina es grande. | 4.Nuestros parques son preciosos. | 5. Mi universidad es prestigiosa.

CHAPTER 7: REFLEXIVE VERBS

PRACTICE 7.1

A. 1. Te llamas Tomás. | 2 Me llamo José. | 3. Se llama Elena. | 4. Se llaman Paula y Teo. | 5. Nos llamamos Martín y Laura. | 6. Se llaman Pablo y Mirta.

B. 1. Se despierta a las 8:00 a.m. | 2. Se lava los dientes a las 8:10 a.m. | 3. Se baña a las 8:15 a.m. | 4.Se afeita a las 8:25 a.m. | 5. Se peina a las 8:30 a.m. | 6. Se viste a las 8:45 a.m. | 7. Se sienta a desayunar a las 9:00 a.m. | 8. Se va al trabajo a las 9:30 a.m.

C. 1. me, se | 2. se | 3. se | 4. te | 5. nos | 6. se | 7. se | 8. os

D. 1. me afeito | 2. te lavas | 3. se despierta | 4. se quita | 5. os sentáis | 6. se bañan

E. 1. Me levanto a las 7:00 a.m. (varies) los sábados. | 2. Me lavo el pelo los lunes (varies) | 3. Me gusta bañarme/ducharme. | 4. Me siento en un sofá (varies). | 5. Sí/No, me peino en la peluquería.

PRACTICE 7.2

A. 1. Yo voy a ir a Estados Unidos. | 2. Martín va a ir a Inglaterra. | 3. Sofía va a ir a Italia. | 4. Teresa y yo vamos a ir a Francia. | 5. Usted y José van a ir a España. | 6. Tú vas a ir a México. | 7. Pablo y María van a ir a Canadá.

B. 1. van a hacer | 2. vamos a ir | 3. Voy a bañarme | 4. Vais a leer | 5. van a viajar | 6. Voy a buscar | 7.va a encontrarse | 8. vamos a hablar

C. 1. va a ganar | 2. va a pedir | 3. va a caerse | 4. va a volar | 5. va a buscar | 6. van a chocar | 7. va a leerla | 8. van a casarse

D. 1. va a visitar | 2. vais a ir | 3. vais a cocinar | 4. voy a cuidar | 5. vamos a salir | 6. vas a ser | 7. Voy a estar | 8. va a ayudar

E. 1. va a ir | 2. Van a viajar | 3. va a conducir | 4. va a manejar | 5. Van a llegar | 6. Van a estar | 7. van a cenar | 8. van a irse

CHAPTER 8: COMPARISONS

PRACTICE 8.1

A. 1. Sofía es menos deportista que Teresa. | 2. Susana es más introvertida que Sofía. | 3. Teresa es menos estudiosa que Susana.

B. 1. Marta es más deportista que Laura. | 2. Roberto es menos deportista que Marta. | 3. Laura es más estudiosa que Marta. | 4. Roberto es más introvertido que Laura. | 5. Laura es más extrovertida que Roberto. | 6. Marta es más morena que Laura. | 7. Marta es menos seria que Roberto.

PRACTICE 8.2

A. 1 mejores | 2. peor | 3. mejor | 4. menor | 5. mayor

B. 1. Los mejores colegios. | 2. Alicia es menor que Paula. | 3. Es el mejor restaurante de la ciudad. | 4.Juan es mayor que Tomás. | 5. Ese museo es peor que aquel.

C. 1. mejor, peor | 2. menor, mayor

PRACTICE 8.3

1. El cuerpo es tan importante como la mente. | 2. Las bananas son tan ricas como las manzanas. | 3.El café es tan estimulante como el té. | 4. La carne es tan sana como el pescado. | 5. Tomás es tan simpático como Sara. | 6. Mi coche es tan rápido como tu coche. | 7. París es tan hermoso como Londres. | 8. Los gatos son tan fieles como los perros.

PRACTICE 8.4

A. 1. tantas | 2. tanto | 3. tantas | 4. tanta | 5. tantos | 6. tantos | 7. tanto

B. 1. En mi colegio no hay tantos estudiantes. | 2. Esteban no come tanta carne. | 3. Teresa no estudia tantas horas por día. | 4. Carlos no mira tantas películas por televisión. | 5. Tú no bebes tanto café como Fernando.

CHAPTER 9: HOW TO ASK QUESTIONS

PRACTICE 9.1

A. 1. Cuánta | 2. Para qué | 3. Dónde | 4. Qué | 5. Cómo | 6. Por qué | 7. Cuándo | 8. Quiénes | 9. Cuál | 10. Cuántos

B. 1. Cuál | 2. Cuál | 3. Qué | 4. Cuáles | 5. Qué | 6. Cuál

C. 1. ¿De dónde? | 2. ¿Adónde? | 3. ¿Dónde? | 4. ¿Dónde? | 5. ¿De dónde? | 6. ¿Dónde? | 7. ¿Adónde? | 8. ¿De dónde? | 9. ¿Adónde? | 10. ¿De dónde?

D. 1. Cuántas | 2. Cuánto | 3. Cuántos | 4. Cuántas | 5. Cuánta | 6. Cuánto | 7. Cuántos | 8.Cuánto

E. 1. ¿De dónde son? | 2. ¿Adónde van? | 3. ¿Dónde están los niños? | 4. ¿Adónde vas? | 5. ¿De dónde vienen? | 6. ¿Dónde está tu mamá?

F. 1. ¿De quién es esta casa? | 2. ¿Quién es Julia Roberts? | 3. ¿De quién son estas medias? | 4. ¿Quién es esa niña? | 5. ¿Quiénes son los mejores jugadores de tenis? | 6. ¿De quién es ese libro?

G. 1. Pilar es profesora. | 2. Tiene 30 años. | 3. Pilar llega en tren y caminando. | 4. Llega a las 7:45 de la mañana. | 5. Pilar almuerza a las 12:00 del mediodía. | 6. Pilar trabaja en un colegio. | 7. Pilar enseña geografía en el colegio. | 8. Una amiga acompaña a Pilar desde la estación de tren. | 9. Pilar come un sándwich y una ensalada.

PRACTICE 9.2

A. 1. Susana viene de Italia en avión. | 2. José y Tomás vienen a buscar manzanas. | 3. Tú vienes a mi fiesta. | 4. Tú y yo venimos al restaurante todos los martes. | 5. Yo vengo de trabajar. | 6. Ellos vienen a París a ver la Torre Eiffel. | 7. Laura viene al hospital para ver al médico.

B. 1. vengo | 2. vienen | 3. vienes | 4. viene | 5. venís | 6. venimos

C. 1. Marcos viene al colegio por la mañana. | 2. Tú y yo venimos a la universidad todos los martes y miércoles. | 3. Ellos vienen a nuestra casa a cenar. | 4. Vosotros/Ustedes venís/vienen al doctor en verano. | 5. María viene al restaurante para comer pescado. | 6. Yo vengo a la fiesta feliz.

CHAPTER 10: ADVERBS TO DESCRIBE ACTIONS

PRACTICE 10

A. 1. mucho | 2. bastante | 3. demasiado | 4. mucho | 5. más | 6. muy | 7. menos

B. 1. Su hermano no está aquí. | 2 No le gustan las manzanas ni las naranjas. | 3. Nunca van al cine. | 4.Tampoco le gusta el ejercicio. | 5. Jamás estudiamos juntos.

C. 1. Siempre | 2. temprano | 3. Luego | 4. nunca | 5. antes | 6. Mientras | 7. Pronto | 8. a tiempo | 9.tarde | 10. temprano

D. 1. inteligentemente | 2. difícilmente | 3. débilmente | 4. felizmente | 5. rápidamente | 6. furiosamente | 7. nerviosamente | 8. sinceramente | 9. verdaderamente | 10. normalmente

E. 1. Sinceramente | 2. totalmente | 3. verdaderamente | 4. cariñosamente | 5. Posiblemente | 6.rápidamente | 7. directamente | 8. pacientemente | 9. puntualmente | 10. tranquilamente

F. 1. felizmente | 2. mucho | 3. difícilmente | 4. tristemente | 5. rápidamente | 6. débilmente | 7.tranquilamente/pacíficamente | 8. Finalmente | 9. Posiblemente. | 10. aproximadamente

G. 1. fuertemente | 2. lentamente | 3. felizmente/alegremente | 4. poco | 5. peor | 6. más | 7. siempre

H. 1. Sí, Elena trabaja tranquilamente en su casa. | 2. Sí, la madre espera nerviosamente a su hijo. | 3.Sí, el periodista critica duramente las noticias. | 4. Sí, Sandra organiza eficientemente los cajones de su habitación. | 5. Sí, Fernando gana felizmente la carrera.

I. 1. Trabajo muy responsablemente. | 2. Tomás y José cocinan muy rico. | 3. La profesora explica mal los problemas. | 4. Ese equipo juega bien al fútbol. | 5. Hoy estamos muy ocupados. | 6. Salgo rápidamente del taxi.

J. 1. Luisa está más cansada que tú. | 2. Pedro habla más claramente que Tomás. | 3. Esta clase es mejor que esa. | 4. El presidente habla apasionadamente. | 5. Conozco bien a su madre. | 6. Jamás se despierta temprano. | 7. El perro siempre come su comida. | 8. Mientras Susana trabaja, Teresa estudia.

CHAPTER 11

PRACTICE 11.1

A. 1. Prefiero la televisión/el cine. | 2. Prefiero aprender español/francés. | 3. Prefiero estudiar lenguas/matemáticas. | 4. Prefiero comer en un restaurante/mi casa. | 5. Prefiero vivir en el campo/la ciudad. | 6. Prefiero la pasta/el pollo. (choices vary according to your preferences)

B. 1. Quiero mantequilla/margarina. | 2. Quiero gelatina/flan. | 3. Quiero sal/pimienta. | 4. Quiero ravioles/ñoquis. | 5. Quiero carne/pescado. | 6. Quiero queso brie/gruyère. | 7. Quiero jugo de manzana/naranja. (choices vary according to your preferences)

C. 1. No, no puede comer sola. | 2. No, no puede pararse sola. | 3. No, no puede caminar sola. | 4. No, no puede subir las escaleras sola. | 5. No, no puede subirse a una silla sola. | 6. No, no puede beber leche sola.

D. 1. tiene | 2. prefieren | 3. viene | 4. queremos | 5. tienen | 6. prefieres | 7. vengo | 8. queréis

PRACTICE 11.2

A. 1. Juan tiene su primer día de colegio. | 2. Juan está nervioso. | 3. Sí, Juan quiere ver a sus amigos. | 4. Juan prefiere ver a sus amigos en el parque. | 5. Pueden venir el sábado a su casa.

B. 1. piensa | 2. pedimos | 3. vuelven | 4. duermo | 5. juegas | 6. volvéis

C. 1. Sí, yo tengo un jardín grande. | 2. Nosotros preferimos el pescado. | 3. No, Laura no consigue pan. | 4. Sí, ellos duermen mucho. | 5. Daniel elige un restaurante chino. | 6. No, nosotros no venimos al museo. | 7. Yo mido un metro sesenta. | 8. Sí, puedo ayudarlo.

D. 1. Elsa no sueña con su exnovio. | 2. Nosotros no dormimos mucho. | 3. Teresa y Miguel no juegan siempre al tenis. | 4. Tú no empiezas a cocinar temprano. | 5. Vosotros no queréis una casa moderna. | 6.Yo no vuelvo tarde del trabajo.

E. 1. pensamos | 2. prefieres | 3. cierran | 4. servimos | 5. jugáis | 6. duermen | 7. vuelvo | 8. piensan

F. 1. Cierro la ventana de la sala. | 2. Empieza sus clases por la mañana. | 3. Almorzáis/Almuerzan en un restaurante francés. | 4. Roberto y María recuerdan a su abuelo. | 5. Juegas al tenis los domingos. | 6.María siempre piensa en sus hijos.

CHAPTER 12

PRACTICE 12.1

1. fueron (ser) | 2. Fuiste (ir) | 3. fuisteis (ser) | 4. fue (ser) | 5. fui (ir) | 6. fuiste (ser) | 7. fuimos (ir) | 8.fuiste (ir) | 9. fuisteis/fueron (ser) | 10. fueron (ir)

PRACTICE 12.2

A. 1. Caperucita Roja fue a ver a su abuela/ Caperucita fue a casa de su abuela. | 2. Se encontró con el lobo. | 3. Un cazador pasó por la casa. | 4. El cazador mató al lobo. | 5. La abuela de Caperucita salió del estómago del lobo.

B. 1. Llamaste | 2. Bebí | 3. Abrimos | 4. ayudaron | 5. bailaron | 6. estudió | 7. Recibisteis | 8. Vieron | 9.Ofrecisteis | 10. soñamos

PRACTICE 12.3

A. 1. empezasteis | 2. Busqué | 3. llegaron | 4. Alcancé | 5. Pagaste | 6. Publiqué | 7. Abracé

B. 1. escribió | 2. Empezó | 3. publicó | 4. Vendió | 5. convirtió | 6. Ganó | 7. cantó | 8. vio

C. 1. él/ella/usted | 2. yo | 3. nosotros | 4. yo | 5. yo | 6. tú | 7. vosotros | 8. ellos/ellas/ustedes | 9.él/ella/usted 10. yo

D.

Infinitive form of verb	hablar	comer	vivir
yo	**hablé**	**comí**	**viví**
tú	**hablaste**	**comiste**	**viviste**
él/ella/usted	**habló**	**comió**	**vivió**
nosotros	**hablamos**	**comimos**	**vivimos**
vosotros	**hablasteis**	**comisteis**	**vivisteis**
ellas/ellos/ustedes	**hablaron**	**comieron**	**vivieron**

E. 1. nos levantamos | 2. te lavaste | 3. os bañasteis | 4. me duché | 5. se afeitaron | 6. se preparó

F. 1. me desperté | 2. tomé | 3. Bebí | 4. comí | 5. estudié | 6. preparé | 7. almorcé | 8. lavé | 9. sequé | 10.jugué | 11. Me acosté | 12. nos despertamos | 13. tomamos | 14. Bebimos | 15. comimos | 16.estudiamos | 17. preparamos | 18. almorzamos | 19. lavamos | 20. secamos | 21. jugamos | 22.Nos acostamos

G. 1. Busqué un empleado. | 2. Empezó el día. | 3. Sacamos el pastel del horno. | 4. Usaron un lápiz. | 5.Os bañasteis en la piscina. | 6. Elena y Luis hablaron por teléfono. | 7. Ofreció sus servicios. | 8.Vivieron bien.

CHAPTER 13: PAST TENSE OF IRREGULAR VERBS

PRACTICE 13.1

A. 1. Di un regalo a mi amigo el sábado. | 2. Teresa y Julio dieron un concierto de piano. | 3. Nosotros hicimos un viaje largo por Canadá. | 4. Vosotros disteis un paseo por el parque. | 5. Ayer hice un pastel para Luisa. | 6. Nosotros le dimos un pastel.

B. 1. fuimos | 2. vivimos | 3. Visitamos | 4. fuimos | 5. Aprendimos | 6. practicamos | 7. hicimos | 8. Vimos | 9. visitamos | 10. comimos | 11. bebimos

C. 1. fui | 2. jugaste | 3. hizo | 4. dimos | 5. fueron | 6. descansasteis

PRACTICE 13.2

A.

Infinitive	dar	hacer	estar	poder	poner	saber
yo	di	hice	estuve	pude	puse	supe
tú	diste	hiciste	estuviste	pudiste	pusiste	supiste
él, ella, usted	dio	hizo	estuvo	pudo	puso	supo
nosotros	dimos	hicimos	estuvimos	pudimos	pusimos	supimos
vosotros	disteis	hicisteis	estuvisteis	pudisteis	pusisteis	supisteis
ellas, ellos, ustedes	dieron	hicieron	estuvieron	pudieron	pusieron	supieron

B. 1. vinieron | 2. Pudimos | 3. Tuvimos | 4. estuvieron | 5. trajeron | 6. Fue | 7. hicimos | 8. Pusimos | 9.nos reunimos | 10. contaron | 11. fuimos

C. 1. fue | 2. fueron | 3. estuvo | 4. quise | 5. Tuvisteis | 6. Viniste | 7. Dijo | 8. pude | 9. estuvo | 10.supisteis

D. 1. viniste | 2. Estuve | 3. tuve | 4. Estuviste | 5. dio | 6. dio

E. 1. El hijo de Elena vino a visitarnos. 2. Estuvo en nuestra casa durante una hora. 3. Nos trajo un regalo. 4. No pudo estar mucho tiempo. 5. Nos dijo adiós y se fue.

PRACTICE 13.3

A. 1. Martín se rio de mis planes. | 2. Mi mamá me pidió un favor. | 3. Yo preferí el helado de chocolate. | 4. Tomás y Juana durmieron muy bien. | 5. El profesor se sintió contento con las notas de los alumnos. | 6. Vosotros servisteis una sopa de tomate. | 7. Tú sonreíste cuando viste a tu amigo.

B. 1. me vestí | 2. te dormiste | 3. pidió | 4. se rio – entendió | 5. preferimos | 6. sirvió | 7. sonrió | 8. os sentisteis

CHAPTER 14: IMPERFECT PAST

PRACTICE 14.1

A. 1. a. cerraba | b. escuchaba | c. miraba | d. quería | e. recibía
2. a. pedías | b. visitabas | c. pensabas | d. entrabas | e. tenías
3. a. preguntaba | b. abría | c. compraba | d. enseñaba | e. volvía

B. 1. veía | 2. iban | 3. era | 4. erais | 5. ibas | 6. veíais

C. 1. Antes lavábamos la ropa a mano. | 2. Antes viajábamos en carreta. | 3. Antes hablábamos cara a cara. | 4. Antes vivíamos en chozas. | 5. Antes escribíamos con máquina de escribir. | 6. Antes cocinábamos con fogatas.

D. 1. De niño vivía en Los Ángeles. | 2. Iba al colegio público. | 3. Tenía dos amigas. | 4. Era un niño inquieto. | 5. Practicaba natación (swimming). | 6. Tenía un gato. (*Answers can vary in this activity*)

E. 1. pasábamos | 2. estaba | 3. iban | 4. jugábamos | 5. almorzábamos | 6. veíamos | 7. Volvíamos/brillaban

F. 1. De joven, Pedro jugaba al fútbol. | 2. De niño, mis primos vivían muy lejos de mi casa. | 3. Durante los veranos, vosotros nadabais en la piscina del club. | 4. Mi abuela bebía leche para dormir. | 5. Yo pasaba los veranos en la casa de mis tíos. | 6. Los domingos, mi abuelo y yo siempre íbamos a almorzar a un restaurante.

PRACTICE 14.2

A. 1. fue | 2. estaba | 3. sacó | 4. apuntó | 5. quería | 6. apareció | 7. se abalanzó | 8. quitó | 9. sujetó

B. 1. se quedaba | 2. salían | 3. dejaban | 4. oyó | 5. Bajó | 6. vio | 7. Tuvo | 8. se movió | 9. gritó | 10. era | 11. entró | 12. vio

C. 1. Cuando la familia paseaba en el parque, el ladrón entró para robar. | 2. Mientras vuestros hijos estaban en el colegio, vosotros hicisteis las compras. | 3. Cuando estabas de viaje, recibiste una oferta laboral. | 4. Cuando estaba en el parque, empezó a llover. | 5. Mientras paseábamos por el bosque, empezó un incendio. | 6. Mientras Horacio estudiaba en la universidad, sus padres vendieron su ropa.

PRACTICE 14.3

1. Era la una en punto cuando Tomás y Daniel se encontraron para almorzar. | 2. Era muy temprano cuando Teresa salió a correr. | 3. Eran las ocho y media cuando llegamos a la fiesta. | 4. Eran las cinco menos cuarto cuando los niños empezaron las clases de tenis. | 5. Eran las nueve cuando llamé al taxi. | 6. Eran las seis de la tarde cuando Roberto apareció en la reunión.

CHAPTER 15: THE VERB SER (TO BE)

PRACTICE 15

A. 1. Luis fue doctor y actor. | 2. Tomás es actor. | 3. Están en una fiesta. | 4. Son actores. | 5. La señora es cantante. | 6. La señora era maestra.

B. 1. Elvis Presley fue de los Estados Unidos. Era estadounidense. | 2. Frida Kahlo fue de México. Era mexicana. | 3. Vincent van Gogh fue de Países Bajos. Era neerlandés. | 4. Albert Einstein fue de Alemania. Era alemán. | 5. Coco Chanel fue de Francia. Era francesa. | 6. Freddy Ricón fue de Colombia. Era colombiano. | 7. Maria Kodama fue de Argentina. Era argentina. | 8. John Lenon fue de Inglaterra. Era inglés.

C. 1. Amy Winehouse fue/era inglesa (identification). | 2. Las sillas eran de plástico (material something was made of). | 3. Ellos eran de Colombia (origin). | 4. Las mesas eran de madera (material something was made of). | 5. La comida fue/era para la niña (for whom something was intended). | 6. Fue lunes (day of the week). | 7. Marcos y Luis fueron/eran abogados (profession). | 8. La fiesta fue en el club (where an event took place). | 9. El perro fue/era de María (possession). | 10. El libro era amarillo (description). | 11. Fue el 14 de febrero (date).

D. 1. era/fue | 2. eran | 3. era/fue | 4. eran | 5. eran/fueron | 6. era/fue

E. 1. Ellos eran/fueron de Alemania | 2. Felix y Alejandra eran/fueron de Argentina | 3. Ellas eran/fueron de Colombia | 4. José era/fue de México | 5. María era/fue de Francia. | 6. Felipe era/fue de Brasil.

F. 1. Eran/Fueron las tres de la tarde | 2. Era/Fue el primero de mayo | 3. Era/fue el 3 de noviembre | 4.Era/Fue miércoles | 5. Eran/Fueron las diez de la mañana | 6. Era/fue domingo

G. 1. Sí, fui simpático de niño. | 2. Sí, eran estudiantes. | 3. No, no era pequeña la casa de Mariana. | 4.Elena era de Inglaterra. | 5. Fue importante estudiar. | 6. Eran las 4:00 p.m.

H. 1. Los perros eran del niño. | 2. El libro era del colegio. | 3. Aquella casa fue del hombre rico. | 4. La moto era del joven. | 5. La comida era del restaurante. | 6. El coche fue del muchacho.

CHAPTER 16: ESTAR (TO BE) AND TENER (TO HAVE)

PRACTICE 16.1

A. 1. Mi casa estaba en Francia (location). | 2. La niña estuvo enferma (health). | 3. Estuvo/Estuve triste (changing mood). | 4. Juan estaba delgado (changing condition). | 5. Nosotros estuvimos aquí (location). | 6. La comida estuvo deliciosa (personal opinion). | 7. Vosotros estuvisteis contentos (changing mood). | 8. Tú estabas cansada luego del ejercicio (changing condition).

B. 1. Tim era español. | 2. El restaurante estaba cerrado. | 3. Las hijas de Pedro eran rubias e inteligentes. | 4. El problema fue muy fácil. | 5. El libro fue interesante. | 6. Tú estuviste furioso. | 7. La banana era amarilla. | 8. Nosotros estábamos felices. | 9. La foto estaba en la silla.

C. 1. era | 2. fue | 3. estuvo | 4. estaban | 5. estaba | 6. estaba | 7. era | 8. estuvo

D. 1. X | 2. X | 3. X | 4. ✓ | 5. X | 6. X | 7. ✓ | 8. X | 9. X | 10. ✓ | 11. X | 12. X

E. 1. Teresa y Miguel estuvieron en el cine. | 2. Vosotros estabais enfermos. | 3. La universidad era buena. | 5. Tú fuiste buena abogada. | 6. Yo era de Perú 8. Las sillas eran de plástico. | 9. Susana fue inteligente. | 11. La moto era de Federico. | 12. Ayer fue miércoles.

PRACTICE 16.2

A. 1. tuvimos | 2. tenían | 3. tenían | 4. tuvo | 5. tuve | 6. tenía | 7. tuvo | 8. tuvimos | 9. tuviste | 10. tenía

B. 1. tenían | 2. tenía | 3. tenías | 4. teníamos | 5. teníais | 6. tenía | 7. tenía | 8. tenían

C. 1. X | 2. X | 3.✓ | 4. ✓ | 5. X | 6. X | 7. X | 8. X

D. 1. Nosotros tuvimos sesenta años. | 2. Ustedes tenían cuarenta años. | 5. Tú tenías quince años. | 6.María tenía seis años. | 7. Tú y Miguel tenían setenta años. | 8. Josefina tenía veintitrés años.

E. 1. tenía | 2. tuvimos | 3. tuvo | 4. tuviste | 5. teníais | 6. tenía | 7. tenían | 8. tuvo | 9. tenía

CHAPTER 17: LIKES AND DISLIKES

PRACTICE 17.1

A. 1. nos | 2. os | 3. les | 4. les | 5. les | 6. me | 7. te | 8. le | 9. le

B. 1. A mí me gustaba/gustó el coche. | 2. A ellos les gustaban/gustaron las cebollas. | 3. A nosotros no nos gustaba/gustó leer. | 4. A ti te gustaban/gustaron las bananas. | 5. A vosotros/ustedes os/les gustaba/gustó trabajar. | 6. A Marcos le gustaba/gustó estudiar. | 7. A Elsa le gustaban/gustaron los tomates. | 8. A mi padre le gustaba/gustó comer. | 9. A mi madre le gustaba/gustó el pescado. | 10. A los chicos no les gustaba/gustó la leche. | 11. A María le gustaba/gustó el pollo.

C. 1. A nosotros nos gustaba/gustó correr. | 2. A los niños no les gustaban/gustaron las verduras. | 3. A mí me gustaban/gustaron esos zapatos. | 4. A Luis y Teresa les gustaban/gustaron las fiestas. | 5. A Elena le gustaba/gustó tocar piano. | 6. A mí me gustaba/gustó el pescado.

D. (Answers may vary) 1. No me gustaba Cristiano Ronaldo, aunque me gustaba Leo Messi. | 2. No me gustó comer pastas, pero me gustó comer hamburguesas. | 3. No me gustaba el café; sin embargo, me gustaba el té. | 4. No me gustó la actriz Judy Dench, pero me gustó la actriz Meryl Streep. | 5. No me gustaba el tenista Medvedev, aunque me gustaba el tenista Federer. | 6. No me gustó estudiar en el comedor, pero me gustó estudiar en la biblioteca. | 7. No me gustaban los gatos, pero me gustaban los perros. | 8. No me gustó viajar en tren; sin embargo, me gustó viajar en coche.

E. 1. les gustaban | 2. os gustaron | 3. te gustaban | 4. nos gustó | 5. me gustaban | 6. le gustaron

F. 1. ¿A nosotros nos gustaban/gustaron las fiestas? | 2. ¿A Teresa le gustaba/gustó su universidad? | 3.¿A ellos les gustaba/gustó recibir gente en su casa? | 4. ¿A mí me gustaba/gustó hacer yoga? | 5.¿A ti te gustaba/gustó el pescado? | 6. ¿A usted le gustaba/gustó viajar?

G. 1. A nosotros nos gustaba/gustó trabajar en esa empresa. | 2. A ustedes les gustaba vivir solos cuando estaban en Paraguay. | 3. A vosotros os gustaba caminar en el parque los sábados. | 4. A Carolina y Luis les gustó subir montañas el lunes. | 5. A ti te gustaba/gustó invitar amigos a tu casa. | 6. A ellos les gustaba/gustó viajar por el mundo.

H. 1. A mí me gustaban los caramelos. | 2. A ti te gustó el pan. | 3. A vosotros os gustaba la leche. | 4. A ti te gustó el café. | 5. A ellos les gustaban las naranjas. | 6. A él le gustó la carne.

I. 1. Al abuelo le gustaba/gustó cocinar. | 2. Al hermano le gustaba/gustó hacer surf. | 3. A la tía le gustaba/gustó leer libros. | 4. A los primos les gustaba/gustó comprar ropa. | 5. Al padre le gustaba/gustó comer y beber. | 6. A la hija le gustaba/gustó buscar caracoles en la orilla. | 7. A la madre le gustaba/gustó la tranquilidad. | 8. A los sobrinos les gustaba/gustó correr por la playa.

PRACTICE 17.2

1. Me gustaría un vaso de agua. | 2. Quiero dormir. | 3. Me gustaría hablar bien español. | 4. Me gustaría ese vestido verde. | 5. Quiero arreglar el techo.

LESSON 18: FUTURE

PRACTICE 18

A. 1. correré | 2. permanecerán | 3. continuará | 4. se volverá | 5. sonarán | 6. Se irán | 7. se renovará | 8.volará | 9. desapareceré | 10. estaré | 11. seguirán

B. 1. Tendré | 2. Sabré | 3. Podré | 4. Saldré | 5. Haré | 6. Compraré | 7. Querré | 8. Compraré | 9. Usaré | 10. Ayudaré

C. 1. Practicarás | 2. Visitarás | 3. Irás | 4. Comerás | 5. Navegarás | 6. Subirás

D. 1. Iremos al cine a las 8:00 p.m. | 2. Cenarán a las 10:00 p.m. | 3. Vendrá al mediodía | 4. Haremos la reunión a las 3:00 p.m. | 5. Saldremos hacia el aeropuerto en la mañana | 6. Podrán ayudarnos a las 7:00 a.m.

E. 1. Seguramente conduciré coches voladores. | 2. Posiblemente podréis comunicaros con los ojos. | 3.Probablemente, Juan y Santiago sabrán cocinar sin ensuciar. | 4. Serás muy viejo. | 5. Viviremos en cápsulas espaciales. | 6. Posiblemente, Martín podrá casarse con un robot.

F. 1. Me gustaría ser diseñadora (designer). | 2. Trabajaré en una oficina sobre el mar. | 3. Me casaré con un hombre aventurero. | 4. Tendré tres hijos. | 5. Ganaré mucho dinero. | 6. Gastaré mi dinero en educar a mis hijos. | 7. Mi pasatiempo será trabajar en el jardín. (answers may vary).

G. 1. Raúl invertirá en la bolsa. | 2. Raúl no pedirá ningún préstamo. | 3. Raúl administrará bien su dinero.| 4. Raúl se adaptará a su presupuesto. | 5. Raúl usará parte del dinero para invertir en la bolsa. | 6. Raúl comprará acciones. | 7. Raúl prestará dinero a un amigo. | 8. Raúl pagará al contado sus compras.

H. 1. A las 7:00 a.m. prepararé el desayuno. | 2. A las 7:30 a.m. saldré al trabajo. | 3. A las 8:00 a.m. tomaré el tren. | 4. A las 8:30 tomaré el tren. | 5. A las 9:00 a.m. me reuniré con el jefe. | 6. A las 9:30 a.m. prepararé un informe. | 7. A las 12:00 a.m. almorzaré. | 8. A las 3:00 p.m. iré a clase de yoga. | 9.A las 4:00 p.m. iré a la estación de tren. | 10. A las 4:20 p.m. tomaré el tren. | 11. A las 5:00 p.m. llegaré a casa. | 12. A las 6:00 p.m. me bañaré. | 13. A las 8:00 p.m. mis amigas vendrán a mi casa. | 14. A las 9:00 p.m. saldremos a tomar algo.

I. 1. dirá | 2. dirán | 3. diré | 4. diremos | 5. diréis | 6. dirás

J. 1. saldrán | 2. Haremos | 3. vendrá | 4. querréis | 5. podrás | 6. pondrá | 7. sabrás | 8. tendréis

CHAPTER 19: SUBJUNCTIVE MOOD – REGULAR

PRACTICE 19

A. 1. preste | 2. coman | 3. suba | 4. hable | 5. escriban | 6. trabaje | 7. ayude | 8. vivan

B. 1. juegues | 2. investigue | 3. empecemos | 4. paguen | 5. busquéis | 6. almuerce

C. 1. recéis | 2. expliquéis | 3. entregue | 4. saquen | 5. llegue | 6. toquéis

D. 1. Te recomiendo que no comas caramelos. | 2. Te recomiendo que no comas pastas. | 3. Te recomiendo que no comas chocolates. | 4. Te recomiendo que no comas pasteles. | 5. Te recomiendo que no bebas alcohol. | 6. Te recomiendo que no bebas gaseosas con azúcar. | 7. Te recomiendo que no bebas leche con chocolate.

E. 1. trabaje | 2. escriba | 3. coma | 4. miremos | 5. leáis | 6. guardes | 7. estudien | 8. escribamos

F. 1. Nos sorprende que ellos compren tantos alimentos. | 2. Es terrible que vosotros creáis en supersticiones. | 3. Es extraño que la luz no prenda. | 4. Es emocionante que Sofía visite a su hermana. | 5. Es maravilloso que Pablo trabaje y estudie al mismo tiempo. | 6. Es increíble que aquellos escaladores suban el Everest en dos meses. | 7. Es un orgullo que Tomás reciba un premio por su pintura. | 8. Es una pena que vosotros discutáis mucho.

G. 1. ¿Qué quieres que aprenda? | 2. ¿Qué quieren que abráis? | 3. ¿Qué quieren/ queréis ustedes que escriba? | 4. ¿Qué quiere la profesora que estudie? | 5. ¿Qué quiere que compren? | 6. ¿Qué quieres que preparemos? | 7. ¿Qué quieren que pague? | 8. ¿Qué queremos que enseñen?

H. 1. Es importante que los candidatos estén bien vestidos. | 2. Es importante que los candidatos se preparen para entrevista. | 3. Es importante que los candidatos lleguen puntualmente a la cita. | 4. Es importante que los candidatos hagan preguntas sobre el trabajo. | 5. Es importante que los candidatos crean en sí mismos. | 6. Es importante que los candidatos respondan con honestidad. | 7. Es importante que los candidatos conozcan la empresa.

I. 1. Me sorprende que mis amigos no me llamen para mi cumpleaños. | 2. Es genial que me inviten a esquiar. | 3. Espero que me suban el sueldo en el trabajo. | 4. Deseo que mi amiga se recupere pronto de su enfermedad. | 5. Es emocionante que la señora Reta ayude a una anciana a cruzar la calle. | 6.Me encanta que lo inviten a jugar al fútbol. (Phrases may vary).

J.

Infinitive	sacar	entregar	comenzar	realizar	apagar	pescar *(fish)*
yo	**saque**	**entregue**	**comience**	**realice**	**apague**	**pesque**
tú	**saques**	**entregues**	**comiences**	**realices**	**apagues**	**pesques**
él/ella/ usted	**saque**	**entregue**	**comience**	**realice**	**apague**	**pesque**
nosotros	**saquemos**	**entreguemos**	**comencemos**	**realicemos**	**apaguemos**	**pesquemos**
vosotros	**saquéis**	**entreguéis**	**comencéis**	**realicéis**	**apaguéis**	**pesquéis**
ellas/ ellos/ ustedes	**saquen**	**entreguen**	**comiencen**	**realicen**	**apaguen**	**pesquen**

CHAPTER 20: SUBJUNCTIVE MOOD – IRREGULAR

PRACTICE 20

A. 1. esté | 2. llame | 3. ganen | 4. lleguemos | 5. se suban | 6. ayude

B. 1. Mariana quiere que vayan al mar. | 2. Pedro quiere que hagan un campamento. | 3. La madre quiere que estén en una isla remota. | 4. El padre quiere que vayan a una ciudad interesante. | 5. La abuela quiere que den un paseo por la costa. | 6. El abuelo quiere que vayan a pescar.

C. 1. Te recomiendo que te levantes temprano. | 2. Te aconsejo que desayunes. | 3. Te recomiendo que no discutas mucho con tus colegas del trabajo. | 4. Te aconsejo que no veas televisión. | 5. Te recomiendo que hagas ejercicio. | 6. Te aconsejo que cocines algunas veces. | 7. Te recomiendo que no comas comida chatarra. | 8. Te aconsejo que no salgas con amigos de noche. | 9. Te recomiendo que no te acuestes tarde. | 10. Te aconsejo que no bebas alcohol. | 11. Te recomiendo que no fumes mucho.

D. 1. consiga | 2. consiga | 3. consigan | 4. consigas | 5. consigamos | 6. consigáis

E. 1. realicemos | 2. busque | 3. llueva | 4. estudie | 5. vengas | 6. nos lavemos | 7. dirija | 8. saquéis | 9.explique | 10. llegue

F. 1. Es bueno que la gente coma más verduras. | 2. Marta está contenta de que su hijo se vaya de viaje.| 3. Es probable que Juan e Iván vengan a cenar. | 4. Espero que vosotros ganéis la elección. | 5.Quieren que los inviten a la fiesta. | 6. Es necesario que salgas afuera a fumar.

G. 1. S | 2. I | 3. S | 4. S | 5. I | 6. S | 7. S | 8. S | 9. I | 10. S | 11. S | 12. I

H. 1. Quiero que el bebé no tenga malos sueños. | 2. Quiero que mi hermana haga ejercicio. | 3. Quiero que mi padre me dé dinero. | 4. Quiero que nuestros tíos sepan esa noticia. | 5. Quiero que mi hijo sea responsable. | 6. Quiero que vosotros vayáis de vacaciones. | 7. Quiero que haya flores en mi casa. | 8. Quiero que Juan no esté solo.

I. 1. críen | 2. continúen | 3. evalúen | 4. espíen | 5. amplíen | 6. averigüe | 7. actúe | 8. se enfríe

J. 1. quiere | 2. duerme | 3. haga | 4. beba | 5. prenda | 6. escuche | 7. lea | 8. baje | 9. se vaya

LESSON 21: IMPERATIVE MOOD

PRACTICE 21.2

1. baile | 2. compre | 3. hable | 4. descanse | 5. entre | 6. regrese | 7. venda | 8. abra | 9. escriba | 10.coma

PRACTICE 21.3

A. 1. llegue | 2. lee | 3. escribid | 4. abran | 5. pensemos | 6. estén | 7. traigamos | 8. olvida

B. 1. Levántense | 2. tomen | 3. Lleguen | 4. siéntense | 5. Organicen | 6. empiecen | 7. pierdan | 8. usen | 9. cierren | 10. vayan

C. 1. vayas | 2. ve | 3. ve | 4. vayas | 5. vayas | 6. ve | 7. ve | 8. ve

D. 1. doble | 2. avance | 3. siga | 4. llegue | 5. continúe | 6. gire

E. 1. comed | 2. bebed | 3. haced amigos | 4. pedid ayuda | 5. descansad | 6. trabajad | 7. hablad con ellos | 8. buscad las mochilas

F. 1. gobierne | 2. cante | 3. cocine | 4. corra | 5. rece | 6. juegue al tenis | 7. nade | 8. estudiad/estudien | 9. tened/tengan paciencia

G. 1. Busque un trabajo. | 2. Trabaje al aire libre. | 3. Sea valiente. | 4. Haga una capacitación. | 5. Averigüe cuáles son los empleos disponibles. | 6. Haga un test vocacional. | 7. Trabaje en una oficina. | 8. Tenga confianza en sí mismo. | 9. Prepare un CV. | 10. Inclúyalo en el CV.

H. 1. mira | 2. pagad | 3. paguen | 4. comencemos o empecemos | 5. mirad | 6. miren | 7. comienza o empieza | 8. paguemos

I. 1. vaya | 2. camine | 3. no se siente | 4. no se quede | 5. párese | 6. no se abroche | 7. no permanezca | 8. muévase | 9. vaya

J. 1. No grites | 2. Practicad | 3. Paguemos, vámonos | 4. Abróchense | 5. Toque | 6. No habléis fuerte | 7.No cruces | 8. Escuchen

LESSON 22: CONDITIONAL MOOD

PRACTICE 22

A. 1. Le regalaría un apartamento a Elena. | 2. Le compraría un coche para su trabajo. | 3. Les daría regalos. | 4. Contrataría una orquesta de músicos para dar un concierto. | 5. Construiría un edificio para albergar a las personas de la calle. | 6. Ofrecería una habitación hermosa y comida rica.

B. 1. encantaría | 2. visitaría | 3. Conocería | 4. Volaría | 5. Probaría | 6. bebería | 7. Recorrería | 8. vería | 9. gustaría

C.

Infinitive form of verb	hablar	comer	vivir
yo	hablaría	comería	viviría
tú	hablarías	comerías	vivirías
él/ella/usted	hablaría	comería	viviría
nosotros	hablaríamos	comeríamos	viviríamos
vosotros	hablaríais	comeríais	viviríais
ellas/ellos/ustedes	hablarían	comerían	vivirían

D. 1. ¿Vendrías a bailar? No, iría a tomar algo. | 2. ¿Harías yoga? No, haría pilates. | 3. ¿Tendrías un perro? No, tendría un gato. | 4. ¿Saldrías de noche? No, saldría de día. | 5. ¿Podrías preparar lasagna? No, podría preparar pollo al horno. | 6. ¿Pondrías dinero en el banco? No, pondría dinero en una compañía de inversiones. | 7. ¿Querrías aprender japonés? No, querría aprender chino. | 8.¿Aprenderías a conducir una lancha? No, aprendería a remar un bote.

E. 1. Hablaría con la dependienta/Iría a buscar la cartera al asiento. | 2. Llamaría a la compañía eléctrica/Prendería muchas velas. | 3. Iría al parque de todos modos/Me quedaría en casa a ver una película. | 4. Lo comería de todos modos/Lo tiraría a la basura. | 5. Llamaría a alguien por mi celular/Gritaría para que me oigan. | 6. Lo dejaría sin comer/Le daría otra cosa para comer. | 7. La dejaría esperar en la fila/La dejaría pasar primero. | 8. Le diría que está gorda/No diría nada.

F. 1. traería | 2. vendríamos | 3. compraría | 4. haría | 5. se ocuparía | 6. pondría | 7. querrían | 8. podría

G. 1. gustaría | 2. preferirían | 3. querría | 4. estaría | 5. querrían | 6. preferirían | 7. estarían | 8.preferiríamos

H. 1. Estarías | 2. estaríamos | 3. sería | 4. Sería | 5. Podríamos | 6. Iríamos | 7. vendría | 8. cabríamos

I. 1. pondríamos | 2. dirías | 3. seríamos | 4. haríais | 5. podrían | 6. vendría | 7. tendríamos | 8. saldría | 9.querría | 10. sabrían | 11. sabría | 12. bajarían

J. 1. gustaría | 2. gustaría | 3. gustaría | 4. gustaría | 5. gustaría | 6. gustaría | 7. gustaría | 8. gustaría

CHAPTER 23: SUPERLATIVES

PRACTICE 23

A. 1. Era la casa más preciosa del mundo. | 2. Era el plato más caliente de todos. | 3. Era la cama más dura de todas. | 4. Era la cama más suave de todas. | 5. La cama más cómoda de todas era la tercera.| 6. Fue el peor susto de su vida.

B. 1. persona bajísima | 2. perros y gatos cariñosísimos | 3. profesor buenísimo | 4. actor guapísimo | 5.periódico buenísimo | 6. ejercicio dificilísimo | 7. amigos simpatiquísimos

C. 1. friísimo | 2. guapísimo | 3. cortísimo | 4. larguísimo | 5. popularísimo | 6. jovencísimos | 7. felicísimos| 8. velocísimos. | 9. ferocísimos |10. amabilísima

D. 1. Estuvo lindísimo. | 2. Estaba friísimo. | 3. Estuvo sabrosísima. | 4. Estuvieron contentísimos. | 5. Fue dificilísimo. | 6. Eran hermosísimos. | 7. Eran baratísimos.

E. 1. George Clooney | 2. El helado | 3. Don Julio | 4. "Abrázame fuerte," de Britney Spears y Elton John | 5. Lionel Messi | 6. La tortuga. (Responses vary)

F. 1. friísima | 2. altísimo | 3. larguísimo | 4. grandísima | 5. riquísima | 6. ferocísimo | 7. lentísimas (Responses vary)

G. 1. Es el sofá más incómodo de la sala. | 2. Es la cantante más popular de América Latina. | 3. Es el animal más ágil de todos. | 4. Es el día más especial del año. | 5. Es la cama más incómoda del apartamento. | 6. Es la calle más estrecha de la ciudad.

H. 1. Sofía Vergara es la actriz más popular del mundo. | 2. Jeff Bezos es el hombre más rico del mundo.| 3. Los suizos son las personas más discretas del mundo. | 4. Los perros son los animales más cariñosos del mundo. | 5. Los exámenes para entrar en Harvard son los más difíciles del mundo. | 6. Tacko Fall es el jugador de baloncesto más alto del mundo. | 7. El Ferrari es el coche más veloz del mundo.

I. 1. El metro de Berlín es el más rápido del mundo. | 2. El niño es el más burlón de la clase. | 3. Es el árbol más pequeño del bosque. | 4. Es el hombre más viejo de la orquesta. | 5. Mónica y Luisa son las empleadas más trabajadoras de la oficina. | 6. La señora Gómez es la profesora más sensible del colegio.

J. 1. Dependiente amabilísimo | 2. Plato calientísimo | 3. Perro fidelísimo | 4. Tormenta fuertísima | 5.Músico sensibilísimo | 6. Comida riquísima | 7. Camino larguísimo

Made in the USA
Columbia, SC
07 September 2024

41990097R00165